KINDNESS TOWARDS ISRAEL

The Jews' Continued Place in God's Plan
in the Era of the Church According to
the Old and New Covenants

ERIC E. ENGLEMAN

Published by Innovo Publishing, LLC
www.innovopublishing.com
1-888-546-2111

Publishing Books, eBooks, Audiobooks, Music, Screenplays, & Courses for the Christian & wholesome markets since 2008.

KINDNESS TOWARDS ISRAEL
The Jews' Continued Place in God's Plan in the Era of the Church According to the Old and New Covenants

Copyright © 2023 by Eric E. Engleman
All rights reserved.

No part of this publication may be reproduced, stored in a retrieval system, or transmitted in any form or by any means electronic, mechanical, photocopying, recording, or otherwise, without the prior written permission of the Author.

Unless otherwise noted, all scripture quotations are taken from the New American Standard Bible®, Copyright © 1960, 1971, 1977, 1995, 2020 by The Lockman Foundation. All rights reserved.

Scripture marked "ESV" is taken from The Holy Bible, English Standard Version. ESV® Text Edition: 2016. Copyright © 2001 by Crossway Bibles, a publishing ministry of Good News Publishers.

Scripture marked "ISV" is taken from the International Standard Version. Copyright © 1995-2014 by ISV Foundation. ALL RIGHTS RESERVED INTERNATIONALLY. Used by permission of Davidson Press, LLC.

Scripture marked "KJV" is taken from the King James Version of the Bible. Public domain.

Scripture marked "NKJV" is taken from the New King James Version®. Copyright © 1982 by Thomas Nelson. Used by permission. All rights reserved.

Scripture marked "BSB" is taken from The Holy Bible, Berean Standard Bible, BSB. Copyright ©2016, 2020 by Bible Hub. Used by Permission. All Rights Reserved Worldwide.

Library of Congress Control Number: 2023907320
ISBN: 978-1-61314-884-6

Cover Design & Interior Layout: Innovo Publishing, LLC

Printed in the United States of America
U.S. Printing History
First Edition: 2023

Has God called you to create a Christ-centered or wholesome book, eBook, audiobook, music album, screenplay, or online course? Visit Innovo's educational center (cpportal.com) to learn how to accomplish your calling with excellence.

BIBLE ABBREVIATIONS

BSB—Berean Study Bible
ESV—English Standard Version
ISV—International Standard Version
NASB—New American Standard Bible
KJV—King James Version
NKJV—New King James Version

CONTENTS

Preface 9
Introduction 13
   Israel: An Allegory of the Church? 15
   Has the Church Always Thought that It Replaces Israel? 18
   The Israel Resurrection Miracle 25

THE OLD TESTAMENT CASE

Introduction 31
In the Beginning 32
The Abrahamic Covenant: "I Will Bless You" 35
Moses and the Conquest: Covenant Kept 43
Covenant Fulfillment After the Conquest 48
Prophecies of a Last-Day Final Fulfillment 55
   Davidic Prophecies of the Eternal Kingdom 57
   Prophecies of the Eternal Kingdom by the Major and Minor Prophets .. 66

THE NEW TESTAMENT CASE: THE GOSPELS

Introduction 101
Jesus's Teaching about the Coming Kingdom 105
   The Kingdom Is a Thing of the Heart 108
   The Kingdom Comes at Christ's Second Coming 112
   Other Hints that Christ's Earthly Kingdom Is Yet to Come 115

THE NEW TESTAMENT CASE: ACTS AND EPISTLES

Introduction 125

Acts and the Epistles Teach Mainly a Spiritual Interpretation
of the Promises 127

In Acts and the Epistles, the Jews Are Not Forgotten 134

THE NEW TESTAMENT CASE: REVELATION

Introduction 153

The Tribulation Events of Revelation Occur Just Before
Christ's Second Coming 154

The Millennial Reign of Christ Is Earthly and Substantially Jewish 164

Conclusion 179

Bibliography 181

Scripture Index 185

PREFACE

My last trip to Israel was full of rich Jewish experiences. On my first night there on the beach in Tel Aviv, one of my feet got tangled up with a jellyfish while I enjoyed an evening swim (that part was not so Jewish!). The next day, as I, in quite a bit of pain, tried to figure out how to take a bus up to the excavation site at Hazor, a very sweet Jewish lady went out of her way to help me get there (that part is very Jewish!). Once there, my domain of digging was under the oversight of two Jewish Hebrew University young ladies who had gobs of charm and, at the same time, kept our rate of dirt extraction (we first had to go down some ten feet to the "Late Bronze Age" level) at a speedy tempo (charm plus productivity: very Jewish!).

When the excavation was over (and I was about ten pounds lighter), a young Jewish couple, whom I met near the top of Mount Hermon, invited me to picnic and swim with them at the Jordan River near the base of the mountain. The climb as well as the time at the river were a delight. A day or two later, I had the pleasure of being served supper at the apartment of one of my dig site colleagues who had previously served as a tank commander in Israel's army. He was very gracious to me but very stern when it came to matters of Israel's security.

After that, I spent a few days in Jerusalem at an old Lutheran "Hospice" and experienced the age-old clamor and musty smells of the ancient city. Evenings were spent on the hospice's balcony, enjoying the warm summer air and the views of the Mount of Olives and the Dome of the Rock, which sits upon the Temple Mount first built by Solomon and still attended—at least at the Western Wall of it—by thousands of Israelites who pray earnestly for the arrival of the Messiah and the establishment of the kingdom prophesied by the prophets so long ago. All so very, very Jewish.

This experience only confirmed what I had felt from childhood: there is something special about the Jews and Israel that is evident now and will always be that way—for the Jews are God's chosen people. As I grew up, I didn't think about that subject much (it was more of a gut feeling), but when I became a Christian in 1990 and, not too long after, went to seminary at a school that puts a high value on the promises made to the Jews and God's certain fulfillment of those promises (Talbot School of Theology), my appreciation for Israel only grew.

While at seminary, however, I learned that most Christian theologians through the eons have understood that the Church replaces Israel in God's great plan; that the literal promises made to Abraham and others after him regarding offspring and land and blessings should only be taken "spiritually" (i.e., figuratively) of, respectively, those who have faith in Christ, heaven, and salvation; and because the Jews in the biblical history and later turned out to be great sinners and, worst of all, killed Jesus, the promises, as taken spiritually, are not fulfilled in them but are fulfilled in the Church.

These "replacement theologians" (who come by several more precise names like "covenant," "amillennial," or "postmillennial" theologians) understand the old promises and prophecies mainly spiritually, and the Jews have by and large forfeited receiving any spiritual fulfillment (salvation) because of their wickedness. So there's nothing left for the Jews and the nation of Israel.

Well, this has bothered me for quite a long time, not mainly because of what I learned in seminary (I didn't understand then much of the "dispensationalism" that was taught at Talbot), but because of my long-held feeling that the Jews and Israel were and always will be special in God's eyes. But I knew in my heart—even for a long time after seminary—that I really didn't understand the issues and so could not make a good biblical argument for the continued validity of Israel. So about four years ago, I decided to finally educate myself on the question. I covered the east wall of my home study with butcher block paper and proceeded to fill it up over a couple years' span with all kinds of notes, mostly from the Bible and some from the main replacement theology and nonreplacement theology books that I read, in order to once and for all either affirm or refute my natural heart for Israel based upon the big picture that was obtained.

The lessons learned from the eastern wall have now been condensed down into this little book, and I hope that it will help you get the big picture too! Here's a little nutshell of what I came to know and what this book will give (mostly biblical) evidence for: God will fulfill what he has *literally* promised to Israel, if just for the reason that he originally made these promises *unconditionally* and also in view of the fact that there is little indication in the Old Testament (OT) that these promises are meant to be taken figuratively (at least, not primarily so). At the same time, the New Testament (NT) clearly shows that the OT patriarchal promises (as well as many later prophecies regarding the end-times) are ultimately fulfilled *figuratively* in the Church—the Church consisting of both Jews and Gentiles.

The OT certainly does not preclude the possibility of a figurative (spiritual) fulfillment of the promises (there are OT hints to this effect), and the NT certainly does not preclude the possibility of a literal fulfillment of those promises (in fact, several texts actively support that possibility). In any case, there's no way that the OT promises and prophecies can be taken to *only* have figurative meaning. Otherwise, we'd have what amounts to a thousand-plus-page allegory on our hands that nowhere gives any signs of being an allegory, which is, literally speaking, absurd. Also, in this case, God would have misled the Jews all these centuries, and, lastly, turning the OT into one giant allegory would throw into severe uncertainty the real meaning of any part of it, for figurative meanings are open to much speculation.

The replacement theologians can relax because the OT was never (primarily, literally) about salvation in the first place; the Jews will not be saved simply because they are sons of Abraham or because they follow the Mosaic Law to the letter. Christ's Church is the place of saved immortal men and women, whether Jew or Gentile. And if the Lord wants the earthly nation of Israel to rise again at some point (maybe she is already in that process) and exist for a very long time peopled by (perhaps not exclusively) mortal sons of Abraham, then what's the big issue? It might be that this "very long time" will be a time when vast numbers of Jews come to faith in Christ and are thus saved from eternal condemnation.

This book counters the main mistake of the replacement theologians, which can be simply explained this way: Because the NT's strong emphasis is on what it takes to be saved (i.e., saved from hell to eternal blessed life), they assume that the OT must have that emphasis too. But because these OT promises and prophecies literally only speak of future earthly, temporal blessings, they must be interpreted only figuratively as representing the "spiritual" higher realities of salvation and heaven. They want to apply these promises and prophecies to the saved and heaven-bound Church, which is not altogether incorrect, but their mistake is that they allow God no room at all to provide some measure of literal fulfillment of these promises and prophecies for the Jews. This book argues that God can fulfill his promises and prophecies both figuratively *and* literally. This view in no way contradicts the NT-clarified doctrine of salvation by grace, through faith, for the literal fulfillment of

PREFACE

those promises and prophecies does not involve anything of immortality but only involves issues of mortal life on earth.

Most agree, after all, that Jesus will one day return, just as he promised. Whether the earth that he returns to remains for another five minutes or for another thousand years, the overall situation, either way, will intensely involve mortal Jewish people, the Jewish land, and the Jewish Savior who long ago cried out to his brothers, "You will not see me again, *until* you say, 'Blessed is he who comes in the name of the Lord.'"[1]

I thank Pastor Randy Burk and his lovely wife, Sandy, for their friendship and encouragement during the time that this book was in process. I thank also Mr. Lance Saltzmann for proofreading an early draft and for his valuable insights. I dedicate the book to the memory of my mother, Nancy Engleman, who loved the Jewish people.

---

[1] Matthew 23:39 (ESV, italics mine)

INTRODUCTION

Before getting started, I'd better define a few terms so as to avoid confusion down the line. First, when I say "Jews" or "Israelites" or "Hebrews," I mean those people who exist today and who existed in the past who are the blood descendants of Abraham, then Isaac, then Jacob (third/second millennium BC). "Jews," of course, can technically denote those who are descendants of Judah, Jacob's third son, from whom is also the Christ. If I use the term in this restricted use, the context should make this clear. The same goes for "Israelites," which can be used in the limited sense of the offspring of Jacob (not Abraham and Isaac). And "Hebrews," technically speaking, should refer to *all* descendants of Eber who was six generations before Abraham; but in this book, that designation will never be used for that enormous group whose blood infuses a mass of unknowing humanity today.[1]

Along the way, we will encounter not a few Bible verses, and some quotes from Bible commentators as well, that indicate that a "Jew" is really only someone—Jew or Gentile—who shares in the faith of Abraham (in Yahweh) or that the true "Israel" of God is the Christian Church. When the Bible or a commentator is using these terms in this "spiritual" sense, I will alert the reader, but I will not use them in this way myself unless I plainly tell the reader that I do so. Needless to say, "Israel" can be used for another name for Jacob and must be used to designate the northern kingdom during the divided monarchy (tenth to eighth centuries BC) and the sovereign nation by that name that exists today.

~*~

> From the standpoint of the gospel they are enemies for your sake, but from the standpoint of God's choice they are beloved for the sake of the fathers; for the gifts and the calling of God are irrevocable. (Saul of Tarsus—Rom 11:28–29)

Is there yet a special place for the Jewish people and for a Jewish nation in the "Promised Land"? Well, if I had said yes to this question a

---

[1.] Of course, if I'm referring to the NT book of "Hebrews," the context will make that clear.

hundred years ago, subsequent history would have proved me a prophet![2] How much more so if I had answered the question affirmatively a thousand years ago or even further back just after the Romans killed most of the Jews in the course of the Bar Kokhba revolt (ca. AD 135) and banished what survivors there were forever from their "beloved city" on pain of death. If I were then to have predicted near two millennia hence a flourishing worldwide Jewish people who excel their human peers in most areas of life and a new Jewish nation called "Israel," the Romans would have branded me a lunatic, and most Christians would have been at the very least very skeptical.

The truth is that God has, in general, protected and blessed the Jews throughout the ages—horrible persecutions notwithstanding—and if he has done this in the past, he will probably do it in the future. If we fly in the stratosphere over Israel's existence from the beginning till now, we see that God blessed Abraham and Isaac. God blessed Jacob and his twelve sons even though they were rascals at times. God brought his "son" out of Egypt despite the fact that they grumbled incessantly, were "stiff-necked and rebellious," and worshipped the idols of the Egyptians and the golden calves. God blessed the Israelites when they came into the Promised Land even though they prosecuted their assigned mission only half-heartedly. God did not forget his chosen people when he banished them to Assyria and Babylon and beyond because of their wickedness. God brought them back to the land, and there he helped them rebuild the temple and the city. Jesus prophesied their desolation and destruction yet, while on the cross, asked the Father to forgive them "for," as he said, "they know not what they do." Even after the Bar Kokhba disaster, the Jews still by and large partook of God's blessings under Roman, then Byzantine, then Muslim rule—although ever restricted, segregated, and oppressively taxed. God preserved and protected them through the Middle Ages and the Reformation, and with the Enlightenment, they experienced freedom hitherto unknown—a freedom that rocketed many of them into the most prominent and influential positions in Western Christian society where most Jews lived.

Today, according to one observer of the Jews, "They make up 0.2 percent of the world population, but 54 percent of

---

[2.] Actually, in 1897, the patriarch of the Zionist movement, Theodor Herzl, recognized after the first Zionist congress in Basel, Switzerland, that he had alone begun the process that would lead to a Jewish homeland no more than fifty years from that date. The nation of "Israel" was founded a few months more than fifty years later (Walter Laqueur, *The History of Zionism* [New York: Schocken Books, 2003], 137).

the world chess champions, 27 percent of the Nobel physics laureates and 31 percent of the medicine laureates. Jews make up 2 percent of the U.S. population, but 21 percent of the Ivy League student bodies, 26 percent of the Kennedy Center honorees, 37 percent of the Academy Award–winning directors...[and] 51 percent of the Pulitzer Prize winners for nonfiction."[3]

I might add that as of today, two out of the nine current US Supreme Court justices are Jewish, and there may be more to come. How could such people survive and tremendously excel (at least in the modern age) unless they were intensely blessed by the Almighty God who made Israel in the first place? And speaking of "Israel," the fact that they have their own "national home" again and call it "Israel" as of 1948 is nothing short of a miracle, which seems to have been wrought by God. More about that a little later.

ISRAEL: AN ALLEGORY OF THE CHURCH?

So *yes*, God has preserved and blessed Israel immensely and will probably do so in the future. Now past history *indicates* the future but doesn't *guarantee* it. So in order to answer our question, "Is there yet a special place for the Jewish people and for a Jewish nation in the 'Promised Land'?" we can only, with certainty, answer the question by considering what God says as recorded in the Bible—the God who first made Israel, gave Israel its promises and prophecies, and knows all that is in store for her.

But answering the question with "certainty" is more easily said than done. Here's why: the OT gives very specific promises to Israel; and if that were all there was, we could, without hesitation, answer yes to the question. Ezekiel, for example, shows that there will be a future temple in which there will be sacrifices.[4] And so it will be. But the NT adds a significant twist to the OT story. In sundry ways, the NT shows that many of the main OT promises are symbols that point to greater realities far more important and real than the literal promises. Ezekiel, as just said, tells us of a future temple; but Jesus indicated that he is God's true

---

[3]. David Brooks, "The Tel Aviv Cluster," *The New York Times* (January 2010). Brooks gets his statistics from Steven Pease's *The Golden Age of Jewish Achievement*.
[4]. Ezekiel 40–47

temple (then and forever), and the apostle Paul taught that each believer is a temple of the Holy Spirit.[5]

We can say that the OT—*when read literally*—nearly always gives promises of earthly blessings, but the NT, in general, understands them figuratively as pointing to heavenly realities. In the OT, the earthly realities, *on the face of it*, are the main subjects of concern: if God's people think and act righteously, then they are blessed with earthly, temporal blessings—like *long* life. In the NT, the heavenly realities are the main subject of concern: if God's people think and act righteously (which includes believing in and obeying Christ), then they are blessed with heavenly blessings—the greatest blessing being *eternal* life.

In view of the NT's focus on eternal blessed life and how to obtain it, it can appear like the earthly concerns of the OT (the "types") are completely transcended and become irrelevant, so much so that even the physical Jewish people, as such, are relativized into insignificance. This especially seems to be so in view of the fact that the Jews nearly universally rejected Jesus of Nazareth as their Messiah and killed him.

The purpose of this book is to demonstrate, through biblical evidence, that a more balanced interpretation is better. Many of the OT end-times prophecies should be understood to point to heavenly realities, but this does not preclude God from providing some degree of literal fulfillment to the blood sons of Abraham, Isaac, and Jacob. This possibility is especially permissible in the eyes of Christians if they understand that the literal fulfillment does not involve (what Christians understand as) "salvation" but only physical earthly blessings. That way, there is no conflict with what the NT teaches about how to be "saved" (as exemplified by what Peter said to the Sanhedrin: "There is no other name under heaven that has been given among men by which we must be saved"[6]).

It is obvious from the NT teaching, as we'll see later, that the Church indeed inherits promises made to Israel inasmuch as they are symbolic of higher realities. But the literal meanings of the promises made to Israel forever belong to Israel, "for," as the apostle Paul said concerning them, "the gifts and the calling of God are irrevocable."[7]

The Church replaces Israel in the fulfillment of the spiritual meanings of the promises but does not replace Israel in the fulfillment of the literal meanings of the promises.[8] Because Christian theologians

---

[5]. John 2:19; 1 Corinthians 6:19

[6]. Acts 4:12

[7]. Romans 11:29

[8]. In view of the fact that many Jews over the eons have come to Christ and that a great conversion of them is indicated in the end-times (Romans 11's olive tree metaphor),

through the ages have felt uneasy about the OT promises being fulfilled in both Israel and the Church—as if fulfillment in the former puts in question the legitimacy of Christianity—they have, during most of the history of the Church, deemed much of the OT to be an allegory of God's mission to reconcile men back to God in order that they might re-access the "tree of life" and thereby achieve eternal blessed life. But, literally speaking, there is no such thing as a real history of a people that is *nothing but* a symbol of something else. It doesn't exist—necessarily—anywhere in all of the world's (nonbiblical) literature.

An *allegory* is a tale of *fictitious* history (e.g., Bunyan's *Pilgrims Progress*, Swift's *Gulliver's Travels*, Hurnard's *Hinds' Feet on High Places*) in which the literal details in many cases represent figuratively other things that have to do with the author's real message. Now it is evidently the case, on the other hand, that God can make allegory out of human history, for he knows human history before it starts and, therefore, can arrange future events such that they can be at some point understood by finite men and woman as figurative of greater realities. But in human literature, this is impossible because men cannot plan and bring to pass future events such that they have far-future figurative meaning. No, not even the most powerful and influential of men can control the future well enough to make the future events consistently and accurately representative of greater things that really exist.

There have been a few individual people who have purposely, for a short time, made their lives an ongoing figurative expression (an allegory) of some higher truths (e.g., the prophets Ezekiel and Hosea—both with God's help), but this is impossible for a large group of people over an extended time. But once again, God can preplan things such that a nation lives out a figurative life. In this case, reality is not just contained in the allegorical fulfillment but is contained in the allegory itself, for the nation really exists, and the promises made by God to that nation really and literally exist.

Speaking very generally, the Church has tended to sweep up the literal meanings of the promises and prophecies of the OT (the "types") into figurative meanings (the "antitypes") that apply only to the Church. The purpose of this book is to untangle the lower realities from the higher ones and to demonstrate that Israel still, by and large, owns the lower ones and the Church, in the main, the higher ones. Put another way, inasmuch as the OT voices pointed toward eternal blessed life with

---

it may be more accurate to say that the Church, for salvation purposes, *displaces* Israel for a season.

God, their testimonies of present and future blessings to Israel—as the NT testifies—are indeed fulfilled by the Church; but the NT leaves the *types* largely undisturbed, such that one cannot dogmatically say that the ethnic Jews no longer are cared for by God or no longer receive his *earthly* blessings.

The NT focuses almost solely on the vastly more important theme of eternal blessed life and how to achieve it, and it so sweeps up into the Church's "inheritance" so much of what was "spiritually" promised to Israel that it can *seem* like all of what was promised to Israel is now the domain of the Church. But carefully understanding the NT shows that what the NT deems as the inheritance of the Church leaves much of what was literally and temporally promised to Israel untouched.

In a word, the literal earthly blessings of prosperity, land, etc. are always to be had by Israel because they were, at the first, promised unconditionally to Israel. The spiritual heavenly blessings of eternal blessed life that these "literal earthly blessings" symbolize are, with the advent of Christ, owned by the Church—whether Jew or Gentile—because the Church is the religious body of those who meet the conditions demanded by God for salvation, viz., faith in God *and* the Son and obedience to the heart of the Law, "love the Lord your God," and "love your neighbor as yourself."[9]

HAS THE CHURCH ALWAYS THOUGHT THAT IT REPLACES ISRAEL?

To a significant extent, yes. During the first three centuries, however, there is some evidence that the Church took the Millennium of Revelation 20 literally and seriously and thus perceived that the Lord Jesus would one day rule in person in Jerusalem. But from what little we have regarding the subject from a few Church fathers, it doesn't seem like they thought much in terms of this era being a time when God would fulfill *literally* promises made long before to the Israelites.[10] The Millennium was

---

[9.] John 14:1; Matthew 22:37–40

[10.] "In the ante-Nicene age, the relationship between Israel and the Church was expressed primarily in terms of faith in Christ and the seed of Abraham. The prevailing view among the millenarian fathers was that Israel as a nation had been set aside by God because of her idolatry and unfaithfulness in Old Testament times and her rejection and crucifixion of Christ. Consequently, according to these early fathers, God's favor was transferred to those among the Gentiles who believed in Christ. Thus as the 'new Israel,' the Church inherited the promises made to the old Israel" (Larry Crutchfield, "The Early

INTRODUCTION

simply to be a time of the Church ruling with Christ over a restored earth, and they left it at that. As far as what the record indicates, the fathers apparently didn't speculate much about the Millennium beyond its mere existence. They didn't, for example, wonder about the status of mortal Jews and Gentiles who survive the Great Tribulation and pass into the era of the Millennium—which in turn would raise the question about the relationship between these mortals and the already immortal resurrected saints in the Millennium.

In general, the fathers thought that the Jews had, by their disbelief and killing of Jesus, disqualified themselves, and so the Church replaced them. Nevertheless, the Millennium that the fathers professed is necessarily (in my view) significantly Jewish in that it will be ruled by Jesus the Jew, twelve Jewish apostles will rule with him over the twelve tribes of Israel,[11] and there will be resurrected blood descendants of Abraham from the OT and Church eras.[12] And this kingdom will be centered in Jerusalem.

Notable historians agree that the early Church considered the Millennium of Revelation 20 to be literal and future. Philip Schaff saw it this way:

> The most striking point in the eschatology of the ante-Nicene age [before the AD 325 council of Nicaea] is the prominent chiliasm, or millennarianism, that is, the belief of a visible reign of Christ in glory on earth with the risen saints for a thousand years, before the general resurrection and judgment.[13]

Church Fathers and the Foundations of Dispensationalism," *Conservative Theological Journal* 2:4 [March 1998]: 25–26).

[11.] Matthew 19:28

[12.] Justin Martyr, in his *Dialogue with Trypho* (chapter 80), especially indicated this: "And Trypho [the Jew] to this replied, 'I remarked to you sir, that you are very anxious to be safe in all respects, since you cling to the Scriptures. But tell me, do you really admit that this place, Jerusalem, shall be rebuilt; and do you expect your people to be gathered together, and made joyful with Christ and the patriarchs, and the prophets, both the men of our nation, and other proselytes who joined them before your Christ came? Or have you given way, and admitted this in order to have the appearance of worsting us in the controversies?' Then I [Justin] answered, 'I am not so miserable a fellow, Trypho, as to say one thing and think another. I admitted to you formerly, that I and many others are of this opinion, and [believe] that such will take place, as you assuredly are aware; but, on the other hand, I signified to you that many who belong to the pure and pious faith, and are true Christians, think otherwise'" (obtained at www.earlychristianwritings.com).

[13.] Phillip Schaff, *The History of the Christian Church* vol. 2 (New York: Charles Scribner, 1914), ("Ante-Nicene Christianity"), 614. Obtained at www.archive.org.

Edward Gibbon, in his history of Rome, observed this fact as well:

> The assurance of...a Millennium was carefully inculcated by a succession of fathers from Justin Martyr, and Irenaeus, who conversed with the immediate disciples of the apostles, down to Lactantius, who was preceptor to the son of Constantine. Though it might not be universally received, it appears to have been the reigning sentiment of the orthodox believers; and it seems so well adapted to the desires and apprehensions of mankind, that it must have contributed in a very considerable degree to the progress of the Christian faith.[14]

And the third to fourth century Church historian Eusebius recorded that the first to second century martyr Papias believed in "a certain millennium after the resurrection, and that there would be a corporeal reign of Christ on this very earth." Eusebius further noted that "[Papias] was the cause why most of the ecclesiastical writers, urging the antiquity of the man, were carried away by a similar opinion."[15] Note that he says *most* of the influential theologians were millenarians.

Now it should be admitted that modern dispensationalists (those who believe, among other things, that the Church does *not* replace Israel) make more of this than what is warranted. These early Church fathers believed in a literal Millennium but, in general, understood that the Church, with Christ at its head, would occupy that epoch. In other words, unlike how some dispensationalists paint them, the fathers didn't make the Millennium out to be Jewish, let alone to consist of Jewish Christ rejecters. They didn't address (at least from what we know from their extant writings or from what others said about them) the demographics of those living, yet mortal, in the Millennium vis-à-vis the demographics of the living, yet already resurrected and immortal, in the Millennium (I'll go into some detail about this tricky subject in the Revelation section near the book's end). On the other hand, unlike the allegorizing theologians who came later, the early fathers at least allowed a place for a literal Millennium and thereby tacitly allowed for some measure of *literal* fulfillment of the OT eschatological prophecies.

The attenuation of the idea of the Jews as God's uniquely chosen people begins with the NT teaching, as we will see. Jesus's prophecy

---

[14.] Edward Gibbon, *The History of the Decline and Fall of the Roman Empire* 1:534 (Philadelphia: H. T. Coates & Co., 1860). Obtained at www.hathitrust.org.

[15.] Christian F. Crusé, trans., *The Ecclesiastical History of Eusebius Pamphilus* book 3, sec. 39 (New York: Thomas N. Stanford, 1856). Obtained at www.archive.org.

regarding the destruction of the Temple and the general desolation of the Jewish nation initiated this attenuation, and Paul's words not long before that destruction confirmed it: "[The Jews] always fill up the measure of their sins. But wrath has come upon them to the utmost."[16]

When the Jews revolted against the Romans in AD 66, few, if any, of the Jewish Christians participated (according to Eusebius they fled east of the Jordan to Pella), and few, if any, were among the million or so starved to death or slain four years later when Titus and his legions conquered Jerusalem and destroyed the Temple.[17] The Jews despised the Christians as a result. Sixty years later, Simon bar Kokhba led a revolt against the Romans and killed many Jewish Christians who refused to join him. Again, the Christians fled Judea (caring more for the true Christ and his heavenly land to come) and were not among the half million or so Jews who died in the conflagration that followed—a conflagration that ended any semblance of Jewish national identity and any attachment of Jews to Jerusalem.[18]

Up till then, there was some regard for the Jews and for their evangelization. But the animosity that resulted from these events prepared the way for the replacement theology that came later. Justin Martyr, for example, believed that Christ would rule at some point for a thousand years in Jerusalem (thereby taking the description of the Millennium in Revelation literally) yet believed that the "Israel" occupying that millennial era—admittedly consisting of some Jews, like the resurrected patriarchs—would be the Church. He told Trypho the Jew: "We, who have been quarried out from the bowels of Christ, are the true Israelitic race."[19] With this replacement mindset initiated, it wasn't long until prominent theologians decided that in order to relieve any tension between the Old and New Testaments, the Old had to be to a major extent allegorized so that the spiritual meaning could fully be realized by the Church.

[16.] 1 Thessalonians 2:16

[17.] Christian F. Crusé, trans., *The Ecclesiastical History of Eusebius Pamphilus* book 3, sec. 5. Obtained at www.archive.org.

[18.] Bernard Lazare, *Antisemitism, its History and Causes* (New York: The International Library, 1903), 53–54. Dion Cassius records: "Five hundred and eighty thousand men were slain in the various raids and battles, and the number of those that perished by famine, disease and fire was past finding out. Thus nearly the whole of Judaea was made desolate" (Earnest Cary, trans., *Dio's Roman History* vol. 8 [London: William Heinemann, 1925], chap. 69. Obtained at www.archive.org).

[19.] Justin Martyr, *Dialogue with Trypho*, chap. 135. Obtained at www.earlychristianwritings.com.

The theologians felt that if the Jews were understood to fulfill the OT promises and prophecies, this would put in question the NT teaching that salvation is only possible through faith in Christ. There has been from very early on in the Church, however, the initial mistake of generally assuming that the OT is in the main about "salvation" from damnation and not so much about "salvation" from earthly hardships due to personal sin and the resultant withholding of God's earthly blessings. It is important to understand this, for it is the root problem which disallows now in many areas of the Catholic and Protestant Churches even the possibility of God yet blessing Jewish people in a homeland of their own.

We have tended in the Church to assume that the whole Bible teaches eternal salvation and the whole Bible makes many descriptions—the OT mainly metaphorically, the NT literally—of the eternal blessed state. But if this is our assumption, we will, of course, do what we can (in our interpretation of the Bible) to not have the Jews obtain salvation as inheritors of the OT promises, for they have rejected Christ, and Christ taught plainly in the NT that no one who rejects him will receive forgiveness come judgment day. So we allegorize not just the promises regarding the return of the Jews to the Edenic restored state (figurative of salvation and heaven), but we also understand the Jews themselves to figuratively represent us—that is, people who love God and who love and obey Jesus Christ.

The Church's view here is not based on common-sense exegesis but upon having the Christian doctrine of soteriology drive interpretation of the whole Bible, even if it goes against the plain OT text. But this would not have happened at the beginning (and would not happen today) if from the start there was no overblowing of the fact that the OT does, in some ways, point figuratively to greater realities beyond what is literally presented.

Early Church theologians perceived varying, yet *limited*, amounts of figurative language in the OT. But with Origen of Alexandria (second to third century), the OT became one giant allegory, and this became the standard view of the Church. To be satisfied with the simple literal first reading of OT Scripture was wrong in his view, but theologians had to search diligently for the deeper meaning:

> For those words which are written are the forms of certain mysteries, and the images of divine things. Respecting which there is one opinion throughout the whole Church, that the whole law is indeed spiritual; but that the spiritual meaning which the law conveys is not known to all, but to those only

on whom the grace of the Holy Spirit is bestowed in the word of wisdom and knowledge.[20]

To stay with the literal meaning of the OT prophecies about the restored kingdom interpreted with the assumption that Revelation's thousand-year reign of Christ is the fulfillment of it was for Origen to turn eschatology into an obsession about the carnal appetites for food, drink, and leisure.[21] This charge was to be echoed by many churchmen after that. A little later, the profoundly influential North African Bishop Augustine of Hippo charged millenarians with the same carnality although he confessed that he had once held the doctrine himself.[22]

Augustine grew up in that Roman era after Emperor Constantine when Christian faith was tolerated, and he served as the bishop at that time (just after Emperor Theodosius I) when Christianity was the mandated religion of the empire. Before this, when Christianity was still illegal and Christians persecuted to the death, theologians greatly anticipated the return of Christ, the resurrection of the saints, and the rule of Christ on earth that would at last bring all the Church's enemies under Christ's feet. But once Christianity blended with the authority of the Roman state—and once the allegorical method of Bible interpretation had become standard—prominent churchmen like Augustine began to understand the Millennium as not a literal thousand year reign of Christ in Jerusalem way in the future but as the current reign of Christ through the Church on earth.

Thus, all that the prophets said about the restored kingdom was interpreted allegorically and understood to be fulfilled in the Church age. The return from exile, for example, was the coming of many during the Church age to Christ. The nations coming to the Jews were the people of the earth submitting to Christ and his leading Christians. The feasting/drinking done in the Millennium was the endless blessings that Christians now shared through the gifts of the Holy Spirit and the resurrection guaranteed and bought by Christ. And so, the Church began to see itself no longer as the persecuted Church that Jesus said would be

---

[20] Origen, *De Principiis* preface (in Schaff's *Ante-Nicene Fathers* vol. 10). Obtained at www.ccel.org.

[21] Origen, *De Principiis* book 2 (in Schaff's *Ante-Nicene Fathers* vol. 10), chap. 2. Origen chastised Christians who looked forward to the carnal pleasures—like marriage and feasting—that are mentioned or implied in several OT prophecies of the final restoration. Obtained at www.ccel.org.

[22] Augustine, *City of God* book 10 (in Schaff's *Nicene and Post-Nicene Fathers* series 1, vol. 2), chap. 7. Obtained at www. ccel.org.

the norm up till his second coming, but the Church that John describes in chapter 20 of the Revelation; that is, the Church that reigns alongside Christ during the millennial reign.

In Augustine's mind, and in subsequent theologians' minds, Jesus had already come with power when the Romans had done God's work of punishment upon the Jews in AD 70, and now Christ ruled on David's throne at the right hand of the Father in millennial authority—a millennial authority that might last a thousand years or maybe longer.[23]

And so, about the time that the Church within the Roman empire became part of the power structure of the empire, the notion of the Church *persecuted*, waiting anxiously for the physical return of Christ and his physical reign on earth in Jerusalem, fell completely from favor and even was deemed heretical. That's the way things remained for a long time—through the middle ages and even on into the Reformation.[24]

Not long after the Reformation was underway, however, not a few theologians began to question the wisdom of the extreme allegorical method and the long-accepted view of the Revelation 20 Millennium (that it represents the current Church age), which seemed, on the face of it, to be at odds with the plain meaning of the text.[25] Still, the Protestant

---

[23.] Schaff writes: "After Christianity, contrary to all expectation, triumphed in the Roman empire, and was embraced by the Caesars themselves, the millennial reign, instead of being anxiously waited and prayed for, began to be dated either from the first appearance of Christ, or from the conversion of Constantine and the downfall of paganism, and to be regarded as realized in the glory of the dominant imperial state-Church. Augustin, who himself had formerly entertained chiliastic hopes, framed the new theory which reflected the social change, and was generally accepted. The apocalyptic millennium he understood to be the present reign of Christ in the Catholic Church, and the first resurrection, the translation of the martyrs and saints to heaven, where they participate in Christ's reign" (Schaff, *History of the Christian Church* vol. 2, 619. Obtained at www.archive.org).

[24.] Ibid. "From the time of Constantine and Augustin chiliasm took its place among the heresies, and was rejected subsequently even by the Protestant reformers as a Jewish dream."

[25.] The English theologian Joseph Mede (b. 1586), for example, said that there was a great problem that results from excessive spiritualizing: "For first, I cannot be persuaded to forsake the proper and usual importment of Scripture language, where neither the insinuation of the text itself, nor manifest tokens of allegory, nor the necessity and nature of the things spoken of (which will bear no other sense) do warrant it. For to do so, were to lose all footing of divine testimony, and instead of Scripture, to believe mine own imagination. Now the 20th of the Apocalypse, of all the narrations of that book, seems to be the most plain and simple, most free from allegory and the involution of prophetic figures" (quoted by Daniel T. Taylor, *The Reign of Christ on Earth; or, the Voice of the Church in all Ages* [Boston: S. Bagster & Sons, 1882], 170. Obtained at www.archive.org. See Taylor's

Church, by and large, remained aligned with the Catholic view, as Protestant doctrinal declarations from the sixteenth and seventeenth centuries show.

But things began to change in the mid-1800s because of the keen thinking and hard evangelistic work of an English-Irish minister named John Nelson Darby. He not only taught and widely propagated the view that God still has in store a literal thousand-year reign of Christ on earth, but that this would be the time when God would make good on all of his (literal) promises made to Israel concerning the Edenic restored state.[26]

Darby built up an awareness of what came to be known as "dispensationalism" first in his Church, the Plymouth Brethren, and then on the continent and in America through his many extended trips there. Prominent men whom Darby influenced went on to regularly hold large-scale conferences at fine resorts to promote the new doctrine, and thousands of Americans attended.

By the end of the nineteenth century, many people in England and America identified themselves as dispensationalists. So strong was the movement that several Bible colleges and seminaries were founded and funded by wealthy converts to the doctrine. And so earnest were its theologians that it caused some division in the leading American denominations—especially the Presbyterians—right at the time at century's end when these denominations needed unity in the face of the onslaught of liberalism.

THE ISRAEL RESURRECTION MIRACLE

So after a millennium-and-a-half hiatus, the Church (admittedly, a small portion of it) once again took seriously the idea of a literal thousand-year messianic kingdom in which the Jewish people and the Promised Land would necessarily be involved and thereby the literal OT promises and prophecies fulfilled. Now it seems to be more than a coincidence that as this mid-to-late-1800s reawakening was underway, there emerged

---

chapters 7 and 8 for a lengthy accounting of the leading millennialists during the seventeenth and eighteenth centuries).

[26.] See John Nelson Darby, *The Hope of the Church of God in Connection with the Destiny of the Jews and the Nations,* lectures 9–10 (London: G. Morrish, lectures given in 1840). Obtained at www.brethrenarchive.org. See also J. N. Darby, *Seven Lectures on the Second Coming of the Lord, Delivered in Toronto in 1863,* lecture 4 (Toronto: Gospel Tract Depository, 1863). Obtained at www.brethrenarchive.org.

independently an interest among European Jews in trying to regain the homeland in Palestine that they had lost so long ago.

At midcentury, several prominent German and Russian Jews decided that Jewish assimilation into their host nations was ultimately futile. Since the great gains in freedom obtained at the start of the century—somewhat a product of the European "enlightenment"—Jews had flourished especially in Germany and France and to a lesser degree in Russia, but now as they became more prominent socially and financially, anti-Semitism grew proportionally. The only solution in the eyes of some Jewish visionaries was for the Jews to find a homeland of their own. These visionaries were, ironically, not orthodox Jews, but socialist humanists who envisioned a utopian and secular socialist Jewish nation that did not have to be—as many of the initial visionaries thought—in Palestine but could be anywhere that Jews could find lasting peace. But the ideas of the first visionaries were, as the historian Walter Laqueur said, "romantic and artificial constructions suspended in mid-air."[27]

The Jewish "Zionist" movement may never have gotten off the ground if it weren't for the vision, audaciousness, and providential luck of an Austro-Hungarian Jew named Theodor Herzl. In the generation just after the original Jewish visionaries just mentioned, he, too, perceived that further attempts at assimilation would fail and that it was only a matter of time before serious persecution against Jews, even in the enlightened parts of Europe, broke out. Herzl, who was already well-known as a journalist and playwright in Vienna, wrote a short book called *Der Judenstaat*— "The Jewish State"—in which he prophesied that one day soon, the Jews would acquire a state of their own, preferably in Palestine. But if need be, it could be in some other suitable land (like Argentina). He then offered ideas about how economically and politically this might be achieved and even speculated about the societal characteristics of the state.

Herzl and his Zionist cause probably would not have gone very far if it were not for the chaplain of the British embassy in Vienna—William Hechler by name, whose theological ideas had been profoundly affected by dispensationalists—who just happened to stroll by a Vienna bookstore that had just put Herzl's book on display. The title immediately caught the eye of the chaplain, so he bought it, read it eagerly and, a few days later, knocked on Herzl's door in order to introduce himself and to offer his assistance in the cause.

Herzl, as it turned out, did not have friends substantially high up in the Austrian or German governments who he might get behind his

---

[27] Laqueur, *The History of Zionism*, 46.

cause, but Hechler told him that he had been, some years before, the tutor for the son of the Grand Duke of Baden—who was also a Christian concerned about the future of the Jews—and that he might be a stepping stone to the Kaiser.

Herzl eventually did meet Wilhelm II in Jerusalem, but the Kaiser made no commitment. More importantly, Herzl had audiences with the Ottoman Sultan in whose dominion was the Promised Land; but here, Herzl was also disappointed. Yet all was not lost. Just the fact that Herzl had courted the Kaiser and the Sultan and other heads of state for the cause of the Jews gave Herzl and his Zionist cause immense respect in the eyes of many Jews and thus set the Zionist program on a respectable permanent footing. Through these remarkable events, the ball politically started rolling for the cause of Jewish Zionism, and Herzl, as a consequence, became its revered patriarch.[28]

The major break that came next was again the seemingly providential combining of Jewish Zionist zealousness and Christian concern for the Jews that emerged as a result of the spread of dispensationalism. After Herzl died, the man who took up the Zionist banner more than any other was the Russian English Jew Chaim Weizmann.

Before and during the war, Weizmann—a chemist who developed chemicals for weapons during the war—worked indefatigably to win the English crown and English Jews to the Zionist cause. The great war dramatically changed the political landscape. As the tide turned against Germany and her Ottoman ally, it looked increasingly like the ancient Turkish empire would be substantially broken up and parceled out to the victors.

In this, Weizmann perceived an opportunity that had not been available to Herzl two decades before. So he pressed British Prime Minister David Lloyd George and Foreign Secretary Henry Balfour for some kind of government statement of sympathy for the Jews and their quest to find a home of their own. This was a long shot, but it just so happened that both George and Balfour were Christians who were both religiously sympathetic to the Zionist mission. And so despite general skepticism in the British government regarding the idea, George and

---

[28.] Ibid., chap. 3. It could be said, as Paul Merkley does, that if Chaplain Heckler had not walked by the bookstore just when the book was put on display and immediately partnered with Herzl to take him to high places, there would have been no explosion of Zionist interest, no Balfour Declaration, no Palestine Mandate, and no state of Israel. Of course, in the final analysis, without the Holocaust, Israel probably would not have risen again—at least not risen with international support (Paul C. Merkley, *The Politics of Christian Zionism 1891–1948* [London: Routledge, 1998], 8).

Balfour managed to pull off a minor miracle when they convinced their colleagues that an official statement concerning this matter would be in the crown's best interest. This statement was soon issued and became known as "The Balfour Declaration." The declaration was short and ambiguous and in no way absolutely committed the British to any particular course of action:

> His Majesty's government view with favour the establishment in Palestine of a national home for the Jewish people, and will use their best endeavours to facilitate the achievement of this object, it being clearly understood that nothing shall be done which may prejudice the civil and religious rights of existing non-Jewish communities in Palestine, or the rights and political status enjoyed by Jews in any other country.

On the other hand, it did set a precedent that would have a long-range effect yet not enough political effect sufficient to establish that "national home" without further incentives that would make the enterprise politically expedient for the powers that were to be in the future.[29]

After the war, the League of Nations directed the British to administrate the land of Palestine—the "Mandate for Palestine" of 1920—until that time when the local peoples could stand on their own. Weizmann and the Zionists hoped that the Jews who were already there would soon be offered a sovereign nation of their own, but it was not yet to be.

It was easy for the British to sympathize with the Jews regarding their desire for a "national home," but a different thing to actually bring it to pass without impinging upon "the civil and religious rights of existing non-Jewish communities"—i.e., the Palestinian Arabs—who had occupied Palestine for many centuries. And so this quandary was the overriding factor between the world wars in Mandatory Palestine. Nevertheless, during that time, not a few Jews emigrated to the Holy Land.

The titanic event that prompted the League of Nations—by that time the "United Nations"—to seriously offer the Jews their own sovereign nation and thus bring the British oversight to a close was the genocide of the Jews committed by the National Socialists (Nazis) and their allies during the Second World War. For a short time after the war, the world took pity on the Jews, and this sympathetic spirit gave Weizmann and other leading Zionists the opportunity to pressure politicians to pressure the UN to finally make the Zionist dream come

---

[29.] Ibid., chap. 4.

true. This worked, and so the UN offered the Jews and the Palestinian Arabs their own separate sovereign states within Palestine.

The Arabs refused this UN-authorized "Plan of Partition," but the Jews eagerly accepted it, and on the same day that the British Mandate expired—May 14, 1948—the Jews declared their independence and the establishment of the sovereign state of "Israel." Chaim Weizmann, who had between the wars continuously campaigned internationally for this moment, was elected the first president. Predictably, a civil war between Jews and Arabs ensued, and many of the latter were killed or pushed out of the lands that the Jews understood belonged to them according to the Partition Plan and, to some extent, according to their sense of religious tradition.[30]

Now let's take stock of all this in view of the main question of the book. Given the history of the appearance and then inevitable disappearance of smaller-scale people groups in the ancient past, and given the great slaughter of the Jews by the Romans in the two Jewish rebellions just after the time of Christ, and given the fact that the Church up till recent times had all but written off the Jews, and, finally, given the fact that the Axis side of the Second World War tried to exterminate them, I now ask: isn't it astonishing that the Jews are such a pronounced people group today and that about half of them live in their own sovereign nation of "Israel"—and not an Israel just anywhere but Israel in the Promised Land?

God promised them "seed" and land, and despite the fact that the Gentiles of the world have tried to deprive them of both, here they are, millions of them, and Israel exists once again. Is their preservation and settlement there only the work of men? Given the big picture, which includes the biblical case that we will now contemplate, I discern the hand of God in it. If this is right, then when and where the Church has denied *any* future for Jews and their Promised Land, the Church has certainly erred.

Weizmann, a secular Jew, all along admonished his fellow Zionists not to fight for their homeland but to allow the Jewish state to arise with the concurrence of the world's nations and through the providence of God.[31] That the UN Partition Plan happened, and that the Jews by

---

[30.] Ibid., chap. 11.

[31.] That Weizmann acknowledged the role of the Almighty is indicated by cables sent soon after the formation of the state of Israel and its selection of Weizmann as president: "My heartiest greetings to you and your colleagues in this great hour. May God give you strength to carry out the task which has been laid upon you and to overcome the difficulties still ahead." And again: "[I] am proud of the great honor bestowed upon me by the Provisional Council of Government of State of Israel in electing me as its first president...."

and large waited for it, is a testimony to Weizmann's wisdom and God's blessing—despite the fact that most in Israel then as well as today do not worship their Maker nor honor his Son. But that is nothing new; they were the same when they came into the Promised Land the first time.

Since the re-creation of Israel, the American Evangelical (i.e., conservative Protestant) Church's appreciation for the Jews and for Israel has grown, although, as of about twenty or thirty years ago, it seems that the zenith has passed. That zenith coincided with the zenith of American Dispensationalism, which probably peaked out just before the *Left Behind* series of books (by Tim LaHaye and Jerry Jenkins) became an international sensation. Sensationalizing the eschatology of Revelation made that science look in the eyes of many like far-out science fiction, and the leaders of the increasingly powerful secular left—along with their Hollywood and news media colleagues—mocked the Church's obsession with Antichrist and Armageddon, and criticized the Church harshly for caring more about the Jews than for the Palestinians.

Now European sympathy for the Jews and for Israel has cooled as the Holocaust memory fades, and half the American political spectrum (Democrat Party) is openly critical of Israel and the Jews there (not of Jews in general, although that might soon change).[32] Christian schools that were founded in America for the purpose of promoting dispensationalism— and did promote that doctrine for upward of a century—have cooled in their dispensationalist zeal, and the Evangelical Church—in the midst of an increasingly hostile culture and ever multiplying distractions—seems to be slipping back into the easy default view of replacement theology. For it takes (as we'll soon see) hard exegetical work to understand the nuances of God's eschatological plan, but it is easy to say that all of what God promised in the OT is spiritually fulfilled in the Church.

So as my tiny contribution to the truth (as best as I understand it), let us now consider what the Bible says about the future of Israel—both the people and the land—and prepare yourself for some "hard exegetical work"!

I dedicate my self to service of land and people in whose cause I have been privileged to labor these many years. I send to Provisional Government and people of Israel this expression of my deepest and most heartfelt affection, invoking blessing of God upon them. I pray that the struggle forced upon us will speedily end and will be succeeded by era of peace and prosperity for people of Israel" (Chaim Weizmann, *Trial and Error: The Autobiography of Chaim Weizmann*, book 2, 1918–1948 [Plunkett Lake Press, 2013], epilogue, Google eBook. Also see his closing words in the last chapter [chap. 45, "The Challenge"]).

32. Laqueur mentions the UN's recent unkindness toward Israel and says this: "If in the decades after World War II blatant anti-Semitism has gone out of fashion, anti-Zionism has become an acceptable, politically correct outlet for it" (Laqueur, *A History of Zionism*, xxiii).

THE OLD TESTAMENT CASE

INTRODUCTION

Before starting, let me say a couple words about how to read the Bible. First, I assume that the Bible, both OT and NT, is the inspired Word of God, without error. Second, I believe that God, who is love and who possesses a mind of infinite order and perfection, has given us a clear statement of his will for our lives. Third, God, who created man's conceptions of language and literature, presents his holy Word through the medium of various literary forms. Fourth, for the Spirit-filled Bible student, the use and purpose of these literary forms are perceptible although they may not be perceptible to those who do not have God's interests in mind. Fifth, in view of God's love and intense desire that "no one should perish," God does not say one thing and mean another unless he signals one way or another that he is doing so. And finally, God keeps his promises; a promise or prophecy may possess figurative meaning, but the literal meaning always has the first priority unless the Scripture plainly tells us otherwise.

God promised land to Abraham, for example, and we know from the NT that the land is figurative of heaven, but the NT doesn't say that this promise is *only* to be taken figuratively.[1] The literal promise is still real, and it still stands. On the other hand, Jesus promised the Samaritan woman at Jacob's well to give her "water" (should she have asked for it), yet we easily see from the context that the water that he was willing to offer was only meant to be taken figuratively as the "water" of eternal life;

---

[1] Hebrews 11:8–16

the literal water promised was only a literary tool, and no more. As we now proceed on into the OT, we must keep these things in mind.

IN THE BEGINNING

Berashith barah Elohim eth hashamayim vuh-eth haeretz—"In the beginning God created the heavens and the earth."[2] With this, we learn that the Bible is about God, and later we learn that God is ultimately the author of the Bible.[3] The Bible is, to a large extent, an autobiography by the One who created everything, including man. God made the "best of all possible worlds."[4] He made it a phenomenally beautiful place with an amazing multitude of creatures and finished it with the crown of the creation: man.

Man, being created in the "image and likeness" of God, was given dominion over the earth and was made to be in fellowship with God forever. Man was designed to love God and submit to God, but this could only happen in the most excellent way if man, like God, could freely choose right from wrong. Tragically for Adam and Eve (and for the entirely of mankind in their loins), they allowed the angelic creature who was already in rebellion against God—Satan—to beguile them into eating the forbidden fruit of the tree of the knowledge of good and evil. And so, the first human sin was manifested by Eve (who blamed the serpent), followed immediately by the second human sin by Adam (who blamed Eve and God), and thus the entire creation became corrupted. The first couple was then ejected from the garden of Eden into the cruel world—for "who is able [among sinful men] to stand before the LORD, this holy God?"[5] The sin of a finite man against the infinite and perfectly holy God necessarily must bring swift judgment upon an infinite crime—an infinite crime that finite man can, in no wise, atone for. He is hopelessly guilty forever.

But Yahweh, being love and not being surprised in the least by this—although no doubt being measurelessly grieved despite the foreknowledge that he had of these proceedings—at the moment of sin put into motion the process that would four millennia hence remedy that sin and allow man to be reconciled to God. The first indication of this is Genesis 3:15 where, just after pronouncing judgment upon

---

[2] Genesis 1:1
[3] "All Scripture is inspired by God" (2 Timothy 3:16).
[4] Gottfried von Leibniz
[5] 1 Samuel 6:20

Satan, God informs the evil one, "I will put enmity between you and the woman, and between your seed and her seed; He shall bruise you on the head, and you shall bruise him on the heel."

Christians call this the "proto-evangel," and rightly so, for here is the entire "good news" in embryonic form foretold: The arch evildoer of the universe, the angel Satan, will one day be dealt a death blow. This death blow will be dealt by some far future descendent of the woman (and the man) whose "heel" will be "bruised" in the process.

What is the story that the Bible tells? It is this story of the bloodline from Adam and Eve onward that passes through many generations until it arrives at the Messiah, the Savior, the "seed" of Eve of whom it was said, "The Lord has caused the iniquity of us all to fall on him," and through that "we are healed."[6] All the events and people and prophecies of the Bible are in some way or another related to this bloodline that culminates in Christ.

Directly in the bloodline (among many others) are Noah, Abraham, Judah (whence we get the name "Jew"), King David, and, of course, Joseph and Mary, the parents of Jesus. Because the "Gentiles" ever impinge upon this holy bloodline all through its history, the Bible has much to say about them too. It is very important to see here that right from the prophetic start, God promises through a prophecy that the decree "you will surely die" will one day be annulled. The "seed" of the woman speaks figuratively of Christ, but at the same time, it speaks of the real seed that would be the real historical men—Noah, Abraham, Judah, etc.—who would be manifested in the epoch between Eve and Christ. These intermediates would be no less real than Jesus.

Now this "cloud of witnesses" that is in between Adam/Eve and Christ is not a superfluous part of the story—not at all—for God has "an appointed time for everything," especially for the lives of those who were part of the story of the holy bloodline that led to Christ. In the first nine generations before the flood, we learn just how corrupt mankind can be; there was "only evil continually" and "the earth was filled with violence."[7] After the flood, we learn that God will never again kill all mankind via drowning, and this promise we can certainly take literally.[8]

Ten generations after the flood we come to the patriarch Abraham and his wife, Sarah, through whom the royal bloodline passes (with

---

[6.] Isaiah 53:5–6
[7.] Genesis 6:5, 11
[8.] Genesis 8:21, 9:8–17

Isaac and Jacob to follow).[9] Beginning with them, God begins to build a family that will soon grow to be a nation ("Israel") that will spread the hitherto almost completely unknown knowledge of the one true God Yahweh through the land of Canaan and eventually through much of the Middle Eastern world.

When the intellectual development of the Gentiles has grown substantially through the epochs of the Egyptians, Assyrians, Babylonians, Persians, Greeks, and Romans, and when the awareness of monotheism has percolated sufficiently through the world, then will come the moment that will be perfect for the first advent of the Messiah. If Jesus came before or after the perfect appointed time, everything that happened in the life of Jesus that had to happen in order for him to provide the atonement for men's sins would not have happened, and we'd still be lost in our sins. Also, if all the events that went before, and the timing of, the coming of Christ were not perfect, the Church would not have been established upon a permanent foundation, and we'd have no Church today.

So the story that the OT tells is an integral and necessary part of the history of how God reconciles man back to himself. And in this historical recounting, the Bible is very careful to record in minute detail what God commits himself to do—all along assuming that he is faithful to fulfill to the letter all that he has promised.

When God said that the seed of Eve would one day crush the head of Satan, he spoke an unconditional prophecy/promise. Regardless of whatever might happen from then on, this would surely happen. It was also an unconditional promise when God swore, at the end of the deluge, that he would never again destroy the world by a flood.[10] We know at the present date that God has done much toward the fulfillment of the former promise through Jesus's atoning work on the cross, and regarding God's faithfulness concerning the latter promise, there has been no global deluge since then. Now we come to another unconditional promise, and this one will bear significantly upon our question of the future of the Jews and Israel. This promise (actually several promises) is known as the Abrahamic Covenant.

[9.] I will always refer in this book to "Abraham" and "Sarah" even though early on in the Genesis narrative, their names were, respectively, "Abram" and "Sarai."

[10.] Isaiah 54:9

THE ABRAHAMIC COVENANT: "I WILL BLESS YOU"

While replacement theologians typically begin their description of the Abrahamic Covenant in Genesis 17, which makes it appear like the covenant is conditional due to God's demand for circumcision, it is far more appropriate to begin our consideration of this covenant at the beginning of Genesis 12 where God first speaks it. In our discussion of this, we must use wisdom and some good old-fashioned common sense, for much depends upon our interpretation of it. Here is the promise as God first gave it:

> Now the LORD said to Abram, "Go from your country and your kindred and your father's house to the land that I will show you. And I will make of you a great nation, and I will bless you and make your name great, so that you will be a blessing. I will bless those who bless you, and him who dishonors you I will curse, and in you all the families of the earth shall be blessed."[11]

Abraham left Ur of Mesopotamia as commanded,[12] sojourned for some years in Haran (upstream on the Euphrates River from Ur), then leaving his father, Terah, behind,[13] journeyed to the Land of Canaan, to the city of Shechem, where,

> The LORD appeared to Abram and said, "To your descendants I will give this land." So he built an altar there to the LORD who had appeared to him.[14]

After this, Abraham and Sarah, who were still without children, spent some time in Egypt. After returning to Canaan and just after Abraham's nephew Lot had decided—because of the growing size of his herds and flocks—to go his own way, God said to the patriarch:

[11.] Genesis 12:1–4a (ESV)

[12.] Stephan, in Acts 7:2–4, tells us that Abraham "was in Mesopotamia, before he lived in Haran," and he implies that it was in Mesopotamia (the region containing Ur) where he received the Genesis 12:1–3 promises and call to move. Genesis seems to say that the call was received in Haran (Gen. 11:31–12:5).

[13.] Terah was possibly already deceased when Abraham left Haran for Canaan, so Stephan's remark (Acts 7:4).

[14.] Genesis 12:7

> Now lift up your eyes and look from the place where you are, northward and southward and eastward and westward; for all the land which you see, I will give it to you and to your descendants forever. I will make your descendants as the dust of the earth, so that if anyone can number the dust of the earth, then your descendants can also be numbered. Arise, walk about the land through its length and breadth; for I will give it to you.[15]

And some years later, after Abraham had rescued Lot from the marauding kings of the East and had given a tenth of the spoils to the enigmatic Melchizedek (priest-king of Salem), Genesis 15 records the following:

> And [the LORD] took him outside and said, "Now look toward the heavens, and count the stars, if you are able to count them." And He said to him, "So shall your descendants be." Then he believed in the LORD; and He reckoned it to him as righteousness. And He said to him, "I am the LORD who brought you out of Ur of the Chaldeans, to give you this land to possess it."[16]

We should notice one more thing. When God gave Abraham the original promise in Ur, he said to the patriarch, "In you all the families of the earth shall be blessed." Many years later when Abraham passed the test on Mount Moriah (he was willing to slay his son Isaac as the LORD had commanded), God repeated the *Ur*-promise in this way: "In your seed all the nations of the earth shall be blessed."[17] This latter form of the wonderful promise confirms that the original "in you" means that some person or persons among Abraham's descendants would one day bless all the nations of the world.

There are several things in these promises that directly relate to the main question of this book. First, we should notice that Abraham will eventually have blood offspring ("seed") that will come from his own body. Second, his offspring will be given the land of Canaan. Third, a person or persons among Abraham's descendants will be a blessing to the world. Now looking at this *literally*, the patriarch did have children, they finally did occupy the Promised Land, and the Israelites/Jews have by and large (then and now) been a big blessing to the world. But, as the NT

---

[15]. Genesis 13:14–17
[16]. Genesis 15:5–7
[17]. Genesis 22:18

makes clear, these promises *also* have figurative ("spiritual") meanings. The true children of Abraham—*for salvation purposes*—are those who have the faith of Abraham (Gal. 3:7), the land that they inherit is eternal life with God in heaven (Heb. 11:16), and the "seed" (singular) who makes salvation possible (and thereby blesses "all nations") is Jesus of Nazareth (Gal. 3:16), who is the son of Abraham according to the flesh.

More will be said about these figurative meanings of the Abrahamic Covenant when we cover the NT data. For now, just let it be known that in the historical record of Israel in the OT, these promises, to some extent, were indeed literally fulfilled; they continue to be fulfilled today too. The NT does not deny the fact and validity of this literal fulfillment, but the *literal* fulfillment long-range importance and relevance pales in comparison to the realities of the *figurative* fulfillment—if just for the reason that temporal life in Palestine is of *relatively* little importance compared to eternal life with God.

Now is this covenant conditional or unconditional? Before answering that, let me first say how important it is to get our answer right, for an answer one way or the other has serious repercussions for our topic. If the covenant is unconditional (as nonreplacement theologians say), then it can be said (according to the covenant's literal terms) that general blessings and the land of Canaan will go to Abraham and to his physical descendants. If, on the other hand, the covenant is conditional (as replacement theologians say), then it can be said that inasmuch as Abraham's descendants did not meet the conditions of the covenant, they forfeited any right to the promised blessings and the Promised Land. If the covenant is unconditional, then we have the problem of the Jews fulfilling the covenant and the Church fulfilling it as well (more on this problem later).

If the covenant is conditional, then it is easy for Christian theologians to say that the Jews, having broken the covenant, are rejected and that the righteous people in the Church are now—according to NT teaching—the recipients of the blessings. That is, the Church replaces Israel.

In the elements of the covenant that I have shown just above, there is nothing of conditionality, with the possible exception of the initial command of God for Abraham to leave Ur, which was issued just before the promises were made. This prompts some to deem the whole Abrahamic Covenant conditional.[18] In a sense, I suppose that this is true. On the other hand, for all intents and purposes, once Abraham left Ur

---

18. Oswald T. Allis, *Prophecy and the Church* (Eugene: Wipf and Stock, 2001), 56.

and went to Canaan, the promises that God made were then sure to happen. In fact, the patriarch did leave Ur and never looked back.

So unconditional were God's promises of "seed" and the seed's future possession of Canaan that God intensely solemnized what he promised through a dread-inducing, covenant-sealing ceremony (Gen. 15) that was so one-sided in its commitment and long-range effect that God had Abraham sleep through the entire proceedings.[19] When the patriarch, who was still childless after some years after his arrival in Canaan, complained to the Lord that his slave Eliezer would end up his heir, God reassured him that he would one day have "seed" that would be as numerous as the stars of heaven. But when he continued to doubt (specifically about God's promise of land), Yahweh had Abraham kill and divide several animals into pieces, and then the following happened:

> Now when the sun was going down, a deep sleep fell upon Abram; and behold, terror and great darkness fell upon him. God said to Abram, "Know for certain that your descendants will be strangers in a land that is not theirs, where they will be enslaved and oppressed four hundred years. But I will also judge the nation whom they will serve, and afterward they will come out with many possessions. As for you, you shall go to your fathers in peace; you will be buried at a good old age. Then in the fourth generation they will return here, for the iniquity of the Amorite is not yet complete." It came about when the sun had set, that it was very dark, and behold, there appeared a smoking oven and a flaming torch which passed between these pieces. On that day the Lord made a covenant with Abram, saying, "To your descendants I have given this land, From the river of Egypt as far as the great river, the river Euphrates."[20]

First to note here is that this expression of the covenant (which is essentially a repeat of what had been previously promised) is completely *unilateral*. There was no side of the bargain that Abraham had to uphold, none at all, so God had him sleep through the ceremony.[21] In expressing the covenant, God mentions that Abraham's descendants would be "strangers in a land that is not theirs" (i.e., Egypt for four centuries), but then they would surely leave there and return to Canaan. And so

---

[19.] Perhaps all of this was only seen by Abraham in a "vision" (Gen. 15:1).
[20.] Genesis 15:12–18
[21.] Abraham might have seen and heard these things in a dream.

committed was God to give the patriarch's descendants the land "from the river of Egypt as far as the great river, the river Euphrates" (a region actually far larger than Canaan), he committed himself to the death penalty should he not bring to pass what he promised.[22] This was the meaning of God, in the physical forms of a "smoking oven" and "flaming torch," passing between the pieces of the slain animals.[23] So for the first several expressions of the covenant given by God to Abraham from when he left Ur to just before he was circumcised twenty years later in the Promised Land, there was no condition put upon Abraham or his seed that would put the fulfillment at risk. God promised it, and come what may, he would fulfill it.

The obviousness of this is why replacement theologians typically ignore or skim over the first twenty or so years of Abraham's residence in Canaan and instead focus on conditions that came later, beginning in Genesis 17 with the condition of circumcision. There, the elements of the Abrahamic Covenant are repeated to the patriarch but with this stipulation:

> God said further to Abraham, "Now as for you, you shall keep My covenant, you and your descendants after you throughout their generations. This is My covenant, which you shall keep, between Me and you and your descendants after you: every male among you shall be circumcised. And

---

[22] See Jeremiah 34:18–20 where men of Zedekiah's court who covenanted with God in a similar ceremony are condemned to death for violating the covenant.

[23] By understanding this as signifying the "death penalty" for failure of God to carry out his terms of the covenant, I am putting the book's theme at risk. For, in this case, *one could say* that when the Jews (through the Romans) killed Christ, that sealed their doom as a national people ("your house is left to you desolate"). If so, then God could no more fulfill his covenant obligations to the Jews; thus, he had to die—which he did, as the second person of the Trinity, the Son of God, who died by crucifixion. In other words, the death of Jesus both precluded the fulfillment of the covenant and at the same moment paid the covenanted price for failure to fulfill the covenant. But these horrors ironically made possible something stupendously wonderful; because the Son of God paid the covenanted nonfulfillment price, the way was opened up to fulfill the terms of the covenant as taken *figuratively*. The blood descendants of Abraham are shut off from God's temporal blessings and from the land, but Abraham's blood descendants (and Gentiles too) who put their faith in Christ are given access to eternal blessed life (in the "city which has foundations, whose architect and builder is God" [Heb. 11:10]) because the blood of Christ (shed at the crucifixion) atones for their sins. So we see that, as the Lord has told us, "God causes all things to work together for good to those who love God" (Rom. 8:28).

you shall be circumcised in the flesh of your foreskin, and it shall be the sign of the covenant between Me and you."[24]

Abraham and his sons were obligated from that point on to practice circumcision, and all male Jews have been under this obligation ever since.[25] There is no deviation from this law until its efficacy *for the purpose of salvation* is questioned by the apostle Paul.[26] There is no question about this ritual's application to sons of Abraham living under the OT dispensation, but it can certainly be asked if this obligation nullifies God's previous promises in case of failure to be circumcised. In view of how God first gave the covenant without conditions, it seems to me that God must fulfill the promises one way or another even while it seems impossible that God could fulfill them for millions of Jews over the eons who have wanted nothing to do with God. Individual sinners might be diverted away from the blessings of the covenant, but God would always have a "remnant" of Jews upon whom he could lavish his blessings (including the blessing of land), even if that remnant was pathetically small.

In other words, from the Christian perspective and in view of what may be allowable by the terms of the covenant, it is safe to say that the blessings listed in the covenant were not necessarily meant to be bestowed upon all of Abraham's descendants but only necessarily on at least some of them. But this "some" would surely be blessed, just as God had promised *unconditionally*.

Before moving on, we should also consider the fact that God not only promised these things to Abraham and put himself under a death obligation should he not keep his promises, but he also sealed the covenant with *an oath*. When Abraham, in Genesis 22, obeyed God and took the knife to sacrifice his beloved and "only" son, Yahweh, seeing that he had passed the test, provided a ram instead, then said:

> By Myself I have sworn…because you have done this thing and have not withheld your son, your only son, indeed I will greatly bless you, and I will greatly multiply your seed as the stars of the heavens and as the sand which is on the seashore; and your seed shall possess the gate of their enemies. In your

---

[24.] Genesis 17:9–11
[25.] Exodus 12:48; Joshua 5:2–9; Luke 2:21; Acts 15:1
[26.] See especially Galatians.

seed all the nations of the earth shall be blessed, because you have obeyed My voice.[27]

The land of Canaan is not mentioned here, but the reconfirmation of the covenant to Abraham's son Isaac shows that the promise of the land of Canaan was contained in the oath made to Abraham. After the Patriarch died, the LORD appeared to Isaac in Gerar (within the Promised Land) and said:

> Sojourn in this land and I will be with you and bless you, for to you and to your descendants I will give all these lands, and I will establish the oath which I swore to your father Abraham. I will multiply your descendants as the stars of heaven, and will give your descendants all these lands; and by your descendants all the nations of the earth shall be blessed; because Abraham obeyed Me and kept My charge, My commandments, My statutes and My laws.[28]

The writer of Hebrews points out that God, in covenanting with Abraham with an oath, had to swear by himself as there was no one higher to swear by.[29] He mentions this in order to encourage Christians with the knowledge that their salvation is secure, for God swore that he would bless Abraham, and, as the NT teaches, those who have the faith like Abraham are truly Abraham's "seed" *for the purposes of salvation*.[30] So there is a higher meaning of these words, and thank God that there is! Yet the literal words still stand, and as the history of the patriarchs and the later Israelites show, God worked hard to fulfill these promises literally for them. While, of course, the people of Israel experienced many hardships because of their sins, it is nevertheless the general case in OT history that the LORD blessed them in the ways that he had at first promised to

---

[27]. Genesis 22:16–18; these are the last words of God to Abraham in the Genesis narrative.

[28]. Genesis 26:3–5; that God swore to give Abraham and his descendants the land is mentioned also in Genesis 26:3; Exodus 33:1; Numbers 14:23, 32:11; and Deuteronomy 1:8. Moses, in fact, understood that Yahweh swore to all three patriarchs—Abraham, Isaac, and Jacob—in the course of speaking the covenant to them: "Remember Abraham, Isaac, and Israel, your servants, to whom you swore by your own self, and said to them, 'I will multiply your offspring as the stars of heaven, and all this land that I have promised I will give to your offspring, and they shall inherit it forever'" (Exod. 32:13).

[29]. Hebrews 6:13–18

[30]. Galatians 3:7, 29

Abraham. Once they were finally settled in the Promised Land, Joshua exulted in how faithful Yahweh had been to keep his promises and said:

> So the LORD gave Israel all the land which He had sworn to give to their fathers, and they possessed it and lived in it. And the LORD gave them rest on every side, according to all that He had sworn to their fathers, and no one of all their enemies stood before them; the LORD gave all their enemies into their hand. Not one of the good promises which the LORD had made to the house of Israel failed; all came to pass.[31]

And nearly a millennium later, the Levites, after the Babylonian exile, could point out the same thing with the tacit hope that God would continue to fulfill what he had promised to the patriarchs.

> You are the LORD, the God who chose Abram and brought him out of Ur of the Chaldeans and gave him the name Abraham. You found his heart faithful before you, and made with him the covenant to give to his offspring the land of the Canaanite, the Hittite, the Amorite, the Perizzite, the Jebusite, and the Girgashite. And you have kept your promise, for you are righteous. You multiplied their children as the stars of heaven, and you brought them into the land that you had told their fathers to enter and possess.[32]

Replacement theologians present this as evidence that the covenant, taken literally, *has been* "fulfilled," and thus, God has met his obligation and there is no further need on his part to continue to dispense blessings to the Jews.[33] The way they should look at this fulfillment mentioned by Joshua and the Levites is to instead take it as evidence that God really did mean what he said literally and that he does fulfill his promises as spoken. But to say that there is no more left for the Jews because the patriarchal covenant has been fulfilled is like saying a man has no further obligation to "love and cherish" his wife after he had met his obligation to love and cherish her on their wedding night. The marriage covenant goes on into perpetuity (or until "death do us part"); the covenant that God made

---

[31] Joshua 21:43–45
[32] Nehemiah 9:7–8, 23 (ESV)
[33] See Hank Hanegraaff, *The Apocalypse Code* (Nashville: Thomas Nelson, 2007), 178–180; Stephan Sizer, *Zion's Christian Soldiers* (Kindle eBook, 2018), chap. 4.

with Abraham likewise goes on into perpetuity, and so "fulfillment" is an ongoing process.[34]

MOSES AND THE CONQUEST: COVENANT KEPT

Now that the central covenant has been established—the Abrahamic Covenant upon which all the other subsequent large-scale biblical covenants hang—it is just a matter of God following through. This he begins to do in a big way with Moses and the brand-new nation of Israel when he leads them out of Egypt, the land of slavery, to the Promised Land, the land of freedom.

Just as God had predicted in Abraham's terrible vision in Genesis 15, the Israelites began their great Exodus after dwelling four hundred years in Egypt (that "iron furnace"[35]). If the original covenant was not meant to be taken literally, then when Moses was originally commissioned by God to lead the people out of Egypt, the "Angel of Yahweh" could have told him to go anywhere. But the covenant was obviously meant to be taken literally by Abraham and by Moses six hundred years later (and by us today). The angel in the burning bush commanded him to lead his fellow Israelites to the Promised Land, and it wasn't much later when Moses learned that their right to this land was based upon the promises previously given to the patriarchs.[36] Moses obeyed God's literal word and did his best to lead his people not just anywhere but to the land of Canaan.

By that time a portion of the covenant had already been significantly fulfilled; Jacob had originally gone to Egypt with seventy souls, but now there were upward of two million. But they were far from being righteous. When Moses first tried to get Pharaoh to let the people go, Pharaoh instead made life harder on the Hebrew slaves, and they in turn got angry at Moses. When Pharaoh finally did let them go after the ten plagues, the people wanted to give up the exodus enterprise out of fear even before the Red Sea was parted. When Moses went up to God on Mount Sinai to receive the Ten Commandments, the people (through Aaron) made the golden calf and commenced to worship it instead of the God who had by that time shown them many stupendous miracles. And after Sinai, God and Moses were ready to lead them to Canaan,

---

[34.] For indications that the Abrahamic Covenant was meant to last forever, see Genesis 13:15, 17:7, 13, 19; 1 Chronicles 16:17; Psalm 105:10; Luke 1:55.

[35.] Deuteronomy 4:20; 1 Kings 8:51

[36.] Exodus 6:8, 33:1; Numbers 32:11; Deuteronomy 1:8, 6:10, 9:5, 30:20, 34:4

but when the bad report of the spies came, the people got cold feet and refused to proceed. All this showed a severe lack of faith and trust in the LORD.

In the last two cases, God wanted to destroy these people who "despised" him, and it seems from the narrative that he would have done so had it not been for Moses's immediate Christlike intercession. In each case, Moses gave the LORD two main reasons why he should not destroy the people. First, he pointed to the solemn covenant that the LORD had made with the patriarchs. Regarding the golden calves incident, he said to Yahweh:

> Remember Abraham, Isaac, and Israel, Your servants to whom You swore by Yourself, and said to them, "I will multiply your descendants as the stars of the heavens, and all this land of which I have spoken I will give to your descendants, and they shall inherit it forever."[37]

A little later when the people refused to invade the Promised Land, Moses again grounded his intercession in the fact that God had "promised them" the land "by oath."[38] Second, Moses highlighted a disturbing consequence if God did not honor the oath: the nations, who were well aware of what he had promised Israel, would accuse Yahweh of malice, infidelity, and weakness. Moses said:

> Why, should the Egyptians speak, saying, "With evil intent He brought them out to kill them in the mountains and to destroy them from the face of the earth"?[39]

> Now if You slay this people as one man, then the nations who have heard of Your fame will say, "Because the LORD could not bring this people into the land which He promised them by oath, therefore He slaughtered them in the wilderness."[40]

In other words, Moses told Yahweh that he would get a bad name if he did not honor the covenant,[41] for the nations knew that Yahweh had solemnly promised to give Israel the land of Canaan. This is not to say that God did not intend a higher spiritual meaning when he promised

---

[37.] Exodus 32:13
[38.] Numbers 14:16
[39.] Exodus 32:12
[40.] Numbers 14:15–16
[41.] This principle is implicit in Ezekiel 20:9, 14, 22, 36:20–23.

the patriarchs the land, but the patriarchs and Moses and, according to Moses, the "nations" rightly understood the primary literal meaning of the terms of the covenant. And so, the Lord was bound to fulfill those exact terms; otherwise, the nations would know that the God of Israel was not a God of his word.

Because the Israelites refused to enter Canaan and attack its residents, God had them wander around the Sinai Peninsula wasteland for forty years. During that period the people from time to time continued to bitterly grumble, and, according to the biblical witness, they continued to worship the gods of the Egyptians, whose idols they had brought along with them. The Lord asked them (through the prophet Amos) seven centuries later:

> Did you present Me with sacrifices and grain offerings in the wilderness for forty years, O house of Israel? You also carried along Sikkuth your king and Kiyyun, your images, the star of your gods which you made for yourselves.[42]

So bad was this tendency of the Hebrews in the wilderness toward idolatry that God had to order his people to quit sacrificing to the "goat demons," after whom they had whored, and instead to bring their sacrifices to the priests at the tabernacle.[43] We should not fail to recall that just before the conquest began, Moabite and Ammonite women, through the agency of the duplicitous prophet Balaam, lured thousands of the Hebrew men into fornication and the worship of the gods of these women. So in view of all this unfaithfulness, Moses, at the end of his command tour, still had to warn the people not to relapse into idolatry when they settled down in the Promised Land:

> [B]eware not to lift up your eyes to heaven and see the sun and the moon and the stars, all the host of heaven, and be drawn away and worship them and serve them, those which the Lord your God has allotted to all the peoples under the whole heaven.[44]

[42.] Amos 5:25–26. In making his historical case of the hard-heartedness of the Jews, Stephen, on trial before the Sanhedrin, quoted the Lord's words spoken through Amos, saying (as per the NASB), "It was not to me that you offered victims and sacrifices forty years in the wilderness, was it, O house of Israel? You also took along the tabernacle of Moloch and the star of the God Rompha, the images which you made to worship" (Acts 7:42–43).

[43.] Leviticus 17:7

[44.] Deuteronomy 4:19

To top it all off, during the forty years of wilderness wandering Israel stubbornly failed to carry out the critical commandment that God had given their patriarch Abraham: "Every male among you shall be circumcised."[45] None of the males born during that period were circumcised, so God had to command that this deficiency be rectified before they entered the Promised Land.[46]

All this goes to show that God initially fulfilled the covenant that he made with the patriarchs, not because the covenant was conditional and the Israelites faithfully obeyed the terms of the covenant but because the covenant was unconditional and God faithfully carried out what he had literally promised to do. Just before Moses died, this is what the prophet knew to be so when he said to Israel:

> Know therefore today that it is the LORD your God who is crossing over before you as a consuming fire. He will destroy them and He will subdue them before you, so that you may drive them out and destroy them quickly, just as the LORD has spoken to you. Do not say in your heart when the LORD your God has driven them out before you, "Because of my righteousness the LORD has brought me in to possess this land," but it is because of the wickedness of these nations that the LORD is dispossessing them before you. It is not for your righteousness or for the uprightness of your heart that you are going to possess their land, but it is because of the wickedness of these nations that the LORD your God is driving them out before you, in order to confirm the oath which the LORD swore to your fathers, to Abraham, Isaac and Jacob. Know, then, it is not because of your righteousness that the LORD your God is giving you this good land to possess, for you are a stubborn people. Remember, do not forget how you provoked the LORD your God to wrath in the wilderness; from the day that you left the land of Egypt until you arrived at this place, you have been rebellious against the LORD.[47]

We must keep in mind that by this time, God had severely multiplied their obligations under the covenant. In the beginning, God told Abraham to leave Ur and then said that he would bless him. Abraham left as ordered and from that time on, Yahweh was committed to follow

---

[45]. Genesis 17:10
[46]. Joshua 5:1–7
[47]. Deuteronomy 9:3–7

through on the promises that he had made. Only much later (at least thirteen years) did God put the requirement of circumcision on Abraham and his offspring. And six centuries after that, God added to Abraham's offspring the obligation to follow all the laws that he gave to Moses on Mount Sinai, along with others that came during the subsequent forty years. Yet their failure to keep all of the laws heaped upon them was not necessarily grounds for being cut off completely from the patriarchal promises, for, if after a season of apostasy the people humbled themselves and repented, the LORD would quickly remember the covenant made to the patriarchs and have mercy. On Mount Sinai, God said this to Moses:

> If they confess their iniquity and the iniquity of their forefathers, in their unfaithfulness which they committed against Me, and also in their acting with hostility against Me…or if their uncircumcised heart becomes humbled so that they then make amends for their iniquity, then I will remember My covenant with Jacob, and I will remember also My covenant with Isaac, and My covenant with Abraham as well, and I will remember the land.[48]

In any case, even if things got so bad that they were evicted from the land and dispersed among the nations, the LORD said:

> Yet in spite of this, when they are in the land of their enemies, I will not reject them, nor will I so abhor them as to destroy them, breaking My covenant with them; for I am the LORD their God.[49]

After Moses died, Joshua took over the leadership of Israel. Even Moses—the humblest man on earth[50]—was not perfect: Because he publicly became angry with the LORD and the people at the waters of Maribah (and as a result did not uphold the LORD "as holy"),[51] Moses was denied entrance into the Promised Land. With this, by the way, we

---

[48.] Leviticus 26:40–42. The Law given at Mount Sinai is generally considered not to be an extension or update of the Abrahamic Covenant. This can be debated. Be that as it may, it should be understood that the Abrahamic Covenant takes precedence over the Mosaic Covenant because it is earlier and is unconditional. Even if the Israelites fail to do their part (which they did) under the Sinai covenant, God must nevertheless one way or another bless them, for, as Paul said, "They are beloved for the sake of the fathers" (Rom. 11:28).

[49.] Leviticus 26:44
[50.] Numbers 12:3
[51.] Numbers 20:2–13

can see limits to what extent the "land" promise is meant to be taken figuratively for a blessed afterlife. Moses was denied entrance, yet he is surely among the eternally blessed "living" whom Jesus had in mind when he said of the LORD, "He is not the God of the dead but of the living."[52]

With the great lawgiver passed on (God greatly honored him by burying him [Deut. 34:6]), Joshua successfully led Israel into the land that God had promised to their ancestors, killing or displacing most of the pagan peoples in the process. When the Israelites had rested from these labors, Joshua rejoiced in how Yahweh had spectacularly fulfilled his promises made to the "fathers."[53] As already pointed out, replacement theologians make much of this, believing that it shows that the patriarchal covenant was then "fulfilled," as if God was no longer under any future obligation to bestow the covenant blessings upon Israel. If that were so, we would not expect any person in the OT narrative after the time of Joshua to express thankfulness for fulfillment of the covenant in his time. But, as we've already seen, by expressing thankfulness to God for his fulfillment of the promises made to the patriarchs, the Levites—a long, long time after Joshua—provided strong evidence of the truth that the Abrahamic Covenant is an eternal covenant whose fulfillment will never be exhausted.[54]

Not only do godly men well after Joshua thank God for keeping the promises given to the patriarchs, but they also appeal to God and the patriarchal covenant so that he will show his mercy and covenantal faithfulness in the future. In other words, fulfillment of the covenant is not a one-time event, but it's something that can always be expected in the future because the covenant is unconditional and eternal. Let us briefly consider several examples of expectations of covenant fulfillment well after Joshua's time.

COVENANT FULFILLMENT AFTER THE CONQUEST

Some four centuries after the conquest, David was finally able to bring the Ark of the Covenant up to Jerusalem.[55] David was, by this time, the

---

[52.] Luke 20:38. We might recall that Moses appeared *alive* with Christ and Elijah on the Mount of Transfiguration (Matt. 17:1–8).

[53.] Joshua 21:43–45

[54.] Nehemiah 9:7–8

[55.] The Ark was taken out of the Tabernacle (at Shiloh) about seventy years before and since then had been in various hands, including the Philistines'.

king over all of the tribes of Israel and desperately wanted Yahweh to have a home in Jerusalem among his people. In view of this success, David had the Levite Asaph and his brothers compose a song of thanksgiving to the LORD. The central wonderful truth of the song is that the great things promised to Abraham, Isaac, and Jacob are what allowed Israel to flourish and will continue to allow them to flourish in the land that God promised them:

> Oh give thanks to the LORD, call upon His name; make known His deeds among the peoples. Sing to Him, sing praises to Him; speak of all His wonders.... Remember His wonderful deeds which He has done, His marvels and the judgments from His mouth.... Remember His covenant forever, the word which He commanded to a thousand generations, the covenant which He made with Abraham, and His oath to Isaac. He also confirmed it to Jacob for a statute, to Israel as an everlasting covenant, saying, "To you I will give the land of Canaan, as the portion of your inheritance."[56]

About 150 years after this (ca. 860 BC), Moab and Ammon invaded Judah with the intent of wiping out Judea and her Davidic monarchy. The godly King Jehoshaphat declared a fast, and many of his people came to the temple in Jerusalem to plead with the LORD for deliverance. There the king, before all the people, lifted up his voice with the following fervent prayer:

> O LORD, the God of our fathers, are You not God in the heavens? And are You not ruler over all the kingdoms of the nations? Power and might are in Your hand so that no one can stand against You. Did You not, O our God, drive out the inhabitants of this land before Your people Israel and give it to the descendants of Abraham Your friend forever?....Now behold, the sons of Ammon and Moab and Mount Seir, whom You did not let Israel invade when they came out of the land of Egypt (they turned aside from them and did not destroy them), see how they are rewarding us by coming to drive us out from Your possession which You have given us as an inheritance. O our God, will You not judge them? For we are powerless before this great multitude who are coming

---

[56.] 1 Chronicles 16:8, 9, 12, 15–18. See also Psalm 105.

against us; nor do we know what to do, but our eyes are on You.[57]

Here, we could almost imagine Jehoshaphat holding and pointing to a copy of the covenant, signed by God and given to Abraham, essentially reminding God of his sworn vow and, therefore, of his obligation to bless them by defeating their enemies and keeping them secure in their land. Out of compassion and covenantal faithfulness, God heard the king's prayer and responded favorably and spectacularly. On the way up to Jerusalem, the soldiers of the marauding armies turned on each other and slaughtered each other to the last man. All Judah had to do was strip the bodies and harvest the spoils.[58]

Seventy or so years later, the Aramean kings Hazael and, after him, his son Ben-Hadad savagely attacked the northern kingdom (Israel), then ruled by Jehoahaz and later his son Joash—both unfaithful kings of Israel. It looked like it might be the end of Israel, but God had mercy on them, as the chronicler tells us because of the promises made to the patriarchs:

> But the LORD was gracious to them and had compassion on them and turned to them because of His covenant with Abraham, Isaac, and Jacob, and would not destroy them or cast them from His presence until now.[59]

God was eminently forbearing with the northern kingdom "until" the nation became so corrupt that there was no remedy. Israel was slowly whittled down by the Arameans and then by the Assyrians. In ca. 723 BC, the Assyrian king Shalmaneser besieged the capitol Samaria and conquered and destroyed the city after three years. The people of Israel were either killed, enslaved, or marched off to distant parts of the Assyrian empire. But this did not mean that the original covenant was no longer in effect. It just meant that God had punished his people, just as he said he would just before he allowed them into the Promised Land the first time.[60]

Meanwhile in Judah, the prophet Micah—even though living under the wicked reign of King Ahaz of Judah (who sacrificed his own son, and refused to accept a stupendous sign when God, through Isaiah,

---

[57.] 2 Chronicles 20:6–12
[58.] 2 Chronicles 20:20–25
[59.] 2 Kings 13:23
[60.] Deuteronomy 28, but see Deuteronomy 30. Also see 2 Kings 17.

offered him one)⁶¹—appealed to the patriarchal covenant in his prophecy of a better future. Exulting in the LORD, Micah said:

> Who is a God like you, pardoning iniquity and passing over transgression for the remnant of his inheritance? He does not retain his anger forever, because he delights in steadfast love. He will again have compassion on us; he will tread our iniquities underfoot. You will cast all our sins into the depths of the sea. You will show faithfulness to Jacob and steadfast love to Abraham, as you have sworn to our fathers from the days of old.⁶²

Here we have a step in the direction of the NT. Yes, as revealed earlier in Micah, the LORD will one day rule on Mount Zion over the regathered people, and every man will sit at peace under his own vine and fig tree;⁶³ but far greater than earthly blessings will be the blessing, expressed here, of forgiveness and elimination of sin—a blessing that enables men to be reconciled to God and to have the death curse reversed.

A little over a century later, God, through Jeremiah, warned the people at the temple with these words as Judah was imploding spiritually and morally:

> Thus says the LORD of hosts, the God of Israel, "Amend your ways and your deeds, and I will let you dwell in this place. Do not trust in deceptive words, saying, 'This is the temple of the LORD, the temple of the LORD, the temple of the LORD.' For if you truly amend your ways and your deeds, if you truly practice justice between a man and his neighbor, if you do not oppress the alien, the orphan, or the widow, and do not shed innocent blood in this place, nor walk after other gods to your own ruin, then I will let you dwell in this place, in the land that I gave to your fathers forever and ever."⁶⁴

Because Jeremiah knew that the primal covenant blessings were meant to be in effect "forever and ever" and because of his compassion for his people, he pled with the LORD, asking:

---

[61]. 2 Chronicles 28:3; Isaiah 7:10–14
[62]. Micah 7:18–20
[63]. Micah 4:4, 7
[64]. Jeremiah 7:3–7

> Have You completely rejected Judah? Or have You loathed Zion? Why have You stricken us so that we are beyond healing?... Do not despise us, for Your own name's sake; do not disgrace the throne of Your glory; remember and do not annul Your covenant with us.[65]

While God refused at that low point in Judah's history to even hear the prayers of the people,[66] he would remember the covenant. God must punish them severely and cast them out of the land, just as he promised he would do if they spurned God and turned to idols.[67] And so, Yahweh said (through Jeremiah):

> Because you have not obeyed My words, behold, I will send and take all the families of the north...and I will send to Nebuchadnezzar king of Babylon, My servant, and will bring them against this land and against its inhabitants and against all these nations round about; and I will utterly destroy them and make them a horror and a hissing, and an everlasting desolation.... This whole land will be a desolation and a horror, and these nations will serve the king of Babylon seventy years.[68]

But, praise the LORD, that would not be the end of the story.

> For behold, days are coming...when I will restore the fortunes of My people Israel and Judah.... I will also bring them back to the land that I gave to their forefathers and they shall possess it.[69]

At the end of those seventy years, the prophet Daniel, who was by then in the service of the kings of Persia, praised God knowing that his covenantal faithfulness would indeed bring his people back to their homeland.

> In the first year of Darius the son of Ahasuerus, of Median descent, who was made king over the kingdom of the Chaldeans—in the first year of his reign, I, Daniel, observed

---

[65] Jeremiah 14:19, 21
[66] Jeremiah 11:14
[67] Leviticus 26:33; Deuteronomy 4:27, 28:64
[68] Jeremiah 25:8–9, 11
[69] Jeremiah 30:3

in the books the number of the years which was revealed as the word of the Lord to Jeremiah the prophet for the completion of the desolations of Jerusalem, namely, seventy years. So I gave my attention to the Lord God to seek Him by prayer and supplications, with fasting, sackcloth and ashes. I prayed to the Lord my God and confessed and said, "Alas, O Lord, the great and awesome God, who keeps His covenant and lovingkindness for those who love Him and keep His commandments, we have sinned...."[70]

Finally, we should remember once more the Levites who labored along with Nehemiah to rebuild the wall of Jerusalem about a century after the seventy years of exile were over. Daniel had praised God for what he confidently *expected God to do* at the end of the seventy years, and the Levites praised God for what *he did do* after the exile ended. The temple was rebuilt, the city partially rebuilt, the wall rebuilt, and many thousands of Jews came back. Exulting in the goodness of God, the Levites—nearly a thousand years after Joshua understood that the Lord had "fulfilled" his covenant—recognized that the Lord had again carried out what he promised to Abraham: "You have fulfilled your promise, for you are righteous."[71]

The following should now be pointed out: the Mosaic Covenant, in my view, is not radically separate from the Abrahamic Covenant. The same could be said about the so-called "Palestinian Covenant" that the Lord made with the Israelites—that pledged land and a new heart if they loved and obeyed God—as they were poised to take the Promised Land.[72] This requires some explaining.

At the first, God promised Abraham unconditionally that he would surely bless him. When God said, "I will bless you," contained therein are all the blessings that God would bestow upon Abraham and his seed forever, including uncountable progeny as well as the land of Canaan. When over two decades later, God commanded Abraham to be circumcised and the promises were repeated, we might understand this as a separate covenant from the original, but it is generally not seen that way because it is obvious that the original unconditional covenant still stands as primary; even if Abraham or his descendants fail to be circumcised, God will, one way or another, carry through with what he unconditionally promised at the first.

---

[70] Daniel 9:1–5a
[71] Nehemiah 9:8. See also Josh 23:14.
[72] Deuteronomy 29–30

The situation with the Mosaic and Palestinian covenants is essentially the same. The former adds to the previous stipulation of circumcision over six hundred additional requirements (the basis being the Decalogue), and the latter adds the requirement to love the Lord. In both of these Mosaic-era covenants, the blessings that result from obedience to the requirements are essentially those that are already contained in the blessings promised unconditionally to Abraham. And so, as these covenants make explicit, even if the people fail to do what they should do and are ejected from the land as a result, God, honoring the patriarchal promises, will bring them back at some point. In other words, there will never come a time when God will ignore and thereby violate the covenant he made with Abraham. If Israel is exiled due to great evil, the Lord will always stand ready to re-fulfill the patriarchal covenant when the people repent.[73]

Moses, knowing this, appealed not so much to God's mercy when he came off the mountain with the Ten Commandments and found the people worshipping the golden calf, but to Yahweh's obligation to bless based upon the legal primacy of the Abrahamic Covenant. God was ready to destroy them because of their failure to do what he had commanded, but Moses appealed to the promises previously made to the patriarchs.

> Remember Abraham, Isaac, and Israel, Your servants to whom You swore by Yourself, and said to them, "I will multiply your descendants as the stars of the heavens, and all this land of which I have spoken I will give to your descendants, and they shall inherit it forever."[74]

And "so," says the next verse, "the Lord changed His mind about the harm which He said He would do to His people." A little later, in the course of dictating the fine points of the Law to Moses, the Lord himself implied that the patriarchal promises would provide the legal basis for bringing the people back from exile after a season of apostasy.

> If they confess their iniquity and the iniquity of their forefathers…or if their uncircumcised heart becomes humbled so that they then make amends for their iniquity, then I will remember My covenant with Jacob, and I will

---

[73.] This is probably why God changes the hearts (Deuteronomy 30:6) of the Israelites. If he didn't, the people would never repent, and so God would find it very difficult to fulfill the promises made to Abraham. If he did fulfill them, he would be blessing eternally wicked people. The Spirit-provided new heart of the New Covenant (Jeremiah 31:31–34) precludes this dilemma from arising.

[74.] Exodus 32:13

remember also My covenant with Isaac, and My covenant with Abraham as well, and I will remember the land.... I will not reject them, nor will I so abhor them as to destroy them, breaking My covenant with them; for I am the Lord their God.[75]

Forty years later, as a part of the aforementioned Palestinian Covenant, the people were commanded to love the Lord and not have anything to do with idols. This would allow Yahweh to be their God just "as he swore to [their] fathers, to Abraham, Isaac, and Jacob."[76] Loving the Lord and obeying his commandments would enable him to keep the Israelites in their homeland. Notice the way that God concludes this covenant:

I call heaven and earth to witness against you today, that I have set before you life and death, the blessing and the curse. So choose life in order that you may live, you and your descendants, by loving the Lord your God, by obeying His voice, and by holding fast to Him; for this is your life and the length of your days, that you may live in the land which the Lord swore to your fathers, to Abraham, Isaac, and Jacob, to give them.[77]

This legal basis is repeated so often in the OT that it seems like dwelling peacefully in the Promised Land is the default situation, and the people are exiled only in the case of extreme apostasy.

So with it in mind that the original covenant given to Abraham is the most potent legal basis for God's conduct with his people—more potent than the conditional covenants that came later—let us now turn to consider many prophecies that demonstrate that the final word with God is not judgment and banishment, but grace and the maintenance of his people in their homeland.

PROPHECIES OF A LAST-DAY FINAL FULFILLMENT

Let us first review the original promises given to Abraham:

Now the Lord said to Abram, "Go forth from your country, and from your relatives and from your father's house, to the

---

[75.] Leviticus 26:40–42, 44
[76.] Deuteronomy 29:13
[77.] Deuteronomy 30:19–20

land which I will show you; and I will make you a great nation, and I will bless you, and make your name great; and so you shall be a blessing; and I will bless those who bless you, and the one who curses you I will curse. And in you all the families of the earth will be blessed."[78]

Once Abraham and family had arrived in Canaan, Gen. 12:7 records:

> The LORD appeared to Abram and said, "To your descendants I will give this land." So he built an altar there to the LORD who had appeared to him.

So far, I have spoken mainly in terms of the Promised Land and the promised progeny. Regarding the latter, when God said, "I will make you a great nation," this primarily showed Abraham that he would have, in time, countless descendants. This legacy was also prophetically foreshadowed when God changed the patriarch's name from Abram to Abraham, from "Exalted Father" to "Father of a People."[79]

In fact, he was told (Gen. 17:4) that he would be the "father of a multitude of nations," and so he was (e.g., Ishmael, Midian, Israel [Jacob], Edom [Esau], etc.). There is no question that Abraham's name has become "great"; indeed his name became great in his own day (see Gen. 23:6). And Abraham's seed has brought countless blessings to the world, especially the blessing of *the* "seed" who, two thousand years after the patriarch, took upon himself the sins of the world. Christ is also the ultimate fulfillment of God's promise that "in you, all the families of the earth will be blessed."

We have thus far considered the patriarchal promises—that they literally speak primarily of earthly blessings, which include the blessing of offspring and the blessing of the physical land of Canaan. We also learned that after the original unconditional promises were made, God put obligations upon Abraham and his descendants (mainly circumcision and later the Law given at Sinai), but these in no way nullified the unconditionality of the original covenant. Plus, we saw how once they were situated in the Promised Land, Joshua understood that the promises had been fulfilled. And not only Joshua, but godly men after his time knew that God was fulfilling his promises then or would fulfill them in the future. Yet it is important for us to know that after all of these

---

[78.] Genesis 12:1–3
[79.] Genesis 17:5

declarations of fulfillment, there was apostasy, judgment, and exile yet to come.

Now because Abraham, Isaac, Jacob, and those recipients of the promises after them were told that the blessings—including the blessing of the land—would go on *perpetually*, one might wonder, given the history of the Jews up till today, if their eternal lot is to forever be "blessed" with the ever-repeating cycle that consists of blessing, sin, apostasy, judgment, exile, repentance, and restoration. Is this what God had in mind when he gave these promises to his beloved people? Fortunately, the answer is "no."

This cycle repeatedly occurred during the 350 or so years after the conquest when "judges" ruled Israel—in fact, for a long time after.[80] But with the coming of Israel's first righteous king, King David, we begin to see in the promises made to him as well as in the songs composed by him—promises and songs regarding his "son," i.e., the Christ—the first significant indication that the day would one day come when the cycle would be broken, and a peaceful, righteous kingdom would exist from that time on.

Davidic Prophecies of the Eternal Kingdom

Before Saul became king (ca. 1050 BC), it doesn't appear like a distinct nation called "Israel" existed in the Promised Land, although during this time, the thirteen tribes occupied the areas of the land of Canaan that had been assigned to them.[81] There were no kings, for God was their king. The highest men (and one woman, Deborah) in the political order were known as "judges." They were usually charismatic military leaders who were raised up by God to call a severely backslidden people to repentance and to lead them in overcoming the enemy invaders that the LORD had unleashed as punishment.

The last of these judges was the prophet Samuel.[82] Late in his prophetical and judicial career, the people decided that they wanted a king to rule over them for they longed to be more like the kingdoms

---

[80.] During the regularly occurring periods of apostasy that occurred during the eras of the judges and the divided monarchy, Israel was not exiled (until the eighth century BC Assyrian and the seventh/sixth century Babylonian exiles), but many nations invaded Israel and made life miserable for them.

[81.] Joseph, Jacob's second to last son, received a double portion that was split between his sons Ephraim and Manasseh (Gen. 48:5). Levi became the priestly tribe and, other than being gifted forty-eight cities (Num. 35:1–8), did not receive a land allotment as the other tribes. Their "inheritance" was the LORD and his service (Num. 18:6, 20–24).

[82.] 1 Samuel 7:15–17

surrounding them.[83] The demand greatly distressed Samuel who felt disrespected and rejected as their leader. But God said something to Samuel that is vital for understanding who the eternal messianic king will ultimately be:

> Listen to the voice of the people in regard to all that they say to you, for they have not rejected you, but they have rejected Me from being king over them. Like all the deeds which they have done since the day that I brought them up from Egypt even to this day—in that they have forsaken Me and served other gods—so they are doing to you also.[84]

A little later, after Saul was anointed king, Samuel rebuked the people asking for a king:

> Even now, take your stand and see this great thing which the LORD will do before your eyes. Is it not the wheat harvest today? I will call to the LORD, that He may send thunder and rain. Then you will know and see that your wickedness is great which you have done in the sight of the LORD by asking for yourselves a king.[85]

So, "Samuel called to the LORD, and the LORD sent thunder and rain that day; and all the people greatly feared the LORD and Samuel."[86] Here, the LORD punished Israel with the destruction of their wheat harvest because they had asked for a *human* king. From Samuel's time on, there will be many prophecies about the coming king of the coming eternal kingdom. Several of these prophecies will strongly indicate that this king will be, in some mysterious way, God in the flesh.[87] Yes, he will be human also, but these prophecies will align with the principle that God plainly inferred when he spoke to Samuel regarding the people's demand for a king. The king who presides over the perpetually blessed kingdom in which the patriarchal promises are ultimately fulfilled must be God in order that "evil" does not reside in the monarchy forever.[88]

---

[83] 1 Samuel 8
[84] 1 Samuel 8:7–8
[85] 1 Samuel 12:16–17
[86] 1 Samuel 12:18
[87] Especially Isaiah 7:14, 9:6; Jeremiah 23:6; Micah 5:2; Zechariah 12:10. See also Psalm 45:6.
[88] Ezekiel 34 and 37 show that God is the shepherd of Israel and "David" is the shepherd of Israel, "and they shall all have one shepherd" (Ezek. 37:24, see also Ezek. 34:23).

THE OLD TESTAMENT CASE

Israel's first king, Saul, turned out to be a bad apple.[89] So God, while Saul was still king, had Samuel anoint David to take Saul's place. For the next several years, David was ever on the run from Saul, who wanted him dead. But Saul was killed while fighting the Philistines, and after another seven years of warring with the remnants of Saul's house, David finally became king of all the tribes.[90] After he had finally brought the Ark of the Covenant up to Jerusalem and had by and large settled the kingdom, David intended to build Yahweh a place to rest among the people, that is, to build him a glorious temple (2 Sam. 7). He told his court spiritual advisor and prophet Nathan about this desire, and the prophet replied: "Go, do all that is in your mind, for the LORD is with you."

But that very night, God indicated to Nathan that he had given concurrence too hastily and instead told him to inform the king of several important things. So Nathan immediately went back to David and spoke to the king all that the LORD commanded him.

First, David was notified that he would not be the one to build God a temple—surely, initially a great disappointment for the king. Second, he was gently informed that it was somewhat presumptuous for him to think that God needed a temple in order to be among his people. He had, after all, been close to his people in the wilderness when a tent was his dwelling. In fact, after the desert tabernacle ceased to be the center of Israelite life,[91] and long before the temple was built, God was close enough to David to raise him from poor shepherd boy to king of all Israel. Third, God said that the day would come when his people Israel would finally find permanent peace.

But the last part of Nathan's prophecy is the most amazing. Nathan, speaking on behalf of the LORD, gave the king this news:

> The LORD also declares to you that the LORD will make a house for you. "When your days are complete and you lie down with your fathers, I will raise up your descendant after you, who will come forth from you, and I will establish his

---

[89.] For the reign of Saul, his persecution of David, and David's rise to power, see 1 and 2 Samuel.

[90.] He was first anointed king of all the tribes in Hebron. Jerusalem was taken shortly thereafter and became Israel's chief city (2 Sam. 5:1–10).

[91.] After entering Canaan, the tabernacle resided first at Gilgal, then was taken up to Shiloh, then to Nob till Saul destroyed the city, then finally to Gibeon where it remained at least till the time of David's foolish census (1 Chron. 21:29). The Ark was removed from the tabernacle (1 Sam. 4) some years before David was born and was never returned.

> kingdom. He shall build a house for My name, and I will establish the throne of his kingdom forever. I will be a father to him and he will be a son to Me; when he commits iniquity, I will correct him with the rod of men and the strokes of the sons of men, but My lovingkindness shall not depart from him, as I took it away from Saul, whom I removed from before you. Your house and your kingdom shall endure before Me forever; your throne shall be established forever."[92]

David had the noble intention of building God a "house," but God tells David that he (God) will build David a house—not a house that one buys and lives in but a dynastic house that will endure forever. This dynastic house of the offspring of David will include a king who will be the one to build God a house—that is, build God a temple in which to dwell—and God "will establish the throne of his kingdom forever."

Now here, it is so very important to see that God has two persons in view in this prophecy. The first person—the "literal" fulfillment if you will—is David's son Solomon, who indeed did build God a temple. The second person—the "spiritual" fulfillment if you please—is Jesus Christ, who indeed builds up the temple, which is his body, the Church.[93] Either way, God is with his people although God's presence in the latter "temple" is far more excellent.

Solomon committed "iniquity," and God chastised him; he died early, and his kingdom was torn asunder upon his death.[94] Christ, on the other hand, was sinless; nevertheless, he was subject to the "strokes of the sons of men," and in his death, God "made Him who knew no sin to be sin on our behalf."[95] By this, he atoned for our sins, and his faithful followers are thereby reconciled back to God.

Solomon was only figuratively the "son" of God; Jesus really was, and is, the Son of God. God says that this special son of both David and God will possess a throne and kingdom that will last "forever." Solomon's throne died when he died, and even if this is taken to mean that his dynasty will go on forever, we must acknowledge the historical fact that the Solomonic dynasty ended in 586 BC when the Babylonians blinded the last Davidic/Solomonic king, Zedekiah, and led him in chains away

---

[92] 2 Samuel 7:11b–16
[93] John 2:19; 1 Corinthians 12:27
[94] 1 Kings 11–12
[95] 2 Corinthians 5:21

to Babylon, never to be heard from again.[96] No descendant of Solomon has been the king of Israel from then until now.

In addition, this son of David and of God, according to the parallel of the prophecy in 1 Chronicles 17, will not only build God's house but will also dwell in God's house forever. The LORD said through Nathan: "I will settle him in My house and in My kingdom forever, and his throne shall be established forever."[97] It is not appropriate to say that Solomon's throne was established forever nor to say that Solomon's throne was in the temple of Yahweh. But this can be said of Christ: he indeed builds God's house, not a temple "made by hands" but Christ's Church in whose hearts the Holy Spirit of God resides (remember God's rebuke of David at the beginning of the prophecy; God does not need a literal temple in order to be with and bless his people). Jesus is genetically the son of David *and* the Son of God who will one day rule over Israel forever. And he, unlike Solomon, does in fact reside in God's house forever in that he—being God—resides now and forever in the hearts of the Christian men and women that comprise his house, his "temple"—the very same house that he made for God to dwell in. Thus, we see that God's plan for a "house" ended up to be far grander than what David had in mind. The words of Paul naturally come to my mind in view of all this:

> Oh, the depth of the riches both of the wisdom and knowledge of God! How unsearchable are His judgments and unfathomable His ways! For WHO HAS KNOWN THE MIND OF THE LORD, OR WHO BECAME HIS COUNSELOR? Or WHO HAS FIRST GIVEN TO HIM THAT IT MIGHT BE PAID BACK TO HIM AGAIN? For from Him and through Him and to Him are all things. To Him be the glory forever. Amen.[98]

As regards the main theme of the book, we learn from this wonderful prophecy that Israel will one day come to a permanent place of blessings and peace and that she will have a king ruling over her who will be human (in that he is the son of David) and divine (in that he is the Son of God). Now let us turn to a couple of Davidic psalms—Psalm 2 and 110—in order to learn a little bit more about the Messiah and his earthly mission.[99]

[96.] Jeremiah 39
[97.] 1 Chronicles 17:14
[98.] Romans 11:33–36
[99.] The superscription of Psalm 110 says, "Psalm of David." Psalm 2 lacks this, but the Church in Acts 4:24–26 attributes it to David.

Psalm 2 tells us that this wonderful Son of God (first introduced in Nathan's prophecy just covered) is also called God's "anointed"—in Hebrew, *mashiach* (from which we get our word "Messiah"), and in Greek, *kristos* (from which we get our word "Christ"). Solomon's anointment with oil (by the priest Zadok and the prophet Nathan)[100] initiated his reign; Jesus's anointment with the Holy Spirit (by God) initiated his public ministry as the "king of the Jews."[101]

In Psalm 110, we further learn that the Messiah is a "priest forever after the order of Melchizedek." When Abraham returned from rescuing his nephew Lot from the four marauding kings, he gave a tenth of the booty to Melchizedek, the king of Salem (Salem was later called Jerusalem), who himself was a "priest of God Most High."[102] The NT book of Hebrews says that this mysterious Melchizedek was "without father, without mother, without genealogy, having neither beginning of days nor end of life, but made like the Son of God, he remains a priest perpetually."[103] Because the Levitical clan was in the loins of Abraham at that time, that priestly clan is subordinate to Melchizedek (says the writer of Hebrews) because that clan participated in the patriarch's submission and tithe to Melchizedek.[104] The Levitical priesthood is therefore inferior because it, unlike the Melchizedekian priesthood, had a beginning and because it submitted (within the loins of Abraham) to Melchizedek.

But Jesus's priesthood is superior in that it had no beginning like Melchizedek's and because it is now in effect "perpetually."[105] With this, however, we are getting into deep Christology, which means we are getting off the theme/question of the book. The Christ-Melchizedek connection is needless to say a baffling one.

Melchizedek, as both Testaments portray him, is certainly an enigmatic figure. All we need to know here is that the Messiah himself will mediate *perpetually* between God and human beings and that his priesthood in time will have the effect of rendering the Levitical priesthood—established by God at Mount Sinai—irrelevant for the purposes of salvation but not necessarily irrelevant for the purposes of God revealing to earthly mortal men how sinful and lost they really are. In other words, it may be the case that God will use the Law in messianic times to continue to get still-mortal human beings—especially Jewish

---

[100] 1 Kings 1:34, 45
[101] Luke 3:22; John 19:19
[102] Genesis 14:17–20
[103] Hebrews 7:3
[104] Hebrews 7:9–10
[105] See Hebrews 7.

ones—to perceive their sinfulness, for the Law only condemns because no one can follow it perfectly.[106] I will write more about the Law's possible function in the Millennium in the closing chapter.

These psalms also tell us something about where the Messiah's kingdom will be based. He will reign "from Zion" (Ps. 110:2) where Yahweh has already installed him as king (Ps. 2:6). Zion is the Jebusite fortress upon a bluff (where Melchizedek long ago reigned) that David conquered and made the chief city of Israel, i.e., Jerusalem, also called "the City of David."[107] The divided-kingdom prophets, as we'll soon see, will tell us more about the blessings that God will shower upon Mount Zion in the messianic era.

Also to be gleaned from these psalms is the fact that the Messiah will conquer all of the nations on earth and bring them into total submission. In Psalm 2, the LORD says to his Son whom he installs on "Zion":

> Ask of Me, and I will surely give the nations as Your inheritance, and the very ends of the earth as Your possession. You shall break them with a rod of iron, You shall shatter them like earthenware.[108]

And Psalm 110:5 describes what "the Lord," i.e., the Messiah, will do in the process of making the "ends of the earth" his possession:

> He will shatter kings in the day of His wrath. He will judge among the nations, He will fill them with corpses, He will shatter the chief men over a broad country.[109]

In view of these facts, God (in Psalm 2) tells the leading men of the earth what they should do:

> Now therefore, O kings, be wise; be warned, O rulers of the earth. Serve the LORD with fear, and rejoice with trembling. Kiss the Son, lest he be angry, and you perish in the way, for his wrath is quickly kindled. Blessed are all who take refuge in him.[110]

[106.] For the Law's function, see Romans 1–7.
[107.] See 2 Samuel 5:7 and 1 Kings 8:1.
[108.] Psalm 2:8–9
[109.] Psalm 110:5–6
[110.] Psalm 2:10–12 (ESV)

There may be spiritual overtones to these psalms, but what they describe literally is the Son of God campaigning—like kings of old have always done—in order to bring as much territory as possible under his authority. Unlike all previous kings, the Messiah's dominion will extend to the "very ends of the earth" (Ps. 2:8). The lesser kings of the earth will be obliged—under pain of death—to "kiss the son," that is, to honor and obey him. Other than the opening scene of Psalm 110 that pictures the Messiah at God's right hand possibly in heaven, the two psalms present a panorama of the future process of the Zion-based Messiah bringing all the nations *on earth* and their kings into submission to his righteous rule.

Before passing on to what the post-Davidic prophets had to say about the future of the Israelites and their land, let's consider briefly a few things that Solomon and two prophets after him had to say about the Messiah.

First, David's son Solomon probably wrote the Psalm that we know as Psalm 72, although it is possible that David wrote it about Solomon. In any case, it is generally acknowledged that this psalm describes not Solomon but the Messiah. Notice here the earthly description of his reign:

> May he also rule from sea to sea and from the River to the ends of the earth. Let the nomads of the desert bow before him, and his enemies lick the dust. Let the kings of Tarshish and of the islands bring presents; the kings of Sheba and Seba offer gifts. And let all kings bow down before him, all nations serve him.[111]

Here, the dominion of the Messiah is again showcased: he will rule over the whole world.

Second, the connection between the Messiah and the future eternal security of Israel is revealed by the LORD through the prophet Jeremiah:

> "Behold, the days are coming," declares the LORD, "When I will raise up for David a righteous Branch; and He will reign as king and act wisely and do justice and righteousness in the land. In His days Judah will be saved, and Israel will dwell securely; and this is His name by which He will be called, 'The LORD our righteousness.'"[112]

[111.] Psalm 72:8–11
[112.] Jeremiah 23:5–6

An amazing thing about this prophecy is the name of the "righteous Branch" of David, i.e., the Messiah: the name given to him by God is "the Lord our righteousness." In Hebrew, the name is *Yahwehzedkanu*, which is the only name given to a man in the OT that contains the entire name of God, *Yahweh*. Many names contain the shortened form of the divine name, *Yah* (e.g., Isai*ah*, Jeremi*ah*, Zedeki*ah*, Eli*jah*), but only the Messiah's special name as presented here contains all of God's name, *Yahweh* (revealed to Moses at the burning bush [Exod. 3:15])—surely a sign of his divinity. The home of this Davidic "Branch" will be "the land" where "Judah" and "Israel" will live forever in peace.

And lastly, the Lord, speaking through Ezekiel while the prophet was exiled in Babylon, tells in chapter 37 of that day when God's Spirit will animate his people, and Judah and Israel will be rejoined as "one nation in the land, on the mountains of Israel." The Lord then declares:

> My servant David will be king over them, and they will all have one shepherd; and they will walk in My ordinances and keep My statutes and observe them. They will live on the land that I gave to Jacob My servant, in which your fathers lived; and they will live on it, they, and their sons and their sons' sons, forever; and David My servant will be their prince forever. I will make a covenant of peace with them; it will be an everlasting covenant with them. And I will place them and multiply them, and will set My sanctuary in their midst forever.[113]

The name "David" here is representative of the son that will come from him who will reign forever, that is, representative of the Messiah. Chapter 37 is chock-full of God-given promises regarding the messianic times.[114]

[113.] Ezekiel 37:24–26

[114.] Lamar Cooper lists them: "There were thirteen promises made to Israel in 37:15–28 that illustrated God's determination to revive, revitalize, restore, and reestablish the nation of Israel. First, God will personally find Israel and gather the people from among the nations (v. 21a). Second, God will bring them again into their land that will be restored to them (v. 21b). Third, God will make one nation of the two that had been in the land (v. 22a). Fourth, God will set one king over the nation (v. 22b, 24a). Fifth, God will ensure the unity of the restored kingdom that will never again be divided (v. 22c). Sixth, God will ensure that the people will never again serve idols (v. 23a). Seventh, God will save them, cleanse them, and establish an intimate personal relationship with them (v. 23b). Eighth, God will enable them to walk in obedience to his law (v. 24b). Ninth, God will establish them in their land forever (v. 25). Tenth, God will establish his new covenant of peace with them (v. 26a; cf. 34:25; Jer. 31:31–34). Eleventh, God will multiply them in the land, and they will enjoy prosperity with peace (v. 26b). Twelfth, God will establish his

In the text above we have a couple that are germane to our project: Note that the "ordinances" and "statutes" to be adhered to in that day are probably those of the Mosaic Law. This possibility is made stronger by the fact that God's "sanctuary," i.e., the Temple, will again be in the midst of Israel. And note that "David" will rule over his people "forever"—a people who will forever dwell in the same land that was given to Jacob and the same land where their "fathers" dwelt.

With these Davidic-related prophecies, we see a recurring theme of the Messiah ruling his own Israelite people who dwell in the Promised Land, and ruling as well the Gentiles who are spread out even "to the ends of the earth." Now let's turn to the prophets of the divided kingdom and Babylonian exile eras. They will give us much more information about the earthly conditions that will obtain during the Millennium.

Prophecies of the Eternal Kingdom by the Major and Minor Prophets

Just before Moses died at the edge of the Promised Land, he told his people what blessings they would receive if they loved and obeyed God, and he also sternly warned them of the curses they would receive if they did not (Deut. 28). The list of curses and consequences of apostasy are hard to read now and must have been shocking to the original hearers.

Moses told them that every area of life would be cursed and degraded. There would be pestilence, consumption, fever, blight, mildew, drought, famine, boils, tumors, scabs, itching "from which you cannot be healed," and blindness. And as a result of being attacked and besieged by foreign armies, there would be starvation, cannibalism, children taken away as slaves, madness, death everywhere, and eventual exile to faraway nations for the few survivors. "Among those nations," said Moses, "you shall find no rest, and there will be no resting place for the sole of your foot; but there the LORD will give you a trembling heart, failing of eyes, and despair of soul."[115] God made good on these warnings—really, prophecies—off and on during the period of the judges and during the era of the divided monarchy that followed the reigns of David and Solomon. But they were fully fulfilled in the events surrounding the Assyrian and Babylonian exiles, and the same could be said about the

---

sanctuary among them and personally dwell there forever (vv. 26c, 27). Thirteenth, God will make Israel a testimony to the nations of his saving grace (v. 28)" (Lamar E. Cooper, *Ezekiel* vol. 17 of *The New American Commentary* [Nashville: Broadman & Holman, 1994]; Ezek. 37:24–28).

[115.] Deuteronomy 28:65

dispersions resulting from the revolts against the Romans circa AD 70 and 135. The "trembling [of] heart, failing of eyes, and despair of soul" has continued to the present day.

But Moses didn't leave it at that and said this:

> I call heaven and earth to witness against you today, that I have set before you life and death, the blessing and the curse. So choose life in order that you may live, you and your descendants, by loving the LORD your God, by obeying His voice, and by holding fast to Him; for this is your life and the length of your days, that you may live in the land which the LORD swore to your fathers, to Abraham, Isaac, and Jacob, to give them.[116]

If Israel would just repent and turn their hearts to God, God would forgive them and reestablish them in the land that he had promised to the patriarchs long before. And so, during the time of the judges, the Israelites were reestablished in their land at the end of each of the seven cycles of blessings and curses.

Four centuries after Moses, Yahweh confirmed the principle to Solomon through a dream in the night:

> If I shut up the heavens so that there is no rain, or if I command the locust to devour the land, or if I send pestilence among My people, and My people who are called by My name humble themselves and pray and seek My face and turn from their wicked ways, then I will hear from heaven, will forgive their sin and will heal their land.[117]

This principle was repeated in a multitude of ways by the prophets who ministered after Solomon on through the time of the Babylonian exile. Like Moses's presentation of the blessings was short compared to the curses, the prophets we turn to now warned far more than they encouraged. Thankfully, after we briefly touch on the warnings, the blessings that the prophets described that have to do with the final restored state of Israel will be our focus. We know that many of the blessings that the prophets prophesied of the post-exilic restoration will be those of the final eternal restored state because they did not materialize when the Jews came back from Babylon nor have they materialized since then until now. In any

---

[116.] Deuteronomy 30:19–20
[117.] 2 Chronicles 7:13–14

case, until the Jews *en masse* obtain a "circumcised heart" through the bestowal of God's Spirit, there will be no permanent restoration to an idyllic Promised Land.

Not only did the prophets foretell the near-term restoration (i.e., the return from Babylon) and the long-term final restoration, but they also foretold near-term disasters due to apostasy as well as the end-time disaster due to the massive apostasy that would be underway then. This universe-shaking judgment depicted in the OT is called by several prophets "the day of the LORD." Of this day, the prophet Isaiah said:

> Behold, the day of the LORD is coming, cruel, with fury and burning anger, to make the land a desolation; and He will exterminate its sinners from it. For the stars of heaven and their constellations will not flash forth their light; the sun will be dark when it rises and the moon will not shed its light. Thus I will punish the world for its evil and the wicked for their iniquity; I will also put an end to the arrogance of the proud and abase the haughtiness of the ruthless. I will make mortal man scarcer than pure gold and mankind than the gold of Ophir.[118]

As horrible as the destructions of Judah were by the Babylonians and the Romans, this "day of the LORD" far transcends these in awfulness and scale. Zephaniah also described this day:

> Near is the great day of the LORD, near and coming very quickly; listen, the day of the LORD! In it the warrior cries out bitterly. A day of wrath is that day, a day of trouble and distress, a day of destruction and desolation, a day of darkness and gloom, a day of clouds and thick darkness, a day of trumpet and battle cry against the fortified cities and the high corner towers.[119]

And Joel:

> Blow a trumpet in Zion, and sound an alarm on My holy mountain! Let all the inhabitants of the land tremble, for the day of the LORD is coming; surely it is near, a day of darkness and gloom, a day of clouds and thick darkness.[120]

[118.] Isaiah 13:9–12
[119.] Zephaniah 1:14–16
[120.] Joel 2:1–2a

Finally, the angelic messenger told Daniel:

> Now at that time Michael, the great prince who stands guard over the sons of your people, will arise. And there will be a time of distress such as never occurred since there was a nation until that time; and at that time your people, everyone who is found written in the book, will be rescued.[121]

Within this "time of distress"—which probably lasts several years, not just one "day"—not only are the enemies of Israel judged severely but Israel is too. Regarding the former, the LORD says through Joel:

> For behold, in those days and at that time, when I restore the fortunes of Judah and Jerusalem, I will gather all the nations and bring them down to the valley of Jehoshaphat. Then I will enter into judgment with them there on behalf of My people and My inheritance, Israel, whom they have scattered among the nations; and they have divided up My land.[122]

And regarding the judgment of Israel, the LORD says through Ezekiel:

> I will bring you out from the peoples and gather you from the lands where you are scattered, with a mighty hand and with an outstretched arm and with wrath poured out; and I will bring you into the wilderness of the peoples, and there I will enter into judgment with you face to face. As I entered into judgment with your fathers in the wilderness of the land of Egypt, so I will enter into judgment with you.... I will make you pass under the rod, and I will bring you into the bond of the covenant; and I will purge from you the rebels and those who transgress against Me; I will bring them out of the land where they sojourn, but they will not enter the land of Israel. Thus you will know that I am the LORD.[123]

In the course of this judgment (where the LORD will be seen "face-to-face"), many of the surviving people of Israel will repent when they see the Messiah's scars and realize what they did to the Messiah at his first advent. Yahweh, in the record of Zechariah, describes this repentance:

---

[121] Daniel 12:1
[122] Joel 3:1–2
[123] Ezekiel 20:34–38

> I will pour out on the house of David and on the inhabitants of Jerusalem, the Spirit of grace and of supplication, so that they will look on Me whom they have pierced; and they will mourn for Him, as one mourns for an only son, and they will weep bitterly over Him like the bitter weeping over a firstborn.[124]

But notice that this sorrow only occurs as a result of the "Spirit of grace and supplication" that God pours out upon his people. Men and women will repent and come to God and stay attached to God only if God graciously gives them some of his own Spirit.

With this, we now have the primary blessing that will allow all the blessings that God promised to be fulfilled *permanently*. For the only way that they can be permanent is if the people's devotion and obedience to God are permanent, and the only way that will happen is if the people's hearts are changed permanently by the Spirit of God.

This foundational permanent blessing of God is mentioned many times in the OT and, of course, in the NT. It is the giving of God's Spirit to his recalcitrant children who would otherwise have no hope. Only Jeremiah ties the coming of the Spirit with what he uniquely terms the "New Covenant,"[125] but other prophets mention the coming of the Spirit as well.[126] Jeremiah 31 records this blessed fact which gives men and women hope of regaining a right relationship with God and of obtaining salvation:

> "Behold, days are coming," declares the LORD, "when I will make a new covenant with the house of Israel and with the house of Judah, not like the covenant which I made with their fathers in the day I took them by the hand to bring them out of the land of Egypt, My covenant which they broke, although I was a husband to them," declares the LORD. "But this is the covenant which I will make with the house of Israel after those days," declares the LORD, "I will put My law within them and on their heart I will write it; and I will be their God, and they shall be My people."[127]

[124.] Zechariah 12:10

[125.] And of course, the new paradigm under Jesus Christ is called the "New Covenant" (Luke 22:20; 1 Cor. 11:25; 2 Cor. 3:6; Heb. 8:8, 13, 9:15, 12:24).

[126.] See Isaiah 32:15, 44:3; Ezekiel 36:27, 37:14, 39:29; Joel 2:28; Zechariah 12:10. The Messiah's possession of God's Spirit is spoken about in Isaiah 11:2, 42:1, and 61:1.

[127.] Jeremiah 31:31–34

This New Covenant supersedes not the Abrahamic Covenant—that one was unconditional and eternal—but the conditional Mosaic Covenant. Why? Because Israel "broke" that covenant, and as a result, it proved impossible for God to bless them and to keep them in the land promised to the patriarchs. They proved, through their apostasy, not to be the people of God, which is what God promised Israel at Mount Sinai that they would be to him: "I will…walk among you and be your God, and you shall be My people."[128]

So what the New Covenant promises as we see in this text is not so much different than what the Mosaic Covenant promises, except that the Old Covenant did not include the giving of God's Spirit. But the New Covenant does give the Spirit, and thus, it will be assured that the people never again break the covenant, and so God will never again retract his blessings from them. In other words, Yahweh will truly be able to say and eternally maintain what he says here in the New Covenant: "I will be their God, and they shall be My people."

Yahweh, at about the same time, described the New Covenant this way to the Jews through the Babylon-based prophet Ezekiel:

> I will give you a new heart and put a new spirit within you; and I will remove the heart of stone from your flesh and give you a heart of flesh. I will put My Spirit within you and cause you to walk in My statutes, and you will be careful to observe My ordinances. You will live in the land that I gave to your forefathers; so you will be My people, and I will be your God.[129]

The contents are essentially the same as the promise given to Jeremiah. This outpouring of the Spirit is described by the LORD in even more wonderful terms in Ezekiel 37:

> Behold, I will open your graves and cause you to come up out of your graves, My people; and I will bring you into the land of Israel. Then you will know that I am the LORD, when I have opened your graves and caused you to come up out of your graves, My people. I will put My Spirit within you and you will come to life, and I will place you on your own

---

[128.] Leviticus 26:12
[129.] Ezekiel 36:26–28

land. Then you will know that I, the LORD, have spoken and done it.[130]

The primary meaning of the resurrection described here is mainly figurative. Men and women are "born again" by God's Spirit, and their lives are vastly changed for the better. Comparatively speaking, they have gone "from death to life." But this prophecy surely must also speak of literal resurrection: when that day comes, God will truly cause the righteous dead to "come up out of [their] graves." Hallelujah![131]

Finally, notice that there is no condition put upon the people in the New Covenant. It is unconditional, and as God tells us through Jeremiah, it is eternal:

> Behold, I will gather them out of all the lands to which I have driven them in My anger, in My wrath and in great indignation; and I will bring them back to this place and make them dwell in safety. They shall be My people, and I will be their God; and I will give them one heart and one way, that they may fear Me always, for their own good and for the good of their children after them. I will make an everlasting covenant with them that I will not turn away from them, to do them good; and I will put the fear of Me in their hearts so that they will not turn away from Me.[132]

This "everlasting covenant," which is the New Covenant, will be the means by which the Abrahamic Covenant is carried through to completion. Because of the conditions added to the original unconditional Abrahamic Covenant—conditions of circumcision and the six hundred plus laws given at Mount Sinai—God could not make good *in perpetuity* on the unconditional promises made to the patriarchs. Why? Because the descendants of Abraham (or anyone else) have never, at any time, *fully* kept God's conditions. But under the New Covenant (which replaces the Mosaic Covenant but not the Abrahamic), people will have the heart necessary to do what God requires of his people.

Will all Jews in that day have this Spirit-infused "heart of flesh"? Based upon what the OT and the NT teach, in the "age to come," many Jews will be "born again" by God's Spirit and many Gentiles too. The messianic age has begun with Christ's first coming, and as we'll see

---

[130.] Ezekiel 37:12–14
[131.] Daniel 12:1–3
[132.] Jeremiah 32:37–40

later, the New Covenant coming of the Spirit began on the Pentecost after Jesus's death, resurrection, and ascension. But in "the period of restoration of all things about which God spoke by the mouth of his holy prophets"[133]—that is, when Jesus restores the kingdom to Israel at his second coming—it appears that nearly all Jews, and perhaps most Gentiles, will "know the LORD" and serve him. But more about this as the story unfolds in subsequent sections. It is enough to say that the New Covenant coming of God's Spirit ensures that the blessings promised to the patriarchs will be actualized. Now let's look at some of the blessings that the prophets told us would be manifest in that day when Israel is permanently reestablished in her homeland.

One marvelous blessing that follows from the wonderful blessing of the giving of the Spirit is the blessing of the forgiveness of sins. Through the Spirit, people will repent, then God will forgive and make good on his promises to the patriarchs. This forgiveness is mentioned by God as a vital component of the New Covenant:

> "They will not teach again, each man his neighbor and each man his brother, saying, 'Know the LORD,' for they will all know Me, from the least of them to the greatest of them," declares the LORD, "for I will forgive their iniquity, and their sin I will remember no more."[134]

And Micah describes God's final forgiveness of Israel this way:

> Who is a God like You, who pardons iniquity and passes over the rebellious act of the remnant of His possession? He does not retain His anger forever, because He delights in unchanging love. He will again have compassion on us; He will tread our iniquities under foot. Yes, You will cast all their sins into the depths of the sea. You will give truth to Jacob and unchanging love to Abraham, which You swore to our forefathers from the days of old.[135]

This is one of the primary ways that God will show "unchanging love to Abraham": the forgiveness of not only his sins but the sins of his many descendants. Because of Jesus's sacrifice on the cross, all those men and women—before and after the time of the cross—who have the faith of

---

[133]. Acts 3:21
[134]. Jeremiah 31:34
[135]. Micah 7:18–19

Abraham will have their sins thrown "into the depths of the sea." That is truly "good news" for all of us sinners!

After the great Day of the Lord, the survivors will be infused with God's Spirit and, as a result, repent. God will forgive their sins and bring his people back to the land that was promised to their fathers long before. Up till now, there have been Jewish regatherings to the Holy Land, but these "Aliyahs" ("ascents" [to Jerusalem]) have always consisted of a minority percentage of Jews scattered throughout the world.

When King Cyrus of Persia commanded the Jews to "go up" and rebuild the temple five or so centuries before Christ,[136] relatively few heeded the call. When the nation of Israel was reestablished in 1948, there was a large influx, but till this day, the majority of Jews continue to live outside Israel. But the prophets of old told us that in that final and permanent regathering, the Aliyah would be comprehensive: none of God's people would be left behind. Consider now the words of Isaiah:

> Then it will happen on that day that the Lord will again recover the second time with His hand the remnant of His people, who will remain, from Assyria, Egypt, Pathros, Cush, Elam, Shinar, Hamath, and from the islands of the sea. And He will lift up a standard for the nations and assemble the banished ones of Israel, and will gather the dispersed of Judah from the four corners of the earth.[137]

> Thus says the Lord God, "Behold, I will lift up My hand to the nations and set up My standard to the peoples; and they will bring your sons in their bosom, and your daughters will be carried on their shoulders."[138]

> "Then they shall bring all your brethren from all the nations as a grain offering to the Lord, on horses, in chariots, in litters, on mules and on camels, to My holy mountain Jerusalem," says the Lord, "just as the sons of Israel bring their grain offering in a clean vessel to the house of the Lord."[139]

[136.] 2 Chronicles 36:22–23; Ezra 1:1–4. See also the prophecy in Isaiah 44:28 where Cyrus appears to be associated with the future rebuilding of the temple and Jerusalem as well.

[137.] Isaiah 11:11–12

[138.] Isaiah 49:22

[139.] Isaiah 66:20

THE OLD TESTAMENT CASE

Notice the LORD says in this last verse that "they shall bring *all* your brethren," not just some. This fact was also foretold by the LORD through Ezekiel:

> "When I bring them back from the peoples and gather them from the lands of their enemies, then I shall be sanctified through them in the sight of the many nations. Then they will know that I am the LORD their God because I made them go into exile among the nations, and then gathered them again to their own land; and I will leave none of them there any longer. I will not hide My face from them any longer, for I will have poured out My Spirit on the house of Israel," declares the Lord GOD.[140]

God will "leave none of them," whether in "Egypt" or "Shinar" or "the islands of the sea" or New York City! All "the ransomed of the LORD will return and come with joyful shouting to Zion, with everlasting joy upon their heads. They will find gladness and joy, and sorrow and sighing will flee away."[141]

In the first part of the Ezekiel text just quoted is a blessing that should be noted—a blessing not for Israel but for God. Notice that Yahweh says, "When I bring them back...then I shall be sanctified through them in the sight of the many nations." "Be sanctified" is sometimes translated as "be made holy," or words to that effect. It is important to know what God means here because it is one of the weighty reasons why God intends to fulfill the promises made to the patriarchs. So allow me a few lines to explain a principle that I've only touched on before.

Not long after the Israelites received the Law at Mount Sinai, God intended for them to immediately go up and take the land of Canaan for themselves. Unfortunately, most of the spies that had been sent there to gather intelligence for the coming campaign brought back a bad report and thereby turned the hearts of the people against the mission, as well as against Moses.[142]

The people cried out, "Why is the LORD bringing us into this land, to fall by the sword? Our wives and our little ones will become plunder; would it not be better for us to return to Egypt?"[143] So they refused to

---
[140] Ezekiel 39:27–29
[141] Isaiah 35:10
[142] Numbers 13–14
[143] Numbers 14:3

KINDNESS TOWARDS ISRAEL

go up, and they wanted to stone Moses to death. That was the last straw for the Lord, so he prepared to destroy them all. But Moses, being the Christlike interceder that he was, pled with the Lord not to do so, giving him this reason why:

> Now if You slay this people as one man, then the nations who have heard of Your fame will say, "Because the Lord could not bring this people into the land which He promised them by oath, therefore He slaughtered them in the wilderness."[144]

In other words, Yahweh's reputation among the nations was at stake. They had heard about his "fame" and the fact that he had promised the land "by oath"—that is, to Abraham and Isaac (see Gen. 22:16–18, 26:3–5)—but if Yahweh killed all Israel, the nations would dishonor him by saying that Israel's god could not keep his promises, and thus, he is weak and evil. By pointing out this threat to Yahweh's reputation, Moses also reminded him of the patriarchal promises and, thus, his obligation to keep them. That Moses was correct in perceiving that God's reputation was at stake was verified about eight centuries later when Yahweh said, through Ezekiel, that a prime motive for bringing Israel back from exile was the maintenance of his reputation:

> "It is not for your sake, O house of Israel, that I am about to act, but for My holy name, which you have profaned among the nations where you went. I will vindicate the holiness of My great name which has been profaned among the nations, which you have profaned in their midst. Then the nations will know that I am the Lord," declares the Lord God, "when I prove Myself holy among you in their sight. For I will take you from the nations, gather you from all the lands and bring you into your own land."[145]

When Yahweh led Israel into the Promised Land the first time, he told them that it was not because of their righteousness that he did so but because he had promised this to the patriarchs. When Yahweh led Israel back to their land after the Babylonian exile, he did not do it because of their righteousness but so as to "vindicate the holiness of [his] great name." Yahweh could not leave Israel in Babylon permanently, or else it would forever be said that the god of Israel was a weak, covenant-

---

[144.] Numbers 14:15–16
[145.] Ezekiel 36:22–24

breaking god and really not God. What the Lord says here assumes the ongoing validity of the Abrahamic Covenant and his ongoing obligation to permanently fulfill it in the sight of not only Israel but the whole world.

For the whole world is—or should be—concerned about this too, for God promised Abraham not just that he and his descendants would be blessed but that through them, "all the nations of the earth [would] be blessed" as well.[146] And here we come to another big blessing revealed by the prophets. Not only would Israel be brought to the Promised Land to experience God's richest blessings but the Gentile nations would also be drawn there and be profoundly blessed. Micah, for example, said:

> And it will come about in the last days that the mountain of the house of the Lord will be established as the chief of the mountains. It will be raised above the hills, and the peoples will stream to it. Many nations will come and say, "Come and let us go up to the mountain of the Lord and to the house of the God of Jacob, that He may teach us about His ways and that we may walk in His paths."[147]

And Zechariah, just after the Babylonian exile, spoke of a yet-future final Aliyah that would involve all nations:

> "[M]any peoples and mighty nations will come to seek the Lord of hosts in Jerusalem and to entreat the favor of the Lord." Thus says the Lord of hosts, "In those days ten men from all the nations will grasp the garment of a Jew, saying, 'Let us go with you, for we have heard that God is with you.'"[148]

We, as Christians, may get the feeling here that what the prophet described is figuratively fulfilled in joyous men and women coming to Christ and finding salvation in him. There is, of course, truth in this, yet the literal words remain and must be fulfilled. It is easy to "spiritualize" what Zechariah says here; on the other hand, it is harder to do so with what he says at the end of his book (which also has to do with a universal Aliyah):

> Then it will come about that any who are left of all the nations that went against Jerusalem will go up from year to year to worship the King, the Lord of hosts, and to celebrate the Feast of Booths. And it will be that whichever of the

---

[146.] Genesis 22:18
[147.] Micah 4:1–2. See also Isaiah 2:2–3.
[148.] Zechariah 8:22–23

families of the earth does not go up to Jerusalem to worship the King, the LORD of hosts, there will be no rain on them. If the family of Egypt does not go up or enter, then no rain will fall on them; it will be the plague with which the LORD smites the nations who do not go up to celebrate the Feast of Booths. This will be the punishment of Egypt, and the punishment of all the nations who do not go up to celebrate the Feast of Booths.[149]

It looks like both Jews and Gentiles will "go up" to get a taste of what it was like for the Israelites to live in "booths" (i.e., tents) during the forty years of wilderness wanderings. If Egypt or other nations do not participate, then they will endure drought as punishment. And not only Israel but the Gentiles as well will "go up from year to year to worship the King, the LORD of hosts." It's hard to see this as anything other than a literal prophecy of what the nations are obliged to do during the Millennium. The best part about this literal prophecy is that men and women from all over the earth will go to Jerusalem in order "to worship the King, the LORD of hosts" who will be enthroned there. So the Jews and the people of the earth will go up to worship Yahweh, and they will do this, as we'll see next, in order to be intimately close to their rightful Lord and King.

The incident of the Israelites demanding their first king, as we have already seen, taught us that if anyone other than God is king over us, it is an "evil" situation. God told Samuel, who judged the Israelites at the time, "They have not rejected you, but they have rejected Me from being king over them."[150] Samuel later rebuked the people for making such a wicked demand, and God then punished them by destroying their crops.[151] The principle is evident here: only God should be the king of human beings. This is just what the prophets said would be the case when Israel is finally gathered back to her homeland, never again to leave. "At that time," says Jeremiah, "they will call Jerusalem 'the throne of the LORD,' and all the nations will be gathered to it, to Jerusalem, for the name of the LORD; nor will they walk anymore after the stubbornness of their evil heart."[152]

Ezekiel shows that Yahweh will bring his kingdom into existence—and he swears to it!

---

[149]. Zechariah 14:16–19
[150]. 1 Samuel 8:7
[151]. 1 Samuel 12
[152]. Jeremiah 3:17

"As I live," declares the Lord God, "surely with a mighty hand and with an outstretched arm and with wrath poured out, I shall be king over you. I will bring you out from the peoples and gather you from the lands where you are scattered, with a mighty hand and with an outstretched arm and with wrath poured out.... [A]nd you will know that I am the Lord, when I bring you into the land of Israel, into the land which I swore to give to your forefathers."[153]

Yahweh's most beautiful prophecy regarding his future monarchy, however, was reserved for the prophet Zephaniah who ministered during the reign of the good King Josiah not long after the northern kingdom of Israel had been destroyed by the Assyrians.

Shout for joy, O daughter of Zion! Shout in triumph, O Israel! Rejoice and exult with all your heart, O daughter of Jerusalem! The Lord has taken away His judgments against you, He has cleared away your enemies. The King of Israel, the Lord, is in your midst; you will fear disaster no more. In that day it will be said to Jerusalem: "Do not be afraid, O Zion; do not let your hands fall limp. The Lord your God is in your midst, a victorious warrior. He will exult over you with joy, He will be quiet in His love, He will rejoice over you with shouts of joy."[154]

What a day of rejoicing that will be! Yahweh will be king, and there will never again be any reason to be afraid. Ezekiel, speaking the words of the Lord, foretold the same:

For thus says the Lord God, "Behold, I Myself will search for My sheep and seek them out. As a shepherd cares for his herd in the day when he is among his scattered sheep, so I will care for My sheep and will deliver them from all the places to which they were scattered on a cloudy and gloomy day. I will bring them out from the peoples and gather them from the countries and bring them to their own land; and I will feed them on the mountains of Israel, by the streams, and in all the inhabited places of the land.... They will no longer be a prey to the nations, and the beasts of the earth

---

[153]. Ezekiel 20:33-34, 42
[154]. Zephaniah 3:14–17

will not devour them; but they will live securely, and no one will make them afraid."[155]

Daniel, during the Babylonian exile, also told of God's coming kingdom:

> [T]he God of heaven will set up a kingdom which will never be destroyed, and that kingdom will not be left for another people; it will crush and put an end to all…kingdoms, but it will itself endure forever.[156]

King Nebuchadnezzar, once his sanity had been restored and his heart humbled, testified to the same about the God of Israel (as recorded by Daniel): "His dominion is an everlasting dominion, And His kingdom endures from generation to generation."[157] And the Persian King Darius, according to Daniel, made a similar declaration when he saw how "the God of Daniel" had protected the prophet in the lion's den:

> I make a decree that in all the dominion of my kingdom men are to fear and tremble before the God of Daniel; for He is the living God and enduring forever, and His kingdom is one which will not be destroyed, and His dominion will be forever.[158]

Finally, Zechariah sums it up in this way: "And the LORD will be king over all the earth; in that day the LORD will be the only one, and His name the only one."[159]

Now at this point the question may arise in the mind of readers: "It's wonderful that God is king, but what about the Messiah—isn't he supposed to be the king of Israel?" Indeed, a very good question. And with this question, we come to the next tremendous blessing promised by the prophets: the Messiah will come, and he will be the permanent king of Israel—praise the LORD from whom all blessings flow! Before we consider how Yahweh can be king and the Messiah can be king, let us first look at some prophetic verses that have to do with the latter. In the name of brevity, I will highlight only a small portion of what the

---

[155.] Ezekiel 34:11–13, 28
[156.] Daniel 2:44
[157.] Daniel 4:34
[158.] Daniel 6:26
[159.] Zechariah 14:9

prophets said concerning the Messiah. But in what we consider, we will see a mysterious identity between God and the Messiah.

First of all, Micah showed us that the coming "ruler of Israel" was to be born in the lowly town of Bethlehem:

> But as for you, Bethlehem Ephrathah, too little to be among the clans of Judah, from you One will go forth for Me to be ruler in Israel. His goings forth are from long ago, from the days of eternity. Therefore He will give them up until the time when she who is in labor has borne a child. Then the remainder of His brethren will return to the sons of Israel. And He will arise and shepherd His flock in the strength of the LORD, in the majesty of the name of the LORD His God. And they will remain, because at that time He will be great to the ends of the earth.[160]

Worthy of note here is the fact that he will be the "ruler of Israel" and, to put it another way, the "shepherd" of Israel. Micah does not say how long this Shepherd will remain, but he does say that before the Shepherd's birth, he had already existed "from long ago, from the days of eternity." It would seem that the only living being that can exist "from the days of eternity" is God. The indication of the Messiah's divinity given here by Micah is made much more explicit by his contemporary, Isaiah, who also spoke of the Messiah's birth:

> For a child will be born to us, a son will be given to us; and the government will rest on His shoulders; and His name will be called Wonderful Counselor, Mighty God, Eternal Father, Prince of Peace. There will be no end to the increase of His government or of peace, on the throne of David and over his kingdom, to establish it and to uphold it with justice and righteousness from then on and forevermore. The zeal of the LORD of hosts will accomplish this.[161]

Whereas Micah told us of the Messiah's past eternity, Isaiah tells us of his future eternity: "There will be no end to the increase of his government" and he will establish the throne of David "from then on and forevermore."

---

[160]. Micah 5:2–4
[161]. Isaiah 9:6–7

Now recall that God said through Ezekiel (Ezekiel 34:12) that he would be like a "shepherd" to Israel when he brings them back to their land. Yet the prophet has God saying a little further down in chapter 34 that "David," i.e., the Messiah, will be their Shepherd:

> "I will feed My flock and I will lead them to rest," declares the Lord GOD.... "[T]herefore, I will deliver My flock, and they will no longer be a prey; and I will judge between one sheep and another. Then I will set over them one shepherd, My servant David, and he will feed them; he will feed them himself and be their shepherd. And I, the LORD, will be their God, and My servant David will be prince among them; I the LORD have spoken."[162]

Yahweh will be their Shepherd, and the Messiah will be their Shepherd, yet Israel will only have "one shepherd" over them. I take this to be a hint that both God and the Messiah are mysteriously combined in a single Shepherd.

A similar hint can also be discerned in the book of Daniel. Already quoted above are the Spirit-inspired assertions by Daniel, Nebuchadnezzar, and Darius that the day will come when God will establish an earthly kingdom that will smash all previous kingdoms and last forever, never to be destroyed. With this in mind, ponder what Daniel says about the Messiah who appears before God in the course of God (the "Ancient of Days") committing the final world human ruler (the "little horn") to eternal flames:

> I kept looking in the night visions, and behold, with the clouds of heaven One like a Son of Man was coming, and He came up to the Ancient of Days and was presented before Him. And to Him was given dominion, glory and a kingdom, that all the peoples, nations and men of every language might serve Him. His dominion is an everlasting dominion which will not pass away; and His kingdom is one which will not be destroyed.[163]

Not only will God have a kingdom that will be eternal and indestructible, but the Messiah will also rule over a kingdom that is "everlasting" and "will not be destroyed." The only difference is that God sets up his own kingdom (Daniel 2:44: "The God of heaven will set up a kingdom"),

---

[162.] Ezekiel 34:15, 22–24
[163.] Daniel 7:13–14

but the Messiah's kingdom is set up for him ("and to him was given dominion"). The kingdom of the Messiah is "given" to him, obviously, by God. Will there then be two kingdoms on earth, one God's and another the Messiah's? Perhaps the answer can be inferred by considering what these three prophets said:

> Ezekiel: "My servant David will be king over them, and they will all have one shepherd; and they will walk in My ordinances and keep My statutes and observe them."[164]
>
> Zechariah: "And the LORD will be king over all the earth; in that day the LORD will be the only one, and His name the only one."[165]
>
> David: "The LORD is my shepherd, I shall not want."[166]

David will be king, and Yahweh will be king, but there will only be "one shepherd," i.e., king, over them. Inferred is that there will be one kingdom in the eschaton and the king will be the LORD who is also the Messiah—admittedly an identity that goes beyond human reason.

But considering what else the OT says about the Messiah and, of course, what the NT teaches about Christ's divinity, this is a mystery that we must accept, for "who has known the mind of the Lord?"[167] And ponder what God said through Isaiah: "As the heavens are higher than the earth, so are My ways higher than your ways and My thoughts than your thoughts."[168] All we can do is fall on our faces and cry out like Isaiah did when he saw the glory of the Lord Christ: "My eyes have seen the King, the LORD of hosts."[169] This messianic blend of God and man is certainly difficult to fathom; but one great benefit of perceiving this identity is that it satisfies the principle that says that God is our only rightful eternal king.

Now let's carry on and look briefly at several other features of the Millennial Kingdom that the prophets told us about. In that day, we who are true followers of God and his Messiah will be, in a spiritual sense, married to God. His love for us and our love for him will be that

---

[164]. Ezekiel 37:24
[165]. Zechariah 14:9
[166]. Psalm 23:1
[167]. Romans 11:34
[168]. Isaiah 55:9
[169]. Isaiah 6:5. Speaking of Jesus, the apostle John said that Isaiah "saw His glory." John most likely had Isaiah 6 in mind when he said this (John 12:41).

profound. Even in view of all our past sinfulness, God will forgive us and take us unto himself as his own. He says through Hosea:

> "And it shall be, in that day," says the LORD, "that you will call Me 'My Husband,' and no longer call Me 'My Master,' I will betroth you to Me forever; yes, I will betroth you to Me in righteousness and justice, in lovingkindness and mercy; I will betroth you to Me in faithfulness, and you shall know the LORD."[170]

And Isaiah testifies: "As the bridegroom rejoices over the bride, so your God will rejoice over you."[171] This subject is too mysterious and hallowed to comment on, so I will pass on to other features of the Millennium.

God will establish his throne and worldwide headquarters on Mount Zion, that is, Jerusalem. "Thus says the LORD of hosts" through the post-exilic prophet Zechariah:

> "I am exceedingly jealous for Zion, yes, with great wrath I am jealous for her." Thus says the LORD, "I will return to Zion and will dwell in the midst of Jerusalem. Then Jerusalem will be called the City of Truth, and the mountain of the LORD of hosts will be called the Holy Mountain."[172]

From that day forward, Ezekiel tells us that the name of the city will be *Yahwehshama*, "The LORD is There."[173]

And there, the Millennial Temple will be built. Among the first group to return from the Babylonian exile were the prophets Haggai and Zechariah. As a humble temple was being rebuilt then out of the Jerusalem rubble—so humble that it caused some men to cry who had seen the First Temple's glory[174]—these prophets spoke of a time when a truly glorious and permanent temple would be made. Haggai encouraged the Second Temple impoverished workers with these words of God:

> For thus says the LORD of hosts, "Once more in a little while, I am going to shake the heavens and the earth, the sea also and the dry land. I will shake all the nations; and they will come with the wealth of all nations, and I will fill this house

---

[170.] Hosea 2:16, 19–20
[171.] Isaiah 62:5
[172.] Zechariah 8:1–3
[173.] Ezekiel 48:35
[174.] Ezra 3:12; Haggai 2:3

with glory," says the LORD of hosts. "The silver is Mine and the gold is Mine," declares the LORD of hosts. "The latter glory of this house will be greater than the former," says the LORD of hosts, "and in this place I will give peace," declares the LORD of hosts.[175]

Zechariah, about the same time, spoke these amazing words of God about Joshua, who was then High Priest:

Take silver and gold, make an ornate crown and set it on the head of Joshua the son of Jehozadak, the high priest. Then say to him, "Thus says the LORD of hosts, 'Behold, a man whose name is Branch, for He will branch out from where He is; and He will build the temple of the LORD. Yes, it is He who will build the temple of the LORD, and He who will bear the honor and sit and rule on His throne. Thus, He will be a priest on His throne, and the counsel of peace will be between the two offices.'"[176]

The High Priest Joshua indeed played an important part in the building of the Second Temple, but this prophecy is pregnant with messianic and messianic-era meaning. First, we are initially alerted to this by Joshua being called the "Branch," which is an undisputable OT messianic title.[177] Second, Joshua, the High Priest, is crowned as king, and he will "sit and rule on his throne." Nothing from the Bible or history gives any indication that this Joshua became a priest-king; on the other hand, the NT shows us that Jesus is our eternal king as well as priest who always "lives to make intercession for [us]."[178] And lastly, here we have the only OT prophetic allusion to the Messiah's name that he would be given at his birth five centuries later: "Joshua" and "Jesus" in Hebrew (*yehoshua* [sometimes *yeshua*], meaning "the LORD saves") are the same name! This "Joshua" will indeed build his Church and, in the Millennium, build his temple, and from that time on, there will truly be "peace…between the two offices" of priest and king.

[175.] Haggai 2:6–9
[176.] Zechariah 6:11–13
[177.] The Messiah as "Branch" or "Sprout" or "Root" is mentioned in Isaiah 4 and 11, Jeremiah 23 and 33, as well as Zechariah 3 and 6. See my book, *The Divine Messiah*, section entitled "The Messiah is the 'Branch,'" in chapter 2.
[178.] Hebrews 7:25

KINDNESS TOWARDS ISRAEL

In that day when the son of David rules on his throne forever, the enemies of Israel will be no more. So said the Lord to David through the prophet Nathan:

> I will also appoint a place for My people Israel and will plant them, that they may live in their own place and not be disturbed again, nor will the wicked afflict them any more as formerly, even from the day that I commanded judges to be over My people Israel; and I will give you rest from all your enemies.[179]

When this day comes, all of the weapons of war, says Micah, will be turned into farm implements:

> And [the Lord] will judge between many peoples and render decisions for mighty, distant nations. Then they will hammer their swords into plowshares and their spears into pruning hooks; nation will not lift up sword against nation, and never again will they train for war.[180]

And according to Isaiah, even the animals will then be at peace with one another:

> [T]he wolf will dwell with the lamb, and the leopard will lie down with the young goat, and the calf and the young lion and the fatling together; and a little boy will lead them. Also the cow and the bear will graze, their young will lie down together, and the lion will eat straw like the ox. The nursing child will play by the hole of the cobra, and the weaned child will put his hand on the viper's den. They will not hurt or destroy in all My holy mountain, for the earth will be full of the knowledge of the Lord as the waters cover the sea.[181]

No enemies, no killing machinery, and no savage animals. Because of that and probably because of human genome changes that God will make, men and women will then live a very long time. Regarding this, the Lord says:

[179.] 2 Samuel 7:10–11a
[180.] Micah 4:3
[181.] Isaiah 11:6–9

> I will also rejoice in Jerusalem and be glad in My people; and there will no longer be heard in her the voice of weeping and the sound of crying. No longer will there be in it an infant who lives but a few days, or an old man who does not live out his days; for the youth will die at the age of one hundred and the one who does not reach the age of one hundred will be thought accursed.[182]

But far more wonderful than that, God said that the day would finally come when death would suffer death and be no more:

> For the LORD of hosts will reign on Mount Zion and in Jerusalem, and His glory will be before His elders.... The LORD of hosts will prepare a lavish banquet for all peoples on this mountain; a banquet of aged wine, choice pieces with marrow, and refined, aged wine. And on this mountain He will swallow up the covering which is over all peoples, even the veil which is stretched over all nations. He will swallow up death for all time, and the Lord GOD will wipe tears away from all faces, and He will remove the reproach of His people from all the earth; for the LORD has spoken.[183]

Here we have one of only two *overt* OT statements—the other being Daniel 12:1–3—that plainly show that mortal men and women will eventually be immortal. Hallelujah![184] "Let us rejoice and be glad in His salvation!"[185]

Now in view of this, you might be wondering if people in the Millennium will live a long time *or* live forever. It seems like it has to be one or the other. I believe, however, that it is *both*. The Millennium will simply be a continuation of earth history, and so, earthly mortal people surviving the "Day of the LORD" (also called the "Tribulation" in the NT) will enter the Millennium, have mortal children, and eventually suffer mortal death. When the Messiah returns to earth a second time at the beginning of the Millennium, he will bring with him his saints who have shortly before been resurrected. These saints—who consist of many Jews and even more Gentiles—will assist Jesus in administering his

---

[182] Isaiah 65:19–20

[183] Isaiah 24:23b, 25:6–8

[184] Many would understand Job 19:25–27 as plainly revealing that there is blessed life after death for those who, like Job, love God.

[185] Isaiah 25:9

Millennial Kingdom, and they, being immortal, will live on indefinitely. But more about this later when we get to the section near the end of the book about John's Revelation.

The prophets also tell us that the land of Israel—for that matter, the whole earth—will be lush and beautiful beyond compare. Isaiah, for example, says this:

> Indeed, the Lord will comfort Zion; He will comfort all her waste places. And her wilderness He will make like Eden, and her desert like the garden of the Lord; joy and gladness will be found in her, thanksgiving and sound of a melody.[186]

Thus, declares Jeremiah, there will be no lack of food and drink:

> They will come and shout for joy on the height of Zion, and they will be radiant over the bounty of the Lord—over the grain and the new wine and the oil, and over the young of the flock and the herd; and their life will be like a watered garden, and they will never languish again.[187]

The abundance of Israel will be stupendous enough, but there will be even more, says God through Isaiah, as the whole world brings its wealth and produce up to Zion:

> Lift up your eyes round about and see; they all gather together, they come to you. Your sons will come from afar, and your daughters will be carried in the arms. Then you will see and be radiant, and your heart will thrill and rejoice; because the abundance of the sea will be turned to you, the wealth of the nations will come to you.... Your gates will be open continually; they will not be closed day or night, so that men may bring to you the wealth of the nations, with their kings led in procession.... You will also suck the milk of nations and suck the breast of kings; then you will know that I, the Lord, am your Savior and your Redeemer, the Mighty One of Jacob.[188]

When Jesus was on earth, did kings bring him "the wealth of the nations"? Well, not during his three-year ministry preceding his death;

---

[186]. Isaiah 51:3
[187]. Jeremiah 31:12
[188]. Isaiah 60:4–5

but as a baby, the "wise men from the East" brought their valuable gifts and laid them at the feet of the newborn Messiah![189] This was just a tiny taste of things to come once he returns and kings and others bring him "the wealth of the nations."

In the Millennium, the thirteen tribes of Israel will be given new allotments of the Promised Land. Ezekiel tells us about this. The allotments will not be the same as those assigned during the time of Moses and Joshua. Despite the dissimilarities, the basis for their assignment will be the same as before: the ancient patriarchal promises. The LORD, as we see in Ezekiel 47, begins the land assignments with this:

> This shall be the boundary by which you shall divide the land for an inheritance among the twelve tribes of Israel; Joseph shall have two portions. You shall divide it for an inheritance, each one equally with the other; for I swore to give it to your forefathers, and this land shall fall to you as an inheritance.[190]

The "forefathers" to whom Yahweh "swore" to give the land were Abraham, Isaac, and Jacob.[191] The reader is invited to read about the Promised Land allotments in Ezekiel 47:12–48:29. These allotments are geographically very specific; therefore, it is difficult to perceive any figurative meaning in them.

Sandwiched between the tribes then will be the temple of Yahweh which is also the temple of Christ, and it will be the center of the world. Isaiah testifies:

> Now it will come about that in the last days the mountain of the house of the LORD will be established as the chief of the mountains, and will be raised above the hills; and all the nations will stream to it. And many peoples will come and say, "Come, let us go up to the mountain of the LORD, to the house of the God of Jacob; that He may teach us concerning His ways and that we may walk in His paths." For the law will go forth from Zion and the word of the LORD from Jerusalem.[192]

---

[189] Matthew 2:1–12
[190] Ezekiel 47:13–14
[191] Genesis 22:16–18, 26:3–5. Moses understood that God also swore to Jacob to give him and his descendants the land (Exod. 32:13).
[192] Isaiah 2:2–3

Fourteen years after the destruction of Solomon's Temple by the Babylonians, Ezekiel, "in visions of God," was taken to Jerusalem. There, a mysterious angelic being—probably the Angel of the LORD—gave the prophet a personally guided tour of the temple and the temple complex.[193] But this temple was clearly not the temple built by Zerubbabel (the governor) and Joshua (the High Priest) about seventy years later nor its splendid modification under Herod, but this temple that Ezekiel saw is obviously the Millennial Temple.[194] There are many reasons why this is so. As I mention a few of them, noticeable are the many physical details that Ezekiel recounts—many of such fine detail that they cannot possibly be taken figuratively.

The final eight chapters of Ezekiel that contain the prophet's vision of the Millennial Temple begin with this:

> In the twenty-fifth year of our exile, at the beginning of the year, on the tenth of the month, in the fourteenth year after the city was taken, on that same day the hand of the LORD was upon me and He brought me there. In the visions of God He brought me into the land of Israel and set me on a very high mountain, and on it to the south there was a structure like a city.[195]

We first notice that Ezekiel was brought to "a very high mountain," which echoes Isaiah's words: "The mountain of the house of the LORD will be established as the chief of the mountains, and will be raised above the hills."[196] Anyone who has been to Jerusalem can testify that Jerusalem and the Temple Mount sit upon and among hills; but they certainly are not situated upon a "very high mountain" that Isaiah calls "the chief of the mountains." Nor does the "city," i.e., Jerusalem, lie mainly to the "south" of the temple as Ezekiel saw it. This could have been said when David bought the Temple Mount ("Mount Moriah") from Araunah: the "City of David"—previously called Jebus—was just south of Araunah's

---

[193.] Keil and Delitzsch understand Ezekiel's temple guide to be the Angel of the LORD because he speaks as his own person (as a "man") and speaks also in the first person as YHWH. See especially Ezekiel 40:4 and 44:5 (Carl F. Keil and Franz Delitzsch, *Commentary on the Old Testament* [Peabody: Hendrickson, 1996]; Ezek. 40:1–4).

[194.] As far as we know, the glory of God never came into the Second Temple like the glory had entered Solomon's Temple and the tabernacle before that (Lev. 9:23; 2 Chron. 7:1–3). But in Ezekiel's temple vision, the glory of God does return and settles again in the temple—permanently (Ezek. 43:1–7).

[195.] Ezekiel 40:1–2
[196.] Isaiah 2:2

threshing floor and about 150 feet lower.[197] But by the time of Ezekiel four centuries later, urban Jerusalem lay both south and west of the Temple Mount, and later in Jesus's day, the city enclosed the mount on the south, west, and north. Because the temple of Ezekiel's vision is atop a gigantic mountain and because "a structure like a city"—surely Jerusalem although, strangely, he never calls it by that name throughout the temple vision—lies only to the south of the temple, it seems that what Ezekiel is shown by the enigmatic angel is not anything that has yet existed.

The mysterious guide took Ezekiel through the temple courts and through the temple itself. Hundreds of details are presented, and the prophet is told sternly to take careful note of all of them so that he can recount them later to his fellow exiles in Babylon.[198]

Let us consider a few of these details of Ezekiel's temple which are different than the features and rites of the earlier temples that existed in Jesus's time and before. The reason that I mention here mainly details that *differ* from earlier temples is because of what I will discuss in the Revelation section near the end of the book.

There are so many differences between the Mosaic cult and the millennial cult that it can reasonably be said that the latter is not a reestablishment of the former—at least not a *complete* reestablishment. In other words, it can only be said with some exaggeration that the Mosaic Law will be reestablished in the Millennium.[199] As we'll see, some parts of it will, but many vital parts will not. It is important to understand this because the NT, in general, teaches that for gentile Christians, and probably even Jewish ones, the Mosaic Law fades away and eventually "disappears."[200]

A full reestablishment of the Mosaic Law in the Millennium would seem to contradict the NT teaching. But in regard to this question, we must keep in mind that the NT teaching mainly has to do with *salvation*. The Law indeed plays no part in that although it does make men sinful

---

[197] 2 Samuel 24

[198] Ezekiel 40:4, 43:10–11

[199] "The very center of the whole Levitical system revolved around the day of Atonement, with its ritual of sprinkling of the blood of atonement by the High Priest on the mercy seat. It is significant that all the necessary parts of this important ritual—the High Priest, the Ark and mercy seat, and even the day itself—are all omitted from the [Ezekiel] record. The absence of that which was most vital to the Levitical system shows that the millennial age will not see the reestablishment of Judaism" (J. Dwight Pentecost, *Things to Come* [Grand Rapids: Zondervan, 2010], chap. 30, sec. 2, Kindle eBook).

[200] Hebrews 8:13

and prompts some of them to cry out to God for mercy.[201] We will see later (in the Revelation section), however, that parts of the Law will play a legitimate *non*-salvific role at the Millennial Temple in the Millennial Kingdom.

We might recall that the wilderness tabernacle and Solomon's Temple had a number of pieces of cultic furniture within them. In the Holy Place, there was the lampstand, the table of "the Bread of the Presence," the altar of incense, and then the curtain just beyond the incense altar that separated the Holy Place from the Most Holy Place (or Holy of Holies).[202] Behind the curtain, that is, in the Most Holy Place, rested the Ark of the (Mosaic) Covenant. This was the absolute center of Israel's Yahweh worship, for the cover of the Ark—called the "Mercy Seat"—was God's "throne." Inside the Ark were the two tablets of the Ten Commandments, a jar of manna (the miraculous food Israel ate during the forty years in the desert), and the staff of Aaron that miraculously budded (thereby certifying his priestly authority).

This Most Holy Place was the center of Israelite religious life, not only because God was there but also because that was the place where the ceremony took place once a year that covered the sins of the people. This happened on the Day of Atonement when the High Priest would enter the Most Holy Place and sprinkle blood upon the Mercy Seat so as to atone for the sins of himself and for the people. Other than this once-a-year occasion, no one ever entered the Holy of Holies.[203] All of this is missing in the Millennial Temple, with the exception of "the table that is before the LORD," which, given its small dimensions, may be the altar of incense.[204] Nearly nothing of what gave the tabernacle and the First Temple their distinctive cultic identity and necessity exists in the Millennial Temple.

Therefore, it is not surprising that among the yearly events that are mentioned by Ezekiel's guide, the Day of Atonement is missing. Passover and the eating of unleavened bread are mentioned, but he is silent regarding the festivals of Firstfruits, Pentecost, Trumpets, the Day of Atonement, and Tabernacles. Zechariah shows that this last feast will

---

[201.] Romans 7:7–13; Galatians 3

[202.] First Kings 7:49 indicates that Solomon's Temple had several lampstands, not just one.

[203.] Exceptions to this rule occurred, of course, when the wilderness tabernacle and its furnishings—including the Ark—needed to be prepared for transport and when it was re-erected when the LORD once again ordered the Israelites to pitch camp. The First Temple's Holy of Holies also might have had some visitors during renovation projects.

[204.] Ezekiel 41:22

exist in the Millennium (the nations will be punished if they do not participate in the Feast of Tabernacles), so it looks like there is at least one feast not mentioned during Ezekiel's temple tour that will in fact be a part of Millennial Temple life.[205] But the guide's silence regarding the Day of Atonement is striking. If it were part of the millennial festival calendar, it would surely have been mentioned by Ezekiel's guide, for it goes to the heart of Israelite religion and the character of God. Israel worships the God of grace. So the silence regarding it must mean that it really does not exist in millennial times. This is only made more probable by the near-emptiness of the temple's inner sanctum. There is nothing in the temple that would allow the Day of Atonement rites to be carried out (as per the Mosaic Law), and so, atonement for the people cannot be accomplished.[206]

The main sacrifices/offerings of the Mosaic Law are shown to be a part of the Millennial Temple rituals (burnt, sin, meal, peace, guilt, drink),[207] but the officiating priesthood is whittled down to only the descendants of Zadok, who served as High Priest in David's time. It might be recalled that at Mount Sinai God decreed that the tribe of Levi would forever be consecrated as his servants and that the Levite Aaron (Moses's brother) and his descendants would forever serve as priests.[208]

From that time on till the Second Temple was destroyed in AD 70, the descendants of Aaron served as priests officiating at the tabernacle/temple, and the non-Aaronic Levites (simply known as "Levites") were their subordinates, assisting the priests in many ways. In the Millennium, however, all the men who would have been priests in olden times will simply be "Levites," except for those descended from Zadok. Thus, more men of the tribe of Levi will be "Levites," and fewer men of the tribe of Levi, who are also descendants of Aaron, will be "priests." This shrinking of the priesthood can be explained this way: During the divided monarchy, the Levites and the Levitical priests, generally speaking, led Israel away from Yahweh and into idol worship, but the priestly descendants of Zadok stayed true to the LORD. Therefore, God says to Ezekiel in 44:10–16 that the men serving closest to him—that is, as priests—will be restricted

---

[205.] Zechariah 14:16–19
[206.] Leviticus 16, 23
[207.] OT prophets other than Ezekiel mention sacrifices in what appears to be millennial times. See Isaiah 56:7, 60:7; Jeremiah 33:18; and Zechariah 14:16
[208.] Numbers 3:5–10, 18:1–7; Exodus 28:1

to descendants of Zadok. All others will be considered Levites and will perform the Levitical subordinate functions.[209]

Another surprising thing is that Ezekiel's guide never says anything about the High Priest. Apparently, there is none. On the other hand, it does seem that "the Prince" of the Millennial Kingdom functions to some extent in this role. The Prince, as described to Ezekiel, is a somewhat enigmatic and, for the Christian, perplexing person.[210] Some have identified him with Christ, but this is probably incorrect because he is a sinner and seems to be mortal as well.[211] There is no mention of the Messiah or of the Son of God in these Ezekiel chapters about the temple. I tend to believe that the Messiah, as the Son of God—who has "revealed"[212] God and who is "the image of the invisible God"[213]—is so at one with the Father and the Holy Spirit that these three are one, and this "One" Yahweh will, at the beginning of the millennial age, indwell the temple (which will be a symbol of his indwelling of his children). Allow me just a few lines to justify this view, and then I'll return to the person and function of the Prince.

Ezekiel (chapters 10–11) witnessed the departure of the glory of God from the temple just before the Babylonians destroyed it in 586 BC. Later, as Ezekiel is given the temple tour by the angelic guide, he sees untold millennia into the future and witnesses the return of the glory of God to the Millennial Temple. Even though Ezekiel saw in both cases God's glory, what he said specifically in the first case is important, and it must apply also to the second case (the case of God returning to the temple).

Before comparing these two cases, we should first note that the same glory that departed the temple was the same "glory of the God of Israel" that Ezekiel had seen at the beginning of his ministry, "in the plain," that is, the plain by the river Chebar.[214] In that original vision, Ezekiel saw above the eye-laden wheels-within-wheels and the "four living creatures" the "glory of the LORD." He described the "glory" this way:

> Now above the expanse that was over their heads there was something resembling a throne, like lapis lazuli in

---

[209.] The evildoings of the divided kingdom era priests are also mentioned in Ezekiel 22:26.
[210.] Ezekiel 44–46
[211.] Ezekiel 45:8–9, 22, 46:1–18
[212.] John 1:18 (ISV)
[213.] Colossians 1:15
[214.] Ezekiel 1, 3:15, 8:4, 10:15, 20, 22

appearance; and on that which resembled a throne, high up, was a figure with the appearance of a man. Then I noticed from the appearance of His loins and upward something like glowing metal that looked like fire all around within it, and from the appearance of His loins and downward I saw something like fire; and there was a radiance around Him. As the appearance of the rainbow in the clouds on a rainy day, so was the appearance of the surrounding radiance. Such was the appearance of the likeness of the glory of the LORD. And when I saw it, I fell on my face.[215]

Notice that Ezekiel saw a "throne" and "the appearance of a man." What he saw here is also what he saw as the Spirit of God left the temple. And what he saw there is the same thing that he saw in his vision of the Spirit returning to the Millennial Temple:

> Then [the angelic guide] led me to the gate, the gate facing toward the east; and behold, the glory of the God of Israel was coming from the way of the east. And His voice was like the sound of many waters; and the earth shone with His glory. And it was like the appearance of the vision which I saw, like the vision which I saw when He came to destroy the city. And the visions were like the vision which I saw by the river Chebar; and I fell on my face. And the glory of the LORD came into the house by the way of the gate facing toward the east.[216]

What Ezekiel saw of God at the Millennial Temple was the same as what he saw at both the 586 BC temple and his inaugural vision before that.

My purpose in recounting all this is simply to show that there is something human, or humanlike, that Ezekiel discerns in God in all three visions. Germane to this point is John's statement that Isaiah, in his vision of Yahweh "sitting upon a throne, high and lifted up" in his temple, saw "his glory"—that is, the glory of Christ.[217] We also might think of Christ's transfiguration in which his glory "shone like the sun" and Peter, James, and John were "terrified" much like both Isaiah and Ezekiel were respectively "ruined" and "overwhelmed" by their visions.[218]

---

[215] Ezekiel 1:26–28
[216] Ezekiel 43:1–4
[217] Isaiah 6:1 (ESV); John 12:41
[218] Matthew 17:1–13; Isaiah 6:5; Ezekiel 3:15 (ESV)

We shouldn't fail to note God's words to Ezekiel as the Spirit took up permanent residence in the Millennial Temple: "Son of man, this is the place of My throne and the place of the soles of My feet, where I will dwell among the sons of Israel forever."[219] This should remind us of Jesus's statement to his disciples:

> Truly I say to you, that you who have followed Me, in the regeneration when the Son of Man will sit on His glorious throne, you also shall sit upon twelve thrones, judging the twelve tribes of Israel.[220]

In view of this, it appears that the return of God to the temple begins the "regeneration" that Jesus spoke of and that his "throne" is the same throne upon which Yahweh will "dwell among the sons of Israel forever."[221]

Now getting back to the enigmatic Prince, we learn, from what the tour guide tells Ezekiel, that he is a prominent civic and ecclesiastical leader, possibly a descendant of David.[222] He is a quasi-priest although he is never called "priest." And here, among the multitude of literal temple details that cannot possibly be taken figuratively, we learn that the people do not just bring their various offerings to the Zadokian priests, but they bring many of them to the Prince who then distributes them as needed—mainly for the Sabbaths, new moon rituals, and the yearly festivals.[223]

Ezekiel's consistent identification of this man as "Prince," instead of "King," is striking and must be exegetically significant. In general, the OT messianic prophecies depict the Messiah as an absolutely sovereign *king* whose dominion is worldwide. While Ezekiel's use of "Prince" can, in a few places, denote a king,[224] it is clear that he knows the difference, for when he speaks of specific kings of Judah and Babylon, he calls them "king" and not "prince."[225] So it seems to be the case that because the Prince of the Millennial Kingdom is designated as such, then he cannot be the King of the kingdom.

Perhaps he is a Davidic "executive officer" or "prime minister" handling both royal and ecclesiastical duties assigned to him by the King LORD-Messiah. We know from the NT that the Messiah, along

---

219. Ezekiel 43:7a
220. Matthew 19:28
221. Regarding the "regeneration," compare with Peter's words spoken at the temple to his fellow Jews as recorded in Acts 3:19–21.
222. Ezekiel 34:23, 24, 37:24 perhaps refer to this person.
223. Ezekiel 45:13–17, 22–25
224. Ezekiel 12:10–13, 21:25, 38:2–3
225. See Ezekiel 1:2, 17:12, 26:7, 29:2

with many of his saints, during the Millennium will exist in resurrected bodies and be immortal.[226] At the same time, there will continue to be un-resurrected mortal people existing during the Millennium.[227] Perhaps the Prince of Ezekiel's vision will be one of the mortal descendants of King David who survives the Great Tribulation.

At all events, we can see in all of this the uniqueness of the millennial cult. It can only partially be understood as Mosaic, and the myriad of physical and ritual details make it very difficult to perceive it all as only an allegory of the Church.

Now there is one more feature of the Millennial Temple that we must not miss before bringing our investigation of the prophets to a close. And this feature, unlike most of the others of the temple, can very well be understood literally *and* spiritually or perhaps only the latter. In fact, it *begs* to be taken figuratively. In chapter 47 Ezekiel is shown a small spring of crystal clear water, emanating from under the southeast corner of the temple, that runs on east by the altar on through the east gate and cascades down toward the Dead Sea. The spring begins as a trickle, but as it flows east, it rapidly increases in size, such that by the time it reaches the desert east of Jerusalem, it has become an unfordable river.[228] If this river existed today, it would tumble down nearly four thousand feet of elevation loss in only twenty miles or so. But the Temple Mount in the Millennium will be raised up much higher, so the river will cascade down an even steeper incline on its way to the Dead Sea. What a sight that will be![229] The prophet is then told:

> These waters go out toward the eastern region and go down into the Arabah; then they go toward the sea, being made to flow into the sea, and the waters of the sea become fresh. It will come about that every living creature which swarms in every place where the river goes, will live. And there will be very many fish, for these waters go there and the others become fresh; so everything will live where the river goes.[230]

[226.] Revelation 20

[227.] These mortal people will be survivors of the Day of the Lord/Great Tribulation and will be living when Christ returns. They will have children and those children will reproduce, thus populating the Millennium. The population growth will be rapid because of the significantly increased longevity (Isa. 65:20).

[228.] Joel 3:18 and Zechariah 14:8 also mention the water that flows from the Millennial Temple.

[229.] Isaiah 2:2; Micah 4:1; Zechariah 14:10

[230.] Ezekiel 47:8–9

The water begins at the temple, the throne of God, then flows—ever increasing—into the dying world where it brings healing and life. Right away, Jesus's description of himself, given to the woman at the Samaritan well, as the "living water" comes to mind.[231] And we remember John's record of Jesus crying out on the last day of the Feast of Tabernacles:

> If anyone thirsts, let him come to me and drink. Whoever believes in me, as the Scripture has said, "Out of his heart will flow rivers of living water."[232]

To which John explains:

> Now this he said about the Spirit, whom those who believed in him were to receive, for as yet the Spirit had not been given, because Jesus was not yet glorified.[233]

Jesus referred to his body as a "temple," and we know that the Holy Spirit—beginning at Pentecost and continuing today—flows in an ever-increasing stream into the hearts of men and women who turn to him in faith and become the "living stones" of his Holy Temple.[234] And we know from Revelation 22 that a more heavenly form of this river exists in the endless era of the post-Millennium final state, for John saw the river in the "New Jerusalem" after the old heaven and earth were destroyed and, interestingly enough, after the Jerusalem Temple is no more:

> Then he showed me a river of the water of life, clear as crystal, coming from the throne of God and of the Lamb, in the middle of its street. On either side of the river was the tree of life, bearing twelve kinds of fruit, yielding its fruit every month; and the leaves of the tree were for the healing of the nations.[235]

Ezekiel's river should certainly be interpreted to figuratively stand for the blessed eternal life that flows from God via the Holy Spirit into the men and women who love him and do his will.[236]

[231.] John 4:10
[232.] John 7:37–38 (ESV)
[233.] John 7:39 (ESV)
[234.] John 2:19; Acts 2; 1 Corinthians 6:19; 1 Peter 2:5
[235.] Revelation 22:1–2
[236.] God said in Isaiah 44:3–4 (KJV): "For I will pour water upon him that is thirsty, and floods upon the dry ground: I will pour my spirit upon thy seed, and my

But is there any literal fulfillment still possible? It should always be kept in mind that the literal-or-spiritual question can always be asked about any part of Scripture, and the more we interpret one part only spiritually, the more likely it is that we will interpret another part spiritually. If this goes too far, the meaning of Scripture becomes increasingly esoteric, and it gets harder to discern what God has really said to us.

In view of this, we should be very careful not to over-spiritualize God's holy Word; the more we do so, the more we drift from exegetical certainty to uncertainty. It's probably better, in the case before us, to naively believe that there will be an actual water spring emanating from under the Millennial Temple and that there will be a real river running through downtown New Jerusalem. At the same time, given the symbolic meaning of water that is apparent in both Testaments, we can safely perceive that God here intends for us to think about the far greater reality of his saving love that "flows" into the world through the atoning work of Christ and the convicting work of the Holy Spirit. Personally speaking, should I be accepted as one of the "saints" to be with Christ in his kingdom, I would love to explore and fish that river that has its source in the temple, grows ever larger, then pours its pure waters into the Dead Sea, where, according to Ezekiel,

> Fishermen will line its banks—from En-gedi to En-eglaim there will be plenty of room to spread out nets. There will be all sorts of species of fish, as abundant as the fish that live in the Mediterranean Sea. There will be lots of them![237]

I'd love to join those "fishermen" and, with them, praise God for the wonderful saving reality that all this abundance symbolizes!

To conclude this section on the millennial prophecies of the prophets, I'd just like to say that while parts of what they said here and there can certainly be taken figuratively, pointing to spiritual realities far greater than the literal things described, it doesn't seem possible that all of what they said about the restored state can be thus understood.

What Ezekiel said about the temple spring can easily—especially in view of NT teaching—be understood figuratively, but to attempt to do the same with the rest of the hundreds of details about the temple that Ezekiel presents is simply unrealistic. For to try to make spiritual

---

blessing upon thine offspring: And they shall spring up as among the grass, as willows by the water courses."

[237]. Ezekiel 47:10 (ISV)

meanings out of all those physical and ritualistic details would be an agonizingly laborious and fantastically speculative task. I would not want to be the one assigned the miserable job of trying to determine what every table, chamber, window, ornament, gate, pillar, stairway, priestly garment, sacrifice type, land apportionment, and measurement figuratively means. My results would be anything but an *educated* guess!

Yet many—maybe most—Christian theologians would tell us today that most, if not all, of the prophecies that I have covered in this section (and many more) do not literally describe a future Jewish restored state but figuratively only the Spirit-filled and saved Church. If they are right, this means that a significant portion of OT prophecy should only be taken figuratively. Yet there is no OT sign that tells us that we should do this on such a large scale. Does the NT, as God's latest Word, tell us to do this? And does the NT teach us that the promises made to Abraham, Isaac, and Jacob that we have already studied are to be understood in the long run as only applying to the Church? Let's now turn to the NT and find out.

THE NEW TESTAMENT CASE:
The Gospels

INTRODUCTION

Before diving into the NT, let us reflect for a moment on the ground that we have covered. Abraham was promised offspring, blessings, land, and that "all nations" would be blessed through one of his descendants. The last promise is fulfilled in the Messiah, and the first three are fulfilled literally in the history after the time of Abraham.

When Moses brought Israel out of Egypt and prepared them to take the land of Canaan, he told them several times that they would be given the land not because of their righteousness but because of the promises made to the patriarchs.[1]

Once settled in the Promised Land, Joshua said that God had fulfilled his promises made to the patriarchs, and nearly four centuries later, Solomon said the same.[2] Then about five centuries after that, Nehemiah declared that God had again fulfilled his promises.[3] Yet the divided kingdom and exilic era prophets described a time far in the future when God would again make good on his promises and that this fulfillment would never again be interrupted by the terrible cycle of sin/punishment/repentance/restoration that Israel had regularly experienced in the past.

The prophets also prophesied in various ways about the son of David, who is the Son of God, the "Messiah," who would rule over that

---

[1] Deuteronomy 9
[2] Joshua 21:45, 23:14; 1 Kings 8:56
[3] Nehemiah 9:7–8

permanently restored kingdom under the system of a "New Covenant," in which all people would know the LORD because the LORD would give them his Spirit. But it was also prophesied that the Messiah would suffer and die for the sins of mankind. Other than the enigmatic prophecy in Daniel 9, the timing of the coming of the Messiah and of his kingdom was not given. And in view of the fact that there has been another large-scale exile (from Roman times till 1948) since the Babylonian exile, it is obvious that the sixth century BC return to Jerusalem from the Babylonian exile was not the final restoration and that there is an unknown amount of time between when the prophets prophesied and the final restoration of Israel.[4] Also, somewhere between the time of the prophets and that of the final restoration with Messiah ruling, there had to be some point in time when the Messiah—as the prophets foretold—would suffer and offer his life as an atonement for sins. Finally, given the fact that the OT does, in a few places, clearly shine the light of the hope of eternal life (especially Isaiah 25 and Daniel 12), one could reasonably suspect that all of what the OT says has something to do with eternal blessed life and the avoidance of eternal cursed life.

Now we come to the New Testament, which is just our way of saying the "New Covenant." Here, as we'll soon see, there is much that clarifies just what the OT was getting at. There is much that is new and surprising but really not anything that we discover to be radically different on a large doctrinal scale. Speaking very generally, the OT told us that God promised to bless men and that, in fact, all nations would be blessed through the Messiah and the unending peace that he would bring. And all this would somehow have something to do with the overcoming of the death curse. The NT will show us that indeed what was said in the OT is finally fulfilled in the person of Jesus Christ and in the eternal blessed life that he makes available.

Yet the NT will *not* say that the literal meaning of the OT promises and prophecies regarding the future of Israel and her land are no longer valid. The NT will concentrate upon the ultimate spiritual fulfillment that brings the OT hints at eternal life into full bloom. In this, many OT texts that speak about righteousness will be shown in the NT to speak of righteousness *to salvation*.[5] The literal meanings of the OT prophecies

---

[4.] The other major exile/dispersion of the Jews after the Babylonian exile happened in the course of the two Jewish revolts against the Romans, AD 66–73 and 132–136. Between then and 1948, there was no "Israel" or "Judah."

[5.] For example, the OT says (Gen. 15:6) that Abraham's belief in God was "credited to him as righteousness" but does not say that this provided him blessed life after death. Paul, in Galatians 3:6, assumes that this was indeed saving faith and that anyone

THE NEW TESTAMENT CASE: THE GOSPELS

that speak of the permanently restored earthly kingdom will be all but ignored, yet we won't find in the NT any teaching that says explicitly that they are ignored because they are no longer valid.

Despite the NT's occupation with Christ and how to be saved, Jesus, Peter, and Paul will provide brief indications that God still plans to fulfill those prophecies literally. And John's Revelation will indicate the time when this will happen. Right after the "Tribulation" ("Day of the LORD") is over but before the eternal state begins (that contains only blessed immortal people), there will be a thousand-year period—"the Millennium"—when mortal earthly people will exist contemporaneously with immortal resurrected people. The OT is fulfilled *spiritually* in this latter group and *literally* in the former. But even after the Millennium, when there will be a new heaven and a new earth, there will be plenty of Abraham's physical offspring in the New Jerusalem, and that wonderful city—that will be one giant temple of God's presence—will be the new and improved "Promised Land."

No doubt about it, the Gospels put the emphasis on Christ and his atonement and how to achieve the eternal blessed life made available through that atonement. The awareness of life after death, which on the face of it hardly seems to be a concern of the OT, was very much a concern by the time of Christ. Of course, people were aware of it back in OT times; it's just that God decided that his OT Word would not plainly contain very much of the subject. But toward the end of the OT era, the prophet Daniel provided us a clear statement as to the reality of resurrection, either to glory or shame: "Many of those who sleep in the dust of the ground will awake, these to everlasting life, but the others to disgrace and everlasting contempt."[6]

During the intertestamental period (roughly 450 BC till Christ) the Jewish literature showed some signs of a growing awareness of the afterlife,[7] and Josephus tells us that during the latter part of this period,

---

who has faith like Abraham will likewise be saved (saved from eternal suffering to eternal blessedness).

[6] Daniel 12:2

[7] In the Hebrew literature during this time, there is, like the OT, not much said about the afterlife. The mother and her seven sons tortured and killed by Antiochus Epiphanes IV, as recorded in 2 Maccabees 7, believed in the resurrection, both to blessedness and punishment. One of the sons, as he was dying, said to the king: "You accursed wretch, you dismiss us from this present life, but the king of the universe will raise us up to an everlasting renewal of life, because we have died for his laws." Then as the youngest son was tortured to death, he said to Antiochus, "Our brothers, after enduring a brief suffering, have drunk of ever-flowing life under God's covenant, but you, by the judgment of God, will receive just punishment for your arrogance." *The Psalms of Solomon*, chapter 3, has

two of the three main religious parties—the Pharisees and the Essenes—believed in the resurrection; the third party, the Sadducees, did not, but, says Josephus, they could not wear that opinion on their sleeves because the people far and away did believe that the dead were raised.[8]

The intertestamental literature and the views of the three parties just mentioned also, in general, manifest the belief that God would still fulfill his literal promises made to the patriarchs and confirmed by the prophets. It was only a matter of time till the Messiah would come and throw off the yoke of bondage, and Israel would rise to everlasting glory.[9] Whether in Jerusalem or the diaspora, the Jews waited for the Messiah, the restoration of the kingdom, and the great final return.[10] By the time of Jesus's first advent, nationalistic and afterlife concerns were very much on the minds of the people.

These concerns—which in general have to do with our question of literal and/or figurative fulfillment of OT promises and prophecies—can be felt in the first part of the Gospels. For example, Mary and Zechariah (John the Baptist's father), as well as Simeon and Anna at the temple, all knew that the Savior had come to redeem and provide Israel with deliverance from her enemies and, more importantly, to provide "salvation by the forgiveness of their sins."[11] All this would be in fulfillment of, as Zechariah said, God's "holy covenant, the oath which He swore to Abraham our father."[12]

Simeon, with the baby Jesus in his arms, praised God for the "salvation" that the baby would provide for not just Israel but the Gentiles

---

this statement: "The destruction of the sinner [is] forever, and he will not be remembered when [God] shows care for the righteous. This is the portion of sinners forever, but those who fear the Lord will rise up to eternal life and their life [will be] in the Lord's light and it will never cease."

[8] Josephus, *Antiquities*, 18.1.3.

[9] Regarding the early rabbinic view of the kingdom and the Messiah, Edersheim writes: "All that Israel needed: 'study of the Law and good works,' lay within the reach of every one; and all that Israel hoped for, was national restoration and glory. Everything else was but means to these ends; the Messiah Himself only the grand instrument in attaining them. Thus viewed, the picture presented would be of Israel's exaltation, rather than of the salvation of the world.... [T]he purely national elements, which well nigh formed the sum total of Rabbinic expectation, scarcely entered into the teaching of Jesus about the Kingdom of God" (Alfred Edersheim, *Life and Times of Jesus* vol. 1 [New York: E. R. Herrick & Co., 1866], 164). Obtained at www.archive.org.

[10] Edersheim: "That hope pointed them all, wherever scattered, back to Palestine. To them the coming of the Messiah undoubtedly implied the restoration of Israel's kingdom, and, as a first part in it, the return of 'the dispersed'" (*Life and Times of Jesus* vol. 1, 78).

[11] Luke 1:77

[12] Luke 1:72b–73

as well.[13] Even though the Gospel accounts of John the Baptist do not tell us exactly what was on the minds of the multitudes that came to him, it appears certain from the context that they were intensely worried about death and the afterlife.[14] Whatever eternal security they felt by merely being sons of Abraham was exploded by John when he told them that, from the Jordan River stones that lay at his feet, God was "able to raise up children to Abraham."[15] In view of what he said next, John pleaded with them to repent:

> [God's] winnowing fork is in His hand, and He will thoroughly clear His threshing floor; and He will gather His wheat into the barn, but He will burn up the chaff with unquenchable fire.[16]

With John, however, we see a definite change in emphasis compared to the OT. With him, the concern about Jewishness and land decreases and the knowledge of the salvation-providing Savior increases. And because Jesus will be "the lamb of God who takes away the sins of the world" and thereby make salvation possible, John knew that Jesus must "increase" compared to himself.[17]

JESUS'S TEACHING ABOUT THE COMING KINGDOM

The Lord Jesus spoke often about the coming blessed kingdom. He didn't call it "the kingdom of Jerusalem" or "the kingdom of the Jews" or any similar title, but he called it either "the kingdom of God" or "the kingdom of heaven." As can be seen, what he called it indicates that this kingdom is more heavenly than earthly or, perhaps better, more spiritual than fleshly.

As we proceed on here, we should keep in mind that the OT saints are saved (to blessed eternal life) through the blood of Christ just as much as we are saved through his blood. The atonement for their sins occurred after their time; the atonement for our sins occurred before our time. With this in mind (learned from the NT and foreshadowed

---

[13.] Luke 2:30

[14.] After John warned that "every tree that does not bear good fruit is cut down and thrown into the fire," they cried out, "Then what shall we do?" (Luke 3:9–10, 12, 14).

[15.] Matthew 3:9

[16.] Matthew 3:12

[17.] John 3:30

in the OT), we understand that while *unfaithful* Israelites during OT times might have partaken of many of God's blessings as promised to the patriarchs, they would not partake of the figurative/spiritual meaning of the blessings. In other words, even though God in his OT Word emphasized the earthly promises and their earthly fulfillment and many unbelieving Jews partook of the blessings of the earthly fulfillment, it was nevertheless the case that men and women had to believe in and serve God in order to be finally forgiven of their sins and saved in the final judgment.

So the reality of the earthly fulfillment thus revealed in the OT did not take away from the spiritual reality that the OT only hints at. Likewise, the reality of the spiritual fulfillment of God's patriarchal promises and subsequent prophecies does not take away from the reality of the earthly fulfillment that the NT, as we'll see, hints at.

Why does the OT emphasize the earthly and the NT the heavenly? It seems to be the case that God had to bring the Israelites/Jews through a lengthy period of earthly/fleshly/sinful immersion in order to get them to apprehend their sinful condition and yearn for something better. The Law, as Paul says, was a "tutor" that revealed sinfulness and evoked the desire for mercy and help.[18] But in Jesus's time, many people—even many non-Jews—were already looking up, thirsty for mercy and help. The "tutor" had done its work. So for Jesus and the NT writers in general, the time was ripe for bringing the "good news" of the Messiah and the salvation available through him to the attention of the people. Shortly after the Law was given to Israel, the people wanted to kill Moses and they despised God, and so, most were consigned to die in the desert. The time was not "ripe." But shortly after Jesus Christ was revealed to Israel, yes, the Jews had him crucified, but within a few weeks of this, at least five thousand of them had repented and come to saving faith.[19]

Jesus, in general, lifted up the people's gaze to heaven and eternity. His conversation with the Samaritan woman at Jacob's well (John 4) is a good example of this. The woman who he had "chanced" to meet while passing through Samaritan territory had up till then been living immorally and in poverty as she had no (actual) husband. But she was intelligently open to any "good news." When Jesus offered her "living water" (ala Ezekiel 47), she assumed that this "water" was perhaps at the moment in Jacob's well or perhaps at some other water source. Jesus attempted to make the figure of speech more obvious, saying, "Whoever

---

[18.] Galatians 3:24
[19.] Acts 2:41, 4:4

drinks of the water that I will give him shall never thirst, but the water that I will give him will become in him a well of water springing up to eternal life."

This piqued the woman's interest, but she still didn't get it. She asked Jesus for some of that water so she wouldn't have to continue to come daily to the well. At that point, it seems that Jesus figured that a tiny miracle might help the woman to think spiritually instead of thinking only of the flesh. So he told her a little about her hard life, that she had had five "husbands" who were really not her husbands. This really got her attention.

"Sir, I perceive that you are a prophet," said she and then—still looking mostly "earthward"—mentioned that the Samaritans and Jews worshipped on different mountains. But Jesus told her that the day was coming, and actually had arrived, when people would not make Gerizim or Zion the focus of their worship, but they would make God, who is Spirit, their focus. "Those who worship Him," said Jesus to the woman, "must worship in spirit and truth." At this point, the woman's perspective apparently shifted heavenward, for she then expressed a longing for the advent of the Messiah who would make all things clear. Jesus, recognizing that she was now ready, said, "I who speak to you am He."

Right about then, the disciples, who then also had too much of an earthly focus, arrived with some food obtained in town. They were incredulous that Jesus spoke with the woman, a Samaritan woman at that. Jesus refused their food, saying, "I have food to eat that you do not know about." The spiritual import of this having flown over their heads, they figured that someone else had already brought Jesus something to eat.

When reading this story, we typically see this as Jesus trying to get the woman (and throughout the Gospels, his disciples) to get her eyes off temporal earthly things and on to eternal heavenly things. But if we think about it, Jesus and the woman and the disciples all still had to drink and eat in order to keep on functioning in life under the sun, as God designed it. Adam and Eve, even before sinning, drank and ate. So it's probably better to understand that Jesus was trying to get her to put her attention *mainly* on spiritual things but not at the total expense of the earthly things, for they, too, have their own subordinate reality. Jesus expressed this thought elsewhere this way:

> Do not worry then, saying, "What will we eat?" or "What will we drink?" or "What will we wear for clothing?" For the Gentiles eagerly seek all these things; for your heavenly Father knows that you need all these things. But seek first

His kingdom and His righteousness, and all these things will be added to you.[20]

In that "kingdom" one day, Jesus will once again drink the Passover wine and eat the Passover meal, as he told his disciples at the Passover just before his betrayal and crucifixion.[21] It is the kingdom where we may expect with gladness to see the woman who Jesus met at the well—despite the fact that she was a sinner and an untouchable Samaritan.

So Jesus lifted up the perspective of his hearers not to "the kingdom of Jerusalem" nor "the kingdom of the Jews" but to "the kingdom of heaven" and "the kingdom of God." For the people were, as Jesus said to his disciples at the well, "ripe for harvest." But, as we will see, Jesus did not teach that there would be no further place *at all* for Jerusalem and the Jews.

The Kingdom Is a Thing of the Heart

While the OT describes the final restored kingdom in vivid earthly details—Zion will be raised up, the temple will be resurrected, the nations will bring their wealth, food and wine will be in great abundance, etc.—the OT's far greater joy is expressed in the fact that people will be in a close and obedient relationship with the Lord. For all that the OT says about the physical kingdom, it is clear that the only thing that makes the physical kingdom worthwhile at all is the love that people have for God and the intimate love that God has for his people.

The NT is really not much different in this regard. The great emphasis is upon faith, love, and holy living. Jesus and one of the honest Jewish scribes who was, as Jesus said, "not far from the kingdom of God," agreed that the greatest commandments of all are to love God and to love one's neighbor.[22] More than anything else, Jesus taught us to love, but this was nothing radically new for, as Jesus said, the entire Law and prophets (here, he probably meant the entire [OT] Scripture) are grounded in the commands to love God and to love one's neighbor.[23] In other words, love is the driving force behind everything that God does, including the giving of his holy Word as recorded in Scripture. That being said, it is obvious that Jesus's concentration was upon things of the heart and heaven whereas the OT appears to be mainly concerned with

---

[20.] Matthew 6:31–33
[21.] Luke 22:14–18
[22.] Mark 12:28–34. Quoted there is Deuteronomy 6:5 and Leviticus 19:18.
[23.] Matthew 22:34–40

THE NEW TESTAMENT CASE: THE GOSPELS

things of the Law and the earthly fulfillment of the patriarchal promises. But there is more common ground than what first meets the eye.

Let us first consider some things that Jesus said about the kingdom that show that he was primarily concerned about its spiritual realities.[24] A perusal of the Lord's various uses of "kingdom of God" and "kingdom of heaven" shows that people become close to entering that kingdom not when they are in a certain place or even if Jesus is physically close to them but only when they believe in God, humble themselves before him, and begin to develop a tender and open attitude toward the real Messiah, Jesus.

Men begin to enter the kingdom when they have childlike faith, are forgiving and do God's will in general, and possess a level of righteousness superior to the Pharisees.[25] To enter in, one must be (as Jesus told Nicodemus) "born again."[26] In the kingdom, men have eternal blessed life, and thus, it is to be sought after with all one's heart and strength.[27] The kingdom will steadily grow; yet, sadly, most people will refuse to enter in.[28] To put what seems to be the icing on its spiritual characteristic, Jesus told us that this kingdom is "not of this world."[29] We'll ponder what he meant by this a little later. The contexts of these Gospel mentions of the kingdom are enough to show that it mainly has to do with the personal *relationship* between man and God and between man and God's Son, Jesus Christ.

Because the kingdom is a thing of the heart and because most people refuse to believe, relatively few people enter into it. Most Jews in Jesus's day refused to believe, and so he told them that the kingdom would be given to men more deserving—that is, to the Gentiles.[30]

Like with the Jews, a small portion of the Gentiles believe, but because there are vastly more of them than Jews, it has appeared from nearly the beginning that the Church has grown only through Gentile conversion. It seemed at first that Jesus's mission was only to the Jews, for he said that he was sent "only to the lost sheep of the house of Israel," and he sent out his disciples on their mission to the same group.[31] Yet

---

[24]. Here I use "spiritual" not to mean "figurative" but simply to denote what is of the mind and eternal matters versus what is of the flesh and temporal matters.
[25]. Matthew 5:20, 7:21, 18:1–4, 23-35, 19:13–14, 21:28–32
[26]. John 3:3
[27]. Matthew 13:43–45
[28]. Matthew 13:24–30, 31–33, 36–43
[29]. John 18:36
[30]. Matthew 21:43
[31]. Matthew 15:24, 10:5–7

he could not help but have compassion and mercy on the Gentiles too, for he healed and provided the Gospel to Gentiles in the regions of Sidon, Samaria (woman at the well), and the Decapolis east of the Sea of Galilee. In this last region, Jesus probably ministered mostly to Greeks as he multiplied a few fish and loaves to feed four thousand people,[32] and nearer to home, he even indicated that salvation could come to hated Roman soldiers.[33]

But because Jesus's mission was far and away directed at fellow Israelites, he was much more apt to speak of their spiritual state. Their spiritual state, in general, was not good—the times being "ripe" notwithstanding.[34] Few truly trusted God, and fewer still accepted Jesus as the Messiah. Many had no interest in spiritual matters at all. So because the "many" unbelievers of the Jews would soon be overwhelmed by the "few" believers of the Gentiles, Jesus spoke at some length about this shift in the demographics of the kingdom. This shift was described mostly in parables.[35]

After telling the parable of the vineyard owner (the owner's representatives and even his own son were killed by the vineyard managers), Jesus told his Jewish hearers that "the kingdom of God will be taken away from you and given to a people producing the fruit of it."[36] In response to the faith of the Roman centurion in Capernaum, Jesus did not use a parable but prophesied plainly about the displacement of the Jews by the Gentiles:

> I say to you that many will come from east and west, and recline at the table with Abraham, Isaac and Jacob in the kingdom of heaven; but the sons of the kingdom will be cast out into the outer darkness; in that place there will be weeping and gnashing of teeth.[37]

These distressing declarations by Jesus make it appear like the Jews have no hope. And yet we must always remember that many Jews—always "the remnant"—did believe right from the start, and many Jews have come to faith in Christ during all the centuries from then till now. And if

---

[32.] Mark 8:1–9. Mark 7:31 indicates that the feeding of the four thousand was in the Decapolis region, which was populated mainly by Greeks.
[33.] Matthew 8:5–13
[34.] Matthew 8:10; Luke 13:34
[35.] Matthew 21:33–44, 22:2–14; Luke 14:16–24, 19:12–27
[36.] Matthew 21:43
[37.] Matthew 8:11–12

THE NEW TESTAMENT CASE: THE GOSPELS

Paul is right in Romans 9–11, many more will come to faith in the final days (I'll go into some detail on this later).

The kingdom is one of the heart, but most Jews will not partake of it. Thus, the Jewish character of it seems to evaporate. It is a kingdom, as Jesus told the Samaritan woman at the well, where Gerizim and Zion aren't the main things but "spirit" and "truth" of worshipping men and women are. Jesus drove the spiritual idea of the kingdom to the uttermost when he assured Pontius Pilate with these words: "My kingdom is not of this world."[38]

It's important, however, to understand the context here and what Jesus really meant by this. It seems certain that Jesus did not want to give the Romans any grounds for putting him to death. The "blood" had to be upon the heads of his own people.[39] So Jesus here spoke ambiguously. On one hand, the meaning could be that Jesus's kingdom is completely in a different "world" and, therefore, of no concern to the Romans. Pilate apparently perceived this meaning, and Jesus knew that he would. On the other hand, it could also mean that the authority (warrant, originating commission) of Jesus's kingdom is not derived from any earthly power but from the power that is "not of this world"—that is, from God.

We, as Christians, of course know that this second meaning is the true one.[40] Even if Pilate perceived something of this second meaning, it doesn't seem that he apprehended the possible implications. If the sanctioning authority of Jesus's kingdom is "not of this world," then that authority is probably God, and if that is so, then it is the case that God has granted Jesus authority over the world where Jesus and Pilate stood.

From what is given to us in the Gospel accounts of Jesus's appearances before Pilate, it is hard to know just what the governor was thinking; but we do know that he judged Jesus not to be a threat to his or Caesar's authority. In this, however, he was mistaken. Jesus's kingdom does, in fact, encompass the whole world, including Judah, even while it does not derive its existence and authority from anything in the world.[41] If I understood Jesus to mean the first possible meaning of

---

[38] John 18:36 (ESV)

[39] Matthew 27:25

[40] Jesus even telegraphed this meaning to Pilate—which he didn't get—when he said, "You would have no authority over Me, unless it had been given you from above" (John 19:11).

[41] My thoughts here regarding Jesus's statement "My kingdom is not of this world" are based on the interpretations of Donald Carson and Leon Morris. Carson says, "Jesus's reign does not have its source or origin in this world," and Morris, "It does not take its origin from this world" (D. A. Carson, *The Gospel According to John*, vol. 4 of

his "ambiguous" statement to Pilate (that Jesus's kingdom is somewhere other than "this world"), then I certainly wouldn't be writing this book. But if the second meaning mentioned above (that his kingdom authority doesn't derive from this world) is really the case and God has bestowed upon him jurisdiction over earth, then the idea of a future earth-based messianic kingdom is certainly not rendered impossible or inappropriate by what Jesus said to the Roman governor.

By answering Pilate ambiguously (but not dishonestly), Jesus set up a decoy that Pilate went after, and thus, he declared Jesus innocent of the charge of sedition. But in his weakness, Pilate let the most vocal opinion of the Jews drive him to nevertheless have Jesus crucified. The Jews were then prompted to say, "His blood shall be on us and on our children!"[42] Jesus had outfoxed them all, and by the end of the day, God's loving purpose in the whole affair would be "finished."[43]

It is interesting to note that when Jesus, earlier that morning, answered the High Priest's question, "Are you the Christ?"[44] he also gave an ambiguous answer that contained two possible meanings; but in this case, both meanings were true and both easily discernable. His answer, "I am,"[45] on one hand meant "yes"; on the other hand, it meant, "I AM," which notified them in no uncertain terms that the God who spoke to Moses through the burning bush fifteen centuries earlier was the same God speaking to them now.[46] This is the real reason why the Jews wanted Jesus dead. In the end, he was killed not because of sedition against the Roman State but because of "sedition" against the Jewish political-religious establishment: not even God was allowed to establish hegemony over them. So what Jesus said to Pilate was true: "he who delivered Me to you has the greater sin."[47]

The Kingdom Comes at Christ's Second Coming

While Jesus was on earth for a short time two thousand years ago, the kingdom of God/heaven came "near" to Israel in an almost imperceptible way. Yes, a few saw the light of Christ, even a few Gentiles, and the

---

The Pillar New Testament Commentary, ed. D. A. Carson [Leicester: Apollos, 1991], 594; Leon Morris, *The Gospel According to John*, vol. 4 of *The New International Commentary on the New Testament*, ed. Gordon D. Fee [Grand Rapids: Wm. B. Eerdmans, 1995], 680).

[42.] Matthew 27:25
[43.] John 19:30
[44.] Mark 14:61
[45.] Mark 14:62
[46.] Exodus 3:13–14
[47.] John 19:11. Jesus speaks of his return in Matthew 24–25; Mark 13; Luke 21.

kingdom began to grow from the humble, tiny mustard seed into a garden plant large enough for a few songbirds to make their home. But near the end of his ministry, Jesus spoke of a second coming of himself and the kingdom that would burst upon the earth in such blazing glory that men and women would immediately know that the world had forever changed and that they should fall down and worship him as "Lord and God."[48] Beginning with his first advent until his second, the kingdom would slowly grow like the mustard plant; but, as Ezekiel indicated, when the Messiah commenced ruling the final restored kingdom, that kingdom would be like the towering cedar of Lebanon and every bird of the air, large or small, would immediately find their home in its branches or perish.[49]

Jesus signaled that this was the case when he passed through Jericho on his way to Jerusalem for the last time, and he knew that those traveling with him expected that "the kingdom of God was going to appear immediately."[50] In other words, they expected that Jesus would be declared king and that somehow the Roman yoke would be thrown off and the messianic kingdom commenced. They still didn't know that the kingdom would emerge like the humble mustard plant, not like the awesome cedar.

Via a parable (Luke 19:11–27), which is almost plain prophecy, Jesus told them that the kingdom which they envisioned would indeed come, but the "nobleman," i.e., Jesus, would first have to go to "a distant country" to receive it. This probably prompted his hearers to think of the Herodian princes who had traveled to Rome in order to seek royal authority from Caesar Augustus.[51] In the meantime, Jesus, through the parable, informed them that it was their duty to "do business" until he returned. The nobleman would surely return one day, and when he did, he would have all the authority to reward those who had done his work during his absence, to punish those who hadn't, and to execute those who had outright opposed him.

After the triumphal entry into Jerusalem, cleansing the temple, and harshly rebuking the Scribes and Pharisees, Jesus then spoke *plainly* about his second coming and the events leading up to it.[52] Regarding the latter, there would be "wars and rumors of wars," the temple would be destroyed, Jerusalem would be "trampled upon by the Gentiles" for

---

[48] John 20:28
[49] Mark 4:30–32; Ezekiel 17:22–24
[50] Luke 19:11
[51] See Josephus, *The Jewish War* book 2, chap. 2.
[52] Matthew 24–25; Mark 13; Luke 21

a long time, disciples of Christ would be persecuted terribly, and just before his coming, there would come "tribulation" like the world had never seen before.

Then Jesus, referring to Daniel 7, said: "They will see the Son of Man coming in a cloud with power and great glory."[53] And there would be no doubt that the King of all the earth had arrived to assume sovereign control. "For," as Jesus said, "just as the lightning comes from the east and flashes even to the west, so will the coming of the Son of Man be."[54] That Jesus first had to "receive" the kingdom, as he indicated in the parable of the nobleman, is confirmed in Daniel 7 where the prophet said:

> I kept looking in the night visions, and behold, with the clouds of heaven One like a Son of Man was coming, and He came up to the Ancient of Days and was presented before Him. And to Him was given dominion, glory and a kingdom, that all the peoples, nations and men of every language might serve Him.[55]

Upon his glorious return, Christ "will send forth His angels with a great trumpet and they will gather together His elect from the four winds, from one end of the sky to the other."[56] Then "the saints of the Highest One," as Daniel was told, "will receive the kingdom and possess the kingdom forever, for all ages to come."[57] High in the theocratic order will be the apostles of Christ, for he said to them:

> [Y]ou who have followed Me, in the regeneration when the Son of Man will sit on His glorious throne, you also shall sit upon twelve thrones, judging the twelve tribes of Israel.[58]

Lesser saints, who have been faithful in their assignment to "do business" during the king's absence, will receive (as Jesus said in his parable of the talents in Matthew 25:14–30) royal jurisdiction over "cities." And the saints will probably participate in Christ's judgment of the nations, which appears to be the final act in securing the kingdom. There, he will separate the nations "from one another, as the shepherd separates the

---

[53] Luke 21:27
[54] Matthew 24:27
[55] Daniel 7:13–14
[56] Matthew 24:31
[57] Daniel 7:18
[58] Matthew 19:28

sheep from the goats."[59] The nations that were kind to God's people while the king was away will "inherit the kingdom prepared for [them] from the foundation of the world." Those nations that were unkind to God's people will be consigned to the "eternal fire which has been prepared for the devil and his angels."[60]

To sum up Jesus's teaching on the kingdom of God/heaven, it is clear on one hand that it was something during Jesus's first advent that was primarily a matter of the human heart and secondarily a matter of the physical presence of Jesus. As men and women began to see Jesus for who he is and put their trust in him, the kingdom came "near" to them. As more people did this, the kingdom grew quietly and slowly like a mustard plant growing or like yeast working its way through a lump of dough. Yet Jesus told us plainly that the drawing "near" of the kingdom is also to be a stupendous *future* event that will overwhelm the lives of all.[61] Then those who love the king will hear, "Enter the joy of your master," and those who hate the king, "Depart from Me, accursed ones, into the eternal fire."[62]

Other Hints that Christ's Earthly Kingdom Is Yet to Come

We should remember that Jesus was a Jew. He was born into typical Jewish poverty, circumcised on the eighth day, raised by parents who were of the "house and lineage of David,"[63] and even at the tender age of twelve had enough knowledge of Judaism and the scriptures to converse with the teachers in his "Father's house" about the great things of God.[64] He came to his temple as "the messenger of the covenant," as Malachi called him,[65] at the age of twelve and many times later as he grew up and eventually embarked on his three-year ministry.

---

[59] Matthew 25:32

[60] Matthew 25:34, 41

[61] Darrell Bock, regarding Luke 11:14–22, speaks of the kingdom at the time of Christ arriving or having arrived, for Satan, the "strong man," had been "overcome." And so, Jesus could drive out demons—but this was only an early and limited manifestation of the kingdom: "[T]he kingdom's presence, or at least its very close proximity, is tied to the first phase of Jesus's career. What Jesus is suggesting is not that the kingdom has arrived in fullness but that signs of its initial stages have come" (Darrell L. Bock, "The Reign of the Lord Christ," in *Israel and the Church*, edited by Craig A. Blaising and Darrell L. Bock [Zondervan Academic], chap. 1, Kindle eBook).

[62] Matthew 25:21, 41

[63] Luke 2:4 (NKJV)

[64] Luke 2:41–50

[65] Malachi 3:1

He came to the Jerusalem Temple in order to worship the Father and to convince his brothers to do the same so that they might themselves become temples of the Holy Spirit. The turning of the temple worship into a house of merchandizing scandalized his soul for, as David had said long before of Jesus, "zeal" for his Father's house "consumed" him.[66] The apostle John said about Christ: "He came to His own, and those who were His own did not receive Him."[67]

Jesus, in his own words, said that he had come not for the Gentiles but for the "lost sheep of the house of Israel."[68] In comparison with these "sheep," the Gentiles—as he told the Syrophoenician woman—were but little "dogs."[69]

Thus, when it was clear that his "own" people rejected him, Jesus bitterly lamented:

> Jerusalem, Jerusalem, who kills the prophets and stones those who are sent to her! How often I wanted to gather your children together, the way a hen gathers her chicks under her wings, and you were unwilling. Behold, your house is being left to you desolate! For I say to you, from now on you will not see Me until you say, "Blessed is He who comes in the name of the Lord!"[70]

Jesus loved his own people and their holy city Jerusalem. They could have been as blessed and safe as chicks under their mother's wings, but Jesus's heart broke because of their hardness of heart and the doom that would soon come upon them as a result. Their house would soon become "desolate," which seemed, like several of his parables, to spell the end of Israel and the Jews. And because of their rejection of him, they would see him no more—that is, "until" they would learn to say of their true Messiah, "Blessed is He who comes in the name of the Lord."

Very important to observe here is that Jesus did not end his lament with "from now on you will not see me" and leave it at that. No, praise the Lord, he cracked the door on the possibility of a reversal of this decree when he added "until." If the Jews would ever, in the future, accept Jesus as their Messiah and call him "blessed" instead of cursed, then they would see him again—in the flesh. When would this happen?

---

[66] Psalm 69:9; John 2:17
[67] John 1:11
[68] Matthew 15:24
[69] Mark 7:27
[70] Matthew 23:37–39

Most likely when Jesus would come, as Daniel had said, "with the clouds of heaven" in order to establish the kingdom bestowed upon him by the Father—a kingdom in which "all peoples, nations, and languages should serve him," an "everlasting dominion, which will not pass away, and… which shall not be destroyed."[71]

A second important "until" statement of Jesus that strongly indicates that he will one day establish his royal authority over Israel is contained in his Olivet eschatological discourse:

> But when you see Jerusalem surrounded by armies, then recognize that her desolation is near…. These are days of vengeance, so that all things which are written will be fulfilled…. For there will be great distress upon the land and wrath to this people; and they will fall by the edge of the sword, and will be led captive into all the nations; and Jerusalem will be trampled under foot by the Gentiles until the times of the Gentiles are fulfilled.[72]

Most commentators see this as describing the Roman siege of Jerusalem that ended in the city's destruction in AD 70. Since then (and especially so since the Bar Kokhba revolt sixty years later), Jerusalem has been "trampled under foot" by Romans, Byzantines, Arabs, Crusaders, Turks, etc. But there will come a day, says Jesus, when those Gentile days are "fulfilled." Implied here—and confirmed in what he says later in the Olivet discourse—is that a day will finally come when the Holy City will revert back to the Jews. This reversion will correspond to the Jews' recognition that the Messiah Jesus is "blessed" because he "comes in the name of the Lord."

During the Gentile era, the Church does not *completely* bring in the kingdom of God on earth. Replacement theologians generally believe that the messianic kingdom is not a future Jewish affair but is a current Christian (therefore, mostly Gentile) affair that is progressively established during the era of the Gentiles (with Christ ruling through his Church leaders). The problem with this view is that it does not, in general, take literally the OT promises and prophecies that we have already covered nor does it take at face value what Jesus says a little later in the Olivet discourse: viz., that he will bodily return at the end of time and then sit in judgment of the nations of the earth. No, it seems clear here that Jesus meant that *after* the era of the Gentiles, Jerusalem would

---

[71.] Daniel 7:13–14 (NKJV)
[72.] Luke 21:20–24

be once again occupied and ruled by the Jews and that the end of the Gentile era would correspond to Jesus's second coming.

This is not the last "until" that Jesus gave us, for he gave us two more that pertain directly to our kingdom subject. These two were given as Jesus celebrated the Passover with his disciples for the last time. Dr. Luke gives us the details:

> When the hour had come, He reclined at the table, and the apostles with Him. And He said to them, "I have earnestly desired to eat this Passover with you before I suffer; for I say to you, I shall never again eat it until it is fulfilled in the kingdom of God." And when He had taken a cup and given thanks, He said, "Take this and share it among yourselves; for I say to you, I will not drink of the fruit of the vine from now on until the kingdom of God comes."[73]

Just after Jesus said this, he administered the first "Lord's supper," which would be the Passover-like supper that his followers would celebrate during the era of the Gentiles or, to put it another way, the era when he would go away to a "distant country" to receive the kingdom. In the meantime, Jesus would not eat the Passover lamb nor drink wine. But when the "kingdom of God" would one day come, Jesus indicated that the eating of the Passover lamb would resume, as well as the drinking of wine.

Only with difficulty can this be understood to mean that he would do these things during the Church age (which many believe to be the "Millennium") when the kingdom of God grows upon earth while Jesus is at the right hand of the Father in heaven.[74] No, it is clear, especially in

---

[73.] Luke 22:14–18

[74.] Many replacement theologians believe that Christ's Millennial Kingdom is in effect now and that the Church is in the process of bringing all nations under the authority of Christ. This does not accord with some things that Jesus literally taught. Yes, the Church will grow slowly—this is seen in the similes of the mustard seed and leaven—to "the remotest part of the earth"; but in regard to how things would go for Christians once Jesus was gone, it was not a picture of triumphant conquering but one of difficulty and persecution. This is especially indicated by Jesus's statements: "If the world hates you, you know that it has hated Me before it hated you" (John 15:18) and "If they persecuted Me, they will also persecute you" (John 15:20). Jesus did not say that his disciple must "pick up his sword" but that he must "pick up his cross" and follow him. The way the Church has grown has been through much hardship. Christianity was illegal until Constantine. Then from Theodosius for a short time, it was the state religion. But most land was lost in the barbarian invasions, then the rest of the empire was enslaved to the Arab and then Turkish Muslims who put Christians under many burdens. Today, after two thousand years, the Church has some power in parts of the world; but in general, Islam has the

view of his Olivet discourse, that he meant that only upon his glorious *second* physical coming—not in weakness but in awesome power—would he again celebrate the Passover and drink wine. Yet again, we see here the mystery of the kingdom already coming "near" when Jesus first walked the earth yet, at the same time, being something that his disciples patiently had to wait for.

It is interesting to note, as might be recalled, that the only celebrations that were mentioned to Ezekiel as being part of the Millennial Temple's rituals were Passover and its associated Feast of Unleavened Bread. One can't help but notice that physical eating and drinking will occur when the Passover is "fulfilled in the kingdom of God."[75] And Jesus said that those disciples who stood by him would not only one day eat at the king's table, but they would also assist him in ruling the kingdom:

> You are those who have stood by Me in My trials; and just as My Father has granted Me a kingdom, I grant you that you may eat and drink at My table in My kingdom, and you will sit on thrones judging the twelve tribes of Israel.[76]

The "twelve tribes of Israel" here are certainly not the Church but the historical twelve tribes. In that day, all of God's people will have a job to do in the administration of Christ's kingdom.[77]

One more thing that Jesus said about the kingdom happens to be the last thing he said on earth, just before his ascension to heaven. One would think that the last words he spoke would be some of the plainest that he ever spoke. Let's look at Luke's account of this at the beginning of the book of Acts.

> The first account I composed, Theophilus, about all that Jesus began to do and teach, until the day when He was taken up to heaven, after He had by the Holy Spirit given

---

upper hand throughout the Middle East and elsewhere, Hinduism still reigns supreme in India, Buddhism and various other religions rule in the far East, and the West, including the USA, is mostly in the grip of enlightenment humanism. But "in the regeneration," Christ and his saints will rule worldwide and rule absolutely.

[75.] Luke 22:16

[76.] Luke 22:28–30

[77.] Jesus elsewhere says, through a parable, that those who are faithful servants of God—i.e., who effectively multiply their "minas"—will "take charge" of "cities" (Luke 19:17). Consider 1 Corinthians 6:2: "Or do you not know that the saints will judge the world? If the world is judged by you, are you not competent to constitute the smallest law courts?" This fits with Daniel 7's depiction of the saints being given the kingdom, as well as Revelation 20's portrayal of the saints ruling with Christ during the Millennium.

> orders to the apostles whom He had chosen. To these He also presented Himself alive after His suffering, by many convincing proofs, appearing to them over a period of forty days and speaking of the things concerning the kingdom of God. Gathering them together, He commanded them not to leave Jerusalem, but to wait for what the Father had promised, "Which," He said, "you heard of from Me; for John baptized with water, but you will be baptized with the Holy Spirit not many days from now." So when they had come together, they were asking Him, saying, "Lord, is it at this time You are restoring the kingdom to Israel?" He said to them, "It is not for you to know times or epochs which the Father has fixed by His own authority; but you will receive power when the Holy Spirit has come upon you; and you shall be My witnesses both in Jerusalem, and in all Judea and Samaria, and even to the remotest part of the earth."[78]

So here we are forty days after the resurrection, and Jesus has spent much time with the disciples showing many "convincing proofs" of his bodily resurrection and speaking of the "kingdom of God." Given the circumstances, it must be the case that these two subjects were critically important to Jesus and that he wanted the disciples to understand them fully before he arose to the Father. Given the gravity of this moment, it is unlikely in the extreme that here, of all places, the Lord would have spoken figuratively. Actually, he quit speaking that way to the disciples some time before.[79]

The first common-sense contextual thing to know here is that Jesus spent forty days teaching them during a time when they understood the general situation far better than they had understood it before Jesus's resurrection. By now, Peter, after bitter tears, had repented; Thomas, after doubting, had declared to Jesus, "My Lord and my God"; two disciples on the way to Emmaus were illumined by the Lord; the disciples saw Jesus eat fish in Jerusalem, and Jesus served them fish on the shore of Galilee; and, most important of all, Jesus "opened their minds to understand the scriptures," which means that he "opened their minds" to understand correctly, among other things, what the prophets had said about the coming kingdom.[80] Luke tells us that Jesus spoke to them at length about the kingdom during the forty days before the ascension.

[78.] Acts 1:1–8
[79.] Mark 4:33–34; John 16:25–30
[80.] Luke 24:45

THE NEW TESTAMENT CASE: THE GOSPELS

Therefore, when the disciples asked him, "Lord, is it at this time you are restoring the kingdom to Israel?" there was nothing flawed in their thinking, and what they said is precisely what they meant.

They spoke neither ignorantly nor figuratively; Jesus did not answer elusively or figuratively. This interchange was all arrow-straightforward, for Jesus had only a few moments to teach them, and he knew that his last first-advent words to them would be the last first-advent words to us. No, when the disciples asked Jesus if he was going to restore the kingdom at that time "to Israel," there was zero possibility that they meant Israel to stand for something other than literal Israel, for Jesus had just taught them for forty days exactly what the kingdom would someday be. And it is only literal Israel that the kingdom can possibly be restored to, for it was only literal Israel that had been blessed with the Davidic kingdom in the past.[81]

The disciples surely had no misunderstandings about the kingdom as such when they asked Jesus this question. If there were any fault in the question, it was only in that they asked a question that Jesus had already told them he could not answer—for the "time" of the Messiah's return was only known by the Father.[82] Not to nitpick, but they also should have remembered that Jesus told them that many cataclysmic events must first take place—events that obviously had not yet occurred. Jesus's response did not at all discredit their question but only reminded them: "It is not for you to know times or epochs which the Father has fixed by His own authority." In this, Jesus signaled that the question was appropriate—the kingdom would come; but it was not their lot (nor ours) to know when. But it was their lot (and ours!) to tell the world about Jesus and about his imminent return.

As Jesus ascended into the clouds and disappeared, two angels said to the disciples: "This Jesus, who has been taken up from you into heaven, will come in just the same way as you have watched Him go into heaven."[83] This would have only served as confirmation to the disciples that the kingdom that they had in mind when they asked Jesus the question was, at some point, going to become a reality. Jesus would not

---

[81.] Regarding "restoring" in "Lord, is it at this time You are restoring the kingdom to Israel?" the base verb employed here is αποκαθίστημι (*apokathistami*) which means "to restore to an earlier condition" (Gerhard Kittel, ed., *Theological Dictionary of the New Testament* [Grand Rapids: Eerdmans, 1964], s.v. "αποκαθίστημι, αποκατάστασις"). The disciples, being men of Israel, were certainly wondering if the Davidic monarchy would at that time be restored to the Jews (Israelites).

[82.] Mark 13:32

[83.] Acts 1:11b

remain in heaven indefinitely, but he would return bodily just like he had ascended bodily. And then he would establish the kingdom that he and the ancient prophets had spoken about. When they heard this from the angels, they no doubt understood that this would be the fulfillment of Daniel's and Zechariah's prophecies:

> I kept looking in the night visions, And behold, with the clouds of heaven One like a Son of Man was coming.[84]

> In that day [the LORD's] feet will stand on the Mount of Olives, which is in front of Jerusalem on the east; and the Mount of Olives will be split in its middle from east to west by a very large valley, so that half of the mountain will move toward the north and the other half toward the south.... And in that day living waters will flow out of Jerusalem, half of them toward the eastern sea and the other half toward the western sea; it will be in summer as well as in winter. And the LORD will be king over all the earth; in that day the LORD will be the only one, and His name the only one. All the land will be changed into a plain from Geba to Rimmon south of Jerusalem; but Jerusalem will rise and remain on its site from Benjamin's Gate as far as the place of the First Gate to the Corner Gate, and from the Tower of Hananel to the king's wine presses.[85]

The disciples would have remembered Jesus teaching them that he had to go away to a "far country" to receive the kingdom, but he would return "with the clouds of heaven" in overwhelming glory and then sit in judgment of all the nations of the earth. They would have also remembered that Jesus told them that they would rule and reign along with him and that they would dine at his royal table and there partake of the Passover lamb and the fruit of the "king's wine presses."

Yes, they knew in one sense that they were in the kingdom now because they devotedly followed Christ; yet they still expected the Messiah and the kingdom to eventually come "to Israel" in literal fulfillment of the prophets and in fulfillment of all that Jesus had plainly told them.

One more thing before we move on to Acts and the epistles. Everything Jesus said and did revolved around the fact that he was bringing in a New Covenant to supersede the Mosaic Covenant, which Israel had failed to follow. The New Covenant was made possible by his death,

---

[84] Daniel 7:13
[85] Zechariah 14:4, 8–10

THE NEW TESTAMENT CASE: THE GOSPELS

which provided the final atonement for sins that the sacrifices under the Mosaic Covenant were unable to make.[86] The Old Covenant—i.e., the Mosaic Covenant—was initiated with the blood of bulls[87] and the New Covenant with the blood of Christ. The Old Covenant promised blessings and occupation of the Promised Land contingent upon Israel's obedience to it; the New Covenant, which is only mentioned by Jesus by name once in the upper room on the night he was betrayed, brings eternal blessed life after death, contingent upon a person's faith in Christ.[88] Does this then make the literal Old Covenant promises irrelevant?

Jesus does not give us the answer in what he said to his disciples in the upper room. But if we go back to several of the OT statements concerning the conditions under the New Covenant, we see that Israel and the land are still in the picture. For example, right after God informed Jeremiah that there would one day come a reliable and lasting "New Covenant," he then assured the prophet that only if the regular order of the moon, sun, and stars were to end would "the offspring of Israel," as he said, "cease from being a nation before Me forever."[89]

The coming of God's Spirit upon men and the re-creation of their hearts was also described by God to Ezekiel not long after Jeremiah was informed about the New Covenant. The LORD said to the Babylon-based prophet:

> Therefore say to the house of Israel, "Thus says the Lord GOD.... 'I will put My Spirit within you and cause you to walk in My statutes, and you will be careful to observe My ordinances. You will live in the land that I gave to your forefathers; so you will be My people, and I will be your God.'"[90]

The land that God gave to Israel's "forefathers," of course, is the land of Canaan. So we see that for all the New Covenant's soteriological implications, the blood sons of Abraham and their land are not forgotten. And, as we will now see, even though the book of Acts and Paul's epistles are far and away concerned with the eternal blessed life made possible by Christ's atonement and resultant forgiveness of sins, there are hints here and there that show that God still has a place for the Jews and their land.

[86.] Hebrews 10:1–4
[87.] Exodus 24
[88.] Luke 22:20. See also Matthew 26:28; Mark 14:24.
[89.] Jeremiah 31:36
[90.] Ezekiel 36:22, 27–28

THE NEW TESTAMENT CASE:
Acts and Epistles

INTRODUCTION

The OT promises—first given to the patriarchs—were in some ways nonspecific. In God's first promise given to Abraham (Gen. 12:2–3), the LORD promised to "bless" Abraham, to "bless" those who blessed Abraham, and to bring it about that "all the families of the earth" would be "blessed" because of Abraham. Shortly thereafter, God added that the land upon which the patriarch stood—wherein then dwelt the Canaanites—would be given to his "seed."[1]

At this point, Abraham wouldn't have known anything about who his "seed" might be, what the blessings might be, or what being given the land really meant. By the time we get to Moses and the Exodus, however, the meaning of the elements of the Abrahamic Covenant had become better known. Abraham's descendants multiplied greatly and were blessed with God's presence and, as they left Egypt, with material abundance. Also, Gentiles who blessed Israel found themselves blessed by God.

As the history proceeds from there, on through the conquest and the era of the judges up till David and Solomon, the original promises found fulfillment in sundry physical and earthly ways. And the prophets during the divided monarchy and later also spoke of physical and earthly future realities that would fulfill what was promised to the patriarchs. But, admittedly, while there is much that the prophets said that cannot

---

[1] Genesis 12:7

be taken as anything other than future "physical and earthly future realities," there are also elements of their visions of the far future that are somewhat surrealistic or, one could say, otherworldly and thus portend something more than meets the eye.

One suspects that the future kingdom (to put it in the words of Paul) is not really about "eating and drinking, but righteousness and peace and joy in the Holy Spirit."[2] Jesus, as we have seen, confirmed that this is so. The final restoration of the kingdom began to occur when the king, Jesus of Nazareth, came on the scene; but it was not a kingdom that would come with "signs to be observed" but was, and still is, a kingdom of the heart.[3] Every man and woman who comes to faith in Christ will by that act grow the kingdom a little bit. Being a kingdom of the heart, entry into it indeed has nothing to do with "eating and drinking"; yet the Lord told us that one day, after a long physical absence, he would again eat and drink in that kingdom with his disciples.[4]

So now we turn to the book of Acts and the various epistles, and here we will find that the story is much the same. The kingdom grows by people being saved to eternal blessed life, but that requires faith in Christ and obedience to his commands. The emphasis is far and away upon "spiritual Israel," that is, upon those—whether Jew or Gentile—who have faith like Abraham and who thereby escape the terrible judgment to come. But God's concern for the physical descendants of Abraham is not forgotten, and there is a hint or two as well of God's ongoing concern for the Promised Land.

In view of what Jesus said and from what Acts and the epistles (mainly of Paul) will say, it is not surprising that many theologians believe that more or less from Jesus's time forward, the original patriarchal promises as well as the prophets' prophecies of the restored kingdom are only fulfilled in the Church. Their view is not just driven by what appears to be the NT teaching but also by the desire to deconflict the Gospel with the OT Law—that is, to avoid any hint at all that adherence to the Law is a means of salvation *in addition to* salvation through faith in Christ. There is the fear that if it is understood that the promises apply literally to Abraham's blood descendants, then some measure of the figurative/spiritual meaning of the promises applies to them too. This puts salvation too close to the Law that the Jews have been obligated to follow throughout their long history. This proximity of salvation and

---

[2] Romans 14:17
[3] Luke 17:20
[4] Luke 22:14–18

Law is in fact too close for comfort, for then it is easy to slip into the belief that salvation comes through a combination of faith and Law-keeping.

The replacement theologians' fear, however, is largely unwarranted because both the OT and the NT show—the former from silence, the latter from explicit teaching—that nothing of the Law can bring about eternal blessed life for a man or woman after his or her earthly life ends. The NT plainly teaches that the Law could only condemn, for no one could follow it fully, and that the sacrifices accomplished under the Law, while they had some short-term expiatory effect, could not wash a man's conscience clean and provide final elimination of sins and thus salvation.[5] So in truth, the replacement theologian does not have to completely "replace" Israel in order for the Gospel to be protected from the threat of Jews possibly being saved under the Law by doing the works of the Law.

Early in the Church's history, a dark image of the Jews was promulgated, but this was something like a "straw man" that was (probably, mainly unintentionally) set up in order to deconflict the Law from the Gospel. The Jews could not be allowed the *spiritual* blessing, and the best way to ensure that was to play it safe and deny them all blessings. But in the process, the Church inappropriately denied the Jews what was their due—namely, what had been *literally* promised them by God at the time of Abraham and later.

ACTS AND THE EPISTLES TEACH MAINLY A SPIRITUAL INTERPRETATION OF THE PROMISES

The Acts of the Apostles is mostly the record of Paul of Tarsus preaching around the Mediterranean world the good news of Jesus Christ. Acts, through historical narration, and Paul's letters, through direct teaching, provide for us the answer to the question: "What must I do to be saved?" This was the question that the Philippian jailer begged Paul to answer when an earthquake destroyed the prison for which he was responsible. Despite the destruction of the prison, none of the prisoners escaped—a miracle that preserved his life. And he knew that Paul and Silas had something to do with it. Paul answered the jailer, "Believe in the Lord Jesus, and you will be saved." Paul, the saved Jew, said this to the Gentile

---

[5.] In 2 Corinthians 3:7, 9 Paul calls the Law the "ministry of death" and "the ministry of condemnation." For the inability of the Law to take away sins, see Hebrews 10.

jailer who needed salvation. The jailer right away believed, nursed Paul's wounds, and became his spiritual brother in the common faith of Christ.[6]

This event at Philippi was a microcosm of the main concern of all of Paul's teaching as reflected in Acts and his letters—the letters being written within a few years of the Philippi earthquake incident. Salvation, according to Paul, comes when people put their faith in the Messiah, Jesus of Nazareth, who is, truth be known, "God over all, blessed forever. Amen."[7] This is, of course, what Jesus himself taught: "I am the resurrection and the life; he who believes in Me will live even if he dies."[8] This is simple enough. But Paul was a Jew, and for quite a long time after Jesus ascended to the Father, James, John, Peter, and others in Jerusalem continued to teach that all men—especially Jews—needed to follow Christ *and* the Mosaic Law. Although after the Acts 15 Jerusalem council the position of the leaders significantly moderated in regard to the Gentiles, nevertheless, adherence to the Law was expected of Jewish Christians. In any case, most everywhere Paul went and planted churches, Jewish Christians soon appeared with the mission of convincing Paul's new Gentile converts that circumcision and some or all of the Law of Moses had to be followed—in addition to believing in Christ—in order for them to be saved.[9] These were the "Judaizers" who vexed Paul so much that he called them "mutilators" and "dogs" who heaped on the new Christians all that the Jews had hitherto been unable to bear and, therefore, only brought condemnation.[10]

And so, Paul did not just tell us how to be saved in his letters, but he had to explain how salvation was to be viewed in light of what God had said to the Jews—the first "Jew" being Abraham—so that he could demonstrate that salvation had nothing to do with following the Law of Moses or even of submitting to the rite of circumcision.

Paul had to fiercely defend the mainly Gentile churches that he planted from the Jewish Christians who believed that all followers of the Jewish Messiah were obligated to follow the Jewish Law. Paul's defense of faith alone is not difficult to understand. "Abraham believed God," Paul said, even before God demanded circumcision of him, "and it was reckoned to him as righteousness."[11] Paul takes this to mean that because of Abraham's faith, God deemed him righteous—even though he, like

---

[6] See Acts 16
[7] Romans 9:5
[8] John 11:25
[9] See Galatians.
[10] Acts 15:10; Galatians 5:12; Philippians 3:2
[11] Galatians 3:6

all men, was a sinner—such that upon his earthly death, Abraham was saved from eternal condemnation.

Critical to note here is that the patriarch was saved before circumcision was demanded of him and long before conformance to the Sinai Law was demanded of his descendants. He was saved by "grace… through faith…not as a result of works."[12] In his letter to the Romans, Paul labors to demonstrate that the Law that came later could only condemn the Israelites, for the Law was so onerous that not one of them could fully follow it.[13] The Law could only get men to look up and cry out to God and thus prompt in them the faith in God which God was looking for in the first place—the faith in God which Abraham exhibited long before there was the Law and which justified his soul before the God who had said to him, "I am God Almighty; walk before Me, and be blameless."[14]

If this was so with Abraham and the other patriarchs and was also so even with the Jews living under the Law, then how could it be any different with those who recognized the Savior for who he was and put their faith in him? Abraham believed in God, and he graciously received the LORD when he came as a man to the patriarch at the oaks of Mamre. Likewise, Christians believe in God and graciously receive the LORD as he comes to them in the form of the Son of God. This truth applies to all: "Everyone who calls on the name of the LORD shall be saved."[15] Paul's overriding concern in his letters is salvation and what it takes to obtain it. That being so, and taking the lead from Jesus, Paul—with the exception of some of what he says in Romans 9–11 (which we'll cover just below)—interprets the promises given to the patriarchs figuratively, that is, "spiritually."

The "seed" of Abraham—to whom, along with Abraham, the blessings were promised—are, in Paul's eyes, all those whether Jew or Gentile who have the same faith as Abraham.[16] And circumcision is figuratively taken to mean faith or, as the OT prophets put it, circumcision of the heart. Thus, circumcision and Abraham's "seed" are nearly synonymous when taken figuratively.[17] One could go as far as to say that Paul makes the notions of circumcision and the Law, and even the notions of Israel and Jewishness, *irrelevant* for the purposes of salvation.

[12.] Ephesians 2:8–9
[13.] Romans 2–3
[14.] Genesis 17:1
[15.] Joel 2:32 (ESV). See also Romans 10:13.
[16.] Preeminently represented by Christ himself.
[17.] Paul says about the Church, "We are the circumcision."

One can especially think this if one understands that the archetype of the saved person was not a "Jew" but a "wandering Aramean" who was justified in God's eyes before anything of Israel or the Jews came to be.[18]

In his letter to the Galatians (who were under pressure by certain Judaizers to commit themselves to following the Law), Paul shows plainly that Christians should understand the patriarchal promises figuratively and thus realize that they are saved by faith, not by works. In view of the fact that Abraham's righteousness came not by works but through his faith in God, Paul says:

> Therefore, be sure that it is those who are of faith who are sons of Abraham. The Scripture, foreseeing that God would justify the Gentiles by faith, preached the gospel beforehand to Abraham, saying, "All the nations will be blessed in you." So then those who are of faith are blessed with Abraham, the believer.... And if you belong to Christ, then you are Abraham's descendants, heirs according to promise.[19]

Here, as elsewhere, Paul interprets the promises figuratively/spiritually. And so, we know that believers are Abraham's "descendants, heirs according to promise"—the "promise" here being understood to be the "blessing" of eternal blessed life. This means, as Paul says in Philippians 3:3, that believers in Christ "are the true circumcision, who worship in the Spirit of God and glory in Christ Jesus and put no confidence in the flesh." Because Abraham came to saving faith before he was circumcised, he is then, according to Paul, "the father of all who believe without being circumcised, that righteousness might be credited to them."[20] There is irony in this. Most of those circumcised in the flesh do not possess a circumcised heart and are thus eternally lost, but many Gentiles have circumcised hearts and are thus saved, even though they lack the physical circumcision.

Because salvation depends on faith and faith alone, there is no distinction between Jews and Gentiles. God does not show favoritism. Paul, in speaking of the two groups, says the following:

[18.] Deuteronomy 26:5 says that the patriarch Jacob was a "wandering Aramean." If this was so for Jacob, how much more was it so for his grandfather, Abraham, who spent the first half of his life in Ur and Paddan-aram.

[19.] Galatians 3:7–9, 29

[20.] Romans 4:11

> But now in Christ Jesus you who formerly were far off have been brought near by the blood of Christ. For He Himself is our peace, who made both groups into one and broke down the barrier of the dividing wall, by abolishing in His flesh the enmity, which is the Law of commandments contained in ordinances, so that in Himself He might make the two into one new man, thus establishing peace, and might reconcile them both in one body to God through the cross, by it having put to death the enmity.[21]

This combining of "the two into one new man" is, as Paul says in Colossians 3:11, a "renewal" in which "there is no distinction between Greek and Jew, circumcised and uncircumcised, barbarian, Scythian, slave and freeman, but Christ is all, and in all."

With all this emphasis on faith and salvation, Paul understands Christ's kingdom mainly through spiritual eyes. The believer is resurrected to that kingdom in a "spiritual body," for "flesh and blood cannot inherit the kingdom of God."[22] Thus, "the kingdom of God is not [about] eating and drinking, but righteousness and peace and joy in the Holy Spirit."[23] He does not say that the kingdom is earthly but that it is "heavenly."[24] In one instance, Paul indicates that Christ's faithful followers inhabit the kingdom now:

> For He rescued us from the domain of darkness, and transferred us to the kingdom of His beloved Son, in whom we have redemption, the forgiveness of sins.[25]

But in Paul's other mentions of the kingdom, it is something that believers enter after they die.[26] As far as that kingdom being something that will be established at the second coming of Christ, the most Paul says—and the closest he gets to earth regarding man's eternal future—is that the redeemed "will be caught up...in the clouds to meet the Lord in the air, and so...shall always be with the Lord."[27] There are several mentions in the book of Acts that Paul preached and taught extensively

---

[21.] Ephesians 2:13–16
[22.] 1 Corinthians 15:44, 50
[23.] Romans 14:17
[24.] 2 Timothy 4:18
[25.] Colossians 1:13–14
[26.] Acts 14:22; 1 Corinthians 6:9–10, 15:24, 50; Galatians 5:21; Ephesians 5:5; 2 Thessalonians 1:5; 2 Timothy 4:18
[27.] 1 Thessalonians 4:17

about the kingdom of God,[28] but Luke's record unfortunately does not tell us what he said other than that Christians must go through "many tribulations" to get there.[29]

The Lord's brother James, who was a prominent leader in the infant Jerusalem Church, believed that the kingdom was already coming upon them in his day. After hearing Paul justify his mission to the Gentiles (recorded in Acts 15), James declared that Paul's missionary work was a fulfillment of the LORD's prophecy spoken through the prophet Amos of the conversion of the Gentiles that happens concurrently with the reappearance of the house of David:

> "After this I will return, and I will rebuild the tent of David that has fallen; I will rebuild its ruins, and I will restore it, that the remnant of mankind may seek the Lord, and all the Gentiles who are called by my name," says the Lord, who makes these things known from of old.[30]

We can safely assume here that the rebuilding of David's tent *is* the reestablishment of the kingdom of "David," i.e., the kingdom of Christ. About twenty years earlier, Peter, after healing a crippled man at the temple, all but indicated the same when he declared to the amazed crowd: "All the prophets who have spoken, from Samuel and his successors onward, also announced these days."[31] Most likely, Peter here was mainly thinking of the prophets who told of the final restored kingdom—something that Peter felt was beginning to be manifested in his day. On the other hand, Peter indicated in the same sermon that the kingdom would come when Jesus one day returned.[32] I'll speak more about that in a moment.

In Acts and the epistles, because Abraham is deemed our "father" and archetype for salvation purposes, the promises given to him by God are understood in general to be figurative of the blessing of salvation. This is the thing far and away most needful, and so the literal meaning of the promises is nearly completely ignored. Within the figurative meaning of the promises, as it is worked out in the Church, are contained the truths as we have just seen of the true "sons of Abraham," of the indistinguishability of Jews and Gentiles, and of the spiritual nature of the kingdom of God. Also contained therein is the truth that Paul highlights of the irrelevancy

---

[28.] Acts 19:8, 20:25, 28:23, 31
[29.] Acts 14:22
[30.] Acts 15:16–18 (ESV). James's quote here is from Amos 9:11–12.
[31.] Acts 3:24
[32.] Acts 3:20–21

of the Mosaic Law. If Abraham, who lived long before the Law, is our spiritual father, then for the purposes of salvation, we can, as it were, fly over the Law without having to deal with it. We have, as Paul (the Jew!) said of himself, "died to the Law"[33] because we have the faith of Abraham who was saved without the Law and because the Law couldn't save a man but only condemn him.[34]

These truths set out by Paul regarding the Law are confirmed with even more specific emphasis by the writer of the book of Hebrews. There, the Mosaic Law, as far as Christians are concerned, is said to be "ready to disappear."[35] Two main reasons why are given. First, because Jesus, our "great High Priest," has "once for all…offered up himself," there is no need to rely on the sacrifices of the Law.[36] Second, the Law will soon "disappear" because the sacrifices made under the Law could not, in any case, "take away sins."[37] They were only effective for the sins that a man committed "in ignorance."[38] And because they could never make a man "perfect," the Levitical priests had to offer up sacrifices repeatedly and with no hope of completely cleansing the conscience of the offeror.[39] Because Christ's sacrifice atones for a man's sins forever, the sacrifices under the Law are rendered irrelevant. Because the sacrifices under the Law could not "take away sins," they are, in regard to salvation, a moot point.

It seems to me that what Paul and the Hebrews author say about the disappearance of the Law does not mean that it disappears altogether. Yes, for the purposes of salvation, it has no lasting atoning value—in fact, it never did. But concerning God's imposition of the Law upon the Jews for temporal earthly purposes, Christ's atonement does not nullify it. Jesus, after all, said: "Till heaven and earth pass away, one jot or one tittle will by no means pass from the Law till all is fulfilled."[40] He also said: "Heaven and earth will pass away, but My words will not pass away."[41]

We sometimes forget that the Law is the "Word" of God, and God's Word never plainly taught, either in the OT or the NT, that the entire Law is no longer binding on the Jews as an earthly ongoing obligation. We should remember that there is much in the Law that will ever be

---

[33.] Galatians 2:19
[34.] Romans 3:20, 5:20, 7:5–13, 8:1–4; 2 Corinthians 3:7–9; Galatians 3:10–13, 19–25
[35.] Hebrews 8:13
[36.] Hebrews 4:14, 7:27
[37.] Hebrews 10:4, 11
[38.] Hebrews 9:7
[39.] Hebrews 9:9, 10:1–3
[40.] Matthew 5:18 (NKJV)
[41.] Luke 21:33

beneficial for the Jews and, for that matter, all people. Who in their right mind would say that "thou shalt not kill," "love the Lord your God," and "love your neighbor" do not apply to us today?[42]

IN ACTS AND THE EPISTLES, THE JEWS ARE NOT FORGOTTEN

So there is much here that has to do with men and women being saved by faith in Christ, and by that, being transferred into his "heavenly" kingdom of love and peace. There is very little about God's original *literal* promises made to the patriarchs and even less about the literal prophecies that the prophets made concerning the final restored kingdom. What little there is will now be covered—and that little bit is worthy of our attention.

We must remember that *the* concern of the NT is making Christ known so men and women can believe in him and be saved from an eternity of punishment. It could be that the NT's general spiritual interpretation of the OT promises and prophecies does not necessarily mean that there is no further literal fulfillment at all; rather, it could simply mean that the blood relation (with the patriarchs) and the land are relatively unimportant (to put it mildly) compared to the question of how men and women escape eternal condemnation. The spiritual interpretation of the OT is vastly more important than the literal one. Hence, Acts and the epistles have to do with what matters most, for "God is love" and he "desires all men to be saved and to come to the knowledge of the truth."[43]

If the NT said plainly that God is done *permanently* with the Jews and their city and land, then that would be that and you would not be reading this book right now. But it doesn't say that—at least not directly.[44]

[42.] Exodus 20:13 (KJV); Deuteronomy 6:5; Leviticus 19:18

[43.] 1 John 4:8; 1 Timothy 2:4

[44.] As we've already seen, the parables of the vineyard owner (Matt. 21:33–46), the nobleman (Luke 19:11–27), and the banquet (Luke 14:16–24) seem to imply this. Jesus's cursing of the fruitless fig tree (Mark 11:12–14, 20–26) may be the closest thing to a direct condemnation of the Jews that spells the doom of their racial and national hopes, yet that cursing is enigmatic and unexplained enough to make us pause before employing it as a basis of this opinion. The main point does not seem to be the presentation of a figurative complete destroying curse upon all Israel but a warning to the disciples not to be unfaithful like most of their brothers, lest they suffer and die unredeemed and therefore doomed like them. After the fig tree withers, Jesus doesn't say, "Thus Israel will be," but the warning imperative, "Have faith in God" (Mark 11:22; see Isa. 7:9). The death of

THE NEW TESTAMENT CASE: ACTS AND EPISTLES

The NT focus indeed is upon salvation, regardless of race, but as we have seen from what Jesus said, the Jews are not forgotten. And from what we will consider now from Acts and Paul's letter to the Romans, it will become evident that the Jews and their kingdom are still on God's radar screen.

Regarding our subject, the tone of this NT portion is set right at the beginning by Dr. Luke in the first chapter of Acts. Here we are told that after the disciples had been for the proceeding forty days taught by Jesus about the kingdom of God, they asked him the last question that they ever asked him on earth: "Lord, is it at this time You are restoring the kingdom to Israel?"[45]

Even with all their previous earthly and ethnic fixation, as mentioned above, they could not possibly have had a *gross* misconception by now about the kingdom—for now they understood what Jesus's mission was all about, and the Holy Spirit, speaking through Luke, was at pains to inform us that he had taught them thoroughly about the kingdom between his resurrection and his ascension. Did the Holy Spirit tell Luke, and us, this only in order to tell us that they still didn't "get it"? Isn't it more likely that the Spirit told us this so that when they asked, "Lord, is it at this time?" we would understand that they asked the question with mainly correct Christ-informed assumptions? This latter possibility must be the correct one. If it were not, then Jesus would have corrected them then and there so that we too could know not to expect any further kingdom of "Israel." But he didn't do that; instead, he simply told them to begin growing the kingdom (like the mustard plant, the leaven, the net) by being his "witnesses" around Roman Palestine "even unto the uttermost parts of the earth."

In other words, he essentially said: "For now, don't worry about the messianic kingdom as you and your forefathers have typically understood it, but get out there and get people saved, and through that, the kingdom that I've told you about and that you expect—with you ruling along with me in Jerusalem—will surely come yet at a time that only my Father in heaven knows." And to indicate to them that their mission would soon make the kingdom at least in an infant form manifest, Jesus told them that the Holy Spirit would "in not many days" come upon them—something they, by this time, no doubt understood to be a fulfillment of

---

the fig tree here corresponds to the breaking of the Jewish "branches" off Paul's figurative olive tree (Rom. 11:16–25). There, the tree lives on, and the day will come (future to Paul's time when "the fullness of the Gentiles has come in") when many of the broken-off branches will be grafted back in. Then, says Paul, "all Israel will be saved" (v. 26).

[45.] Acts 1:6

what the prophets had foretold about the coming of the Spirit of God and the kingdom's restoration.

About ten days later, the Holy Spirit came upon the gathered disciples with power, such that they began praising God and speaking in foreign tongues. Thus, the kingdom began to be actualized. That this was so was strongly indicated by Peter when he then told the amazed Jewish onlookers that they were witnessing the fulfillment of prophecy. Joel had told of the "Day of the Lord" in which God would pour out his Spirit "on all flesh." If this was the dawning of that "Day," then that meant that the king was now beginning to establish his kingdom, just like Solomon began to establish his kingdom (Peter might have thought) by the execution of those men who had directly opposed him. The "mustard seed" sprouted a little bit that day. "Three thousand souls" put their faith in Christ because of what they saw and because of what Peter said.

A short time later, Peter confirmed that the prophesied kingdom was then beginning to become a reality. He and John, as mentioned earlier, went up to the temple to pray, and on the way in, they healed a beggar who had been lame from birth. Peter then proclaimed to the astonished crowd that all that had occurred with Jesus and the amazing miracles that they were now witnessing were the fulfillment of what the prophets had said from Samuel's time onward.[46]

So we see here that the emphasis right from the beginning of the Church was on manifesting the kingdom through getting people saved. Yet even in this, Peter did not forget about the "regeneration" of Israel that Jesus had spoken of, in which Jesus would "sit upon his glorious throne" and Peter and the other apostles would "sit upon twelve thrones judging the tribes of Israel." While the healed beggar, just mentioned, was still clinging to Peter and John with profound gratitude, Peter said to the crowd:

> [R]epent and return, so that your sins may be wiped away, in order that times of refreshing may come from the presence of the Lord; and that He may send Jesus, the Christ appointed for you, whom heaven must receive until the period of restoration of all things about which God spoke by the mouth of His holy prophets from ancient time.[47]

On one hand, the prophets predicted the days of the early Church—that is, they predicted the emergence of the kingdom that began to appear in

---

[46.] Acts 3:24
[47.] Acts 3:19–21

Peter's day. On the other hand, the "restoration of all things"—that is, the "restoration" of the kingdom of Israel—was understood by Peter to come at a future date when Jesus would return from "heaven." To put this succinctly, the spiritual "restoration" was already occurring, and the literal "restoration" was yet to come.

We have here yet another "until": Jesus is to remain in heaven "until the period of restoration." Peter does not say where Jesus will go when the restoration happens, but given all that the OT prophets said about the kingdom and the Messiah, and what Jesus said as well concerning his glorious return, Peter surely believed that the "restoration" would be of Israel and her rightful messianic king.

In a way, what Peter says here is an answer to the disciples' final question to Jesus, "Lord, is it at this time You are restoring the kingdom to Israel?" In view of what Peter said here by the Spirit, he could have theoretically answered the disciples: "Now is not the time, but when Jesus returns from heaven, he will then restore the Kingdom to Israel." This answer still does not meet their desire to know "when," but it does inform them that until that day, Jesus will remain in heaven, presumably at the right hand of the Father.

The disciples' root word for *restoring* and Peter's root word for *restoration* are the same and the meaning the same: "to restore to an earlier condition."[48] Obviously, the nation of Israel is what is to be restored, along with "David's fallen tent."[49] We should also not fail to note the rough parallel of Jesus's answer to Peter's declaration and question: "Behold, we have left everything and followed You; what then will there be for us?"[50]

> Truly I say to you, that you who have followed Me, in the regeneration when the Son of Man will sit on His glorious throne, you also shall sit upon twelve thrones, judging the twelve tribes of Israel.[51]

---

[48] *Theological Dictionary of the New Testament*, "αποκαθίστημι."

[49] The ardent replacement theologian Stephen Sizer in his book *Zion's Christian Soldiers? The Bible, Israel and the Church*, chap. 4, makes much of Peter's testimony (Acts 3:24) that the prophets had "announced these days," i.e., the days of the first outpouring of the Spirit and the subsequent beginnings of the Church. But regarding Peter's mention of the "period of restoration" that would occur upon Jesus's return from heaven (v. 21), Sizer is silent.

[50] Matthew 19:27

[51] Matthew 19:28

As used here, *regeneration* is nearly synonymous with Peter's use of *restoration*—the former meaning to "return to existence."[52] The "period of restoration of all things about which God spoke by the mouth of His holy prophets from ancient time" mentioned by Peter at the temple is the same "regeneration when the Son of Man will sit on His glorious throne" mentioned by Jesus. In Jesus's day, the kingdom was "near," and in Peter's day, the kingdom was already appearing. Yet for both Jesus and Peter, the kingdom over which Jesus would be king in Israel was something yet to come.

The apparent paradox of the kingdom already fulfilled and, at the same time, yet to be fulfilled could be stated this way: the Church (spiritually) fulfills the patriarchal promises now and the Jews will (literally) fulfill them in the future. This is not hard and fast, for there are plenty of Jews in the Church now, and there will be plenty of Gentiles in the restored kingdom when Jesus returns.

Paul deals with this mystery in Romans 9–11, explaining it through trying hard to account for what is to be made of the patriarchal promises made to the Jews in view of the fact that the promises are fulfilled in the Church. Earlier in Romans, Paul made the case that the Jews, having been stumbled by the Mosaic Law, are lost; yet Christians, having the faith of Abraham, are saved. God, however, made his promises to Abraham and his "seed," not to the Gentiles. So how can he now ignore the Jews and not be guilty of failure to fulfill what he has promised?

As can be seen, this question that Paul deals with has the potential for addressing the main question of this book, viz., will God fulfill his *literal* promises to the Jews even while the Church can be understood as *spiritually* fulfilling those promises? Unfortunately, Paul here does not *plainly* answer this question, but he does handle nicely the general question about how God can honor his promises to the Jews even while the promises are fulfilled in the Church. In other words, Paul handles the question only *spiritually*—i.e., how can the Church be saved, but God not save the Jews? Paul does not deal with the literal promises made to Israel although, as we'll see, there still seems to be a place for those literal promises as we read between the lines of Paul's argument.

Before we consider Paul's thoughts in Romans 9–11, let us look back just for a moment. God made promises to Abraham that had ongoing literal fulfillment in the OT history after him, and the prophets beginning in David's time confirmed that those promises would continue to be fulfilled literally. There were, of course, hints of the possibility of

---

[52.] *Theological Dictionary of the New Testament*, "παλιγγενεσία" (see "γίνομαι").

spiritual fulfillment in that the OT mentioned plainly in a few places that blessed life after death is a reality. John the Baptist and Jesus confirmed that there was indeed a spiritual fulfillment to be had (eternal blessed life) and said in their own unique ways that not all of the physical descendants of Abraham would be saved.

They could have used Paul's words of Romans 9:6: "They are not all Israel, which are of Israel."[53] As we've just seen, Paul took this a shocking (for Jews) step further when he taught that not only are some Jews really not children of Abraham but that some Gentiles in fact are. *But all this is for the purpose of salvation.* This is what the NT focuses on because it is the most important thing. But as we've seen, there are signs here and there that strongly indicate that the literal promises and prophecies are not forgotten by God. Jesus had his several uses of "until,"[54] and Peter, as just mentioned, had an important one too.[55] Now here, Paul will, at the end of his argument, give us an "until" that will, like the others, indicate that God has yet a plan for the Jews and their nation.

What Paul exactly means at every point of his argument in Romans 9–11 is not easy to understand. The reason why is given at the end of chapter 11. The truth of the matter is ultimately a "mystery" that only "the mind of the Lord" can know.[56] That is, the question that Paul deals with here—how can God be seen as honoring his promises to the Jews when they are fulfilled in the Church?—ultimately is not fully understandable by finite human minds.

The commentary that I'm holding in my hands spends more than two hundred pages striving to explain Romans 9–11.[57] But here we will only use a few pages, for the main argument that Paul makes is easy enough to understand. It is this: God has not broken his promises made to Israel because there has always been, and always will be, a "remnant" of Jews who believe and are saved. This argument includes three main components: first, the Jews are loved; second, there will always be a remnant because God sovereignly chooses them; third, the remnant is currently small, but after the chosen among the Gentiles have come in, God will choose many Jews to eternal blessed life. Let's now take a closer look at each of these three components.

[53.] KJV
[54.] Luke 21:24, 22:16, 18
[55.] Acts 3:21
[56.] Romans 11:25, 34
[57.] Douglas J. Moo, *The Epistle to the Romans*, vol. 6 of *The New International Commentary on the New Testament*, ed. Gordon D. Fee (Grand Rapids: Eerdmans, 1996).

Paul begins in chapter 9 by telling us of his anguish regarding his unsaved Jewish brothers. So intense is this anguish that he even goes as far as to say that he would be willing to be damned in their place if that would save them. Now here we can assuredly say that this is a reflection of the love that God has for the Jews. This thought is made sure by Paul's statement in 11:28 that the Jews are "beloved" by God "for the sake of the fathers," i.e., the patriarchs.

We might also remember Jesus lamenting, "Jerusalem, Jerusalem.... How often I wanted to gather your children together, the way a hen gathers her chicks under her wings, and you were unwilling."[58] Paul's love and concern for his brothers is ultimately not frustrated because God does keep his word. "It is not as though the word of God has failed," says Paul, "for they are not all Israel who are descended from Israel."[59] Reading on down through chapter 9, we learn that many who claim to be of Israel really are not because they are not true and obedient believers like Abraham. On the other hand, God has always chosen some of the patriarch's descendants to believe and be saved. God will keep his word to the "Israelites, to whom," Paul says, "belongs the adoption as sons, and the glory and the covenants and the giving of the Law and the temple service and the promises, whose are the fathers, and from whom is the Christ according to the flesh, who is over all, God blessed forever. Amen."[60]

Note here what God has lovingly bestowed upon the Jews: "adoption," "glory," "covenants," and "promises"—all blessings that have some spiritual import (representing salvation). God has also given "the Law" and "the temple service"—blessings that are in the main understood literally. It is important to see here that Paul is deeply concerned about his Jewish brothers, the corporate Israel, and that God has blessed them beyond measure with the blessings just mentioned. Paul goes on to declare that God has indeed honored his word in that there has always been a "remnant," both in the past and at the present time.

In the past, for example, Elijah believed and was told by God that seven thousand men besides the prophet still honored the LORD.[61] And in Paul's time, the apostle pointed out that at the very least, he believed and was saved, thus fulfilling God's promises to the Jews.[62] But notice that among the things that Paul numbers among God's blessings, several

---

[58.] Matthew 23:37
[59.] Romans 9:6
[60.] Romans 9:4–5
[61.] Romans 11:4
[62.] Romans 11:1

of them cannot entirely be applied to the Church: "the covenants and the giving of the Law and the temple service."[63]

To make this simpler, we could roll the "temple service" into "the Law" of which it was a part and then roll "the Law" into the Mosaic Covenant. It's easy to see the possible spiritual meaning in the elements of the Abrahamic Covenant but difficult to perceive spiritual meanings in most of the hundreds of elements of the Mosaic Covenant. In other words, when Paul says that the Mosaic Covenant belongs to Israel, it can only belong to *national* Israel and not to the Gentile-laden Church in which in Paul's day (according to his own teaching) there was diminishing regard for the Law and an increasing regard for the freedom obtained in Christ. If the elements of the Mosaic Covenant still literally belong to Israel, then the elements of the Abrahamic Covenant that can be taken literally—and, in fact, were for centuries after the patriarch—perhaps still belong to Israel in addition to what can be taken spiritually.

The second component that strengthens Paul's assertion that God continues to fulfill his promises made to the Jews is this: Paul, in the second half of chapter 9, shows how God has always *chosen* descendants of Abraham to become recipients of his blessings, according to the promises made to the patriarchs. There will always be a saved remnant because God sovereignly elects them. For example, Isaac was chosen instead of Ishmael and, in the next generation, Jacob instead of Esau.

Paul here goes into a brief description and defense of the election (predestination) doctrine. Because his line of thought here is arguably the most hard-hitting argument for election found in all of Scripture, this is the go-to Bible text that many hardcore predestination-minded pastors and theologians appeal to in order to support their cause. They often overlook the fact that the doctrine is not Paul's main issue but is only employed to support the trustworthiness of God's original promises given to the patriarchs. If God saves Jews from eternal condemnation, the salvation that he provides is not contingent upon the voluntary will of Jewish men and women but only upon his sovereign choice. This being so, the salvation that he can provide, in fulfillment of the promises, is incalculably more reliable than if the fulfillment were left to capricious and corrupt human choice. And thank God that this is so because, as the end of chapter 9 and also chapter 10 show, the Jews, having stumbled over the Law thinking that they can earn salvation apart from faith, have been overall in a long-term condition of infidelity toward God. But if

---

[63.] Romans 9:4

God, by his sovereign choice, can harden their hearts, he can also by his sovereign choice unharden them.

This now takes us to the third component of Paul's overall argument: God will fulfill his promises made to the Jews in that he will eventually bring about a large-scale Jewish revival. Paul explains in chapter 11 that God, through his sovereign choice, has for the time being hardened the hearts of the Jews. He has given them a "spirit of stupor, eyes to see not and ears to hear not." It seems hopeless, but Paul asks:

> [T]hey did not stumble so as to fall, did they? May it never be! But by their transgression salvation has come to the Gentiles, to make them jealous. Now if their transgression is riches for the world and their failure is riches for the Gentiles, how much more will their fulfillment be![64]

The Jews are hardened so that salvation comes to the much more numerous Gentiles, and what a blessing that is! But that's not the end of the story. The massive Gentile salvation will provoke the Jews to "jealousy," which will bring a great "fulfillment" among the Jews, and what an even greater blessing that will be! Paul even sees in his own mission the task of provoking his countrymen to jealousy so that he might "save some of them."[65] That this "fulfillment" means a future mass conversion of the Jews is indicated in Rom 11:15—"their acceptance [will] be but life from the dead"—and especially in what Paul says through his olive tree metaphor found in Rom 11:17–24. Let's consider this olive tree in some detail.

Many faithless Jewish branches have been broken off of the olive tree root of Israel. In other words, many blood descendants of Abraham are broken off from the root and do not partake in salvation. Paul here does not explain exactly what the "root" of the "cultivated olive tree" is, but it is clear enough that it represents Abraham and his descendants who share his faith—i.e., the Israel that is truly Israel.

The natural branches that are originally in the tree are faithful Jews, and the natural branches that have been broken off are faithless Jews. Based on what Paul says earlier about the general hardness of heart of the Jews, it is evident—although Paul does not say it here—that most of the natural branches of the olive tree in Paul's day were in the process of being broken off. But praise be to God, he has permitted faithful Gentiles to be grafted into the olive tree where they are "nourished by the sap" and find salvation. This is not a natural process, but one that is only

---

[64.] Romans 11:11–12
[65.] Romans 11:14

accomplished with difficulty. In other words, it is much more natural for Jews to be saved than for Gentiles to be saved. We might recall here Jesus's words: "Salvation is of the Jews."

This is good news for Paul's Roman Gentile readers; but he warns them: "Do not be conceited, but fear; for if God did not spare the natural branches, He will not spare you, either."

> But if some of the branches were broken off, and you, being a wild olive, were grafted in among them and became partaker with them of the rich root of the olive tree, do not be arrogant toward the branches; but if you are arrogant, remember that it is not you who supports the root, but the root supports you.[66]

If Paul had elaborated on this, he might have said something like the following to his Gentile audience:

> You may think that you are on equal footing with the Jews, or even superior, but the reality is that your eternal destiny is totally dependent upon the Jews—for the knowledge of God and the Christ has come to you via the Jews, and the atonement for your sins, which is necessary for salvation, is only provided by the "seed" of Abraham, Jesus of Nazareth. Thus, your salvation is truly, as Jesus said, "from the Jews." And all this being so, salvation, in God's eyes, is "to the Jew first and also to the Greek." Gentiles are, as the Lord said, in comparison with the Jews, only "dogs."[67]

Based upon what Paul says in Romans 9–11 and elsewhere, I don't think that this hypothetical elaboration is inaccurate. Yes, in his saving activity in the world, "God does not show favoritism."[68] As Paul said in Romans 10:28, "There is no distinction between Jew and Greek." But the tree into which we are unnaturally grafted, and through which we receive the "sap" that saves us from damnation, is thoroughly Jewish.

Given God's special care for the Jews and the wondrous mission that he has given them, it is no surprise that Paul indicates that God is far from being done with the Jews. After telling the Romans that it is a

---

[66.] Romans 11:17–18
[67.] See Matthew 15:26; John 4:22; Romans 1:16.
[68.] Romans 2:11 (BSB)

much more natural thing to graft back in the natural branches (i.e., Jews who repent and believe), Paul says this:

> For I do not want you, brethren, to be uninformed of this mystery—so that you will not be wise in your own estimation—that a partial hardening has happened to Israel *until* the fullness of the Gentiles has come in; and so all Israel will be saved.[69]

Because Paul has already spoken of a future Jewish "fulfillment," which will be like "life from the dead"; because he has just explained the relative ease that it takes for God to graft back in the natural broken-off branches; and finally because of the fact that the Jews will ever be "beloved" by God even while they are "enemies" of the Gospel, it is appropriate to let the "until" here remind us of those eschatological uses of the word by Jesus and Peter that we have previously pondered. With this in mind, we can safely assume that when Paul says that "a partial hardening has happened to Israel *until* the fullness of the Gentiles has come in," he knows—although he doesn't say it—that God will unharden the hearts of the Jews when the Gentile "fullness" is complete. Massive numbers of them will then be grafted back into the olive tree and saved. There will be a Jewish "fulfillment," i.e., a revival, like the world has never seen.

As it turns out, the unique "until" instances that we have considered tell us quite a lot about what will happen when Jesus returns from the "far country" in order to take possession of the "glorious throne": according to Paul, there is a mass conversion of the Jews; the Jews say to Jesus, "Blessed is he who comes in the name of the Lord";[70] Jesus eats the Passover and drinks wine with his disciples;[71] Jerusalem ceases to be "trampled underfoot by the Gentiles";[72] and finally, as Peter said, then will occur "the period of restoration of all things about which God spoke by the mouth of His holy prophets from ancient time."[73] Peter understood that what the prophets prophesied "from ancient times" was then being fulfilled *spiritually* in his day (as he indicates in Acts 2 and 3) and would be fulfilled *literally* in the future "restoration of all things."

Paul in Romans 9–11 goes a long way toward answering the question, "What about God's promises to the Jews?" by showing that

---

[69.] Romans 11:25–26a. Italics mine.
[70.] Luke 13:35
[71.] Luke 22:16–18
[72.] Luke 21:24
[73.] Acts 3:21

Jews are getting saved in his day (including himself), and many more will be saved after the Gentile harvest is over. But at the end of his excursus, he admits that there is still more to the story that he cannot fathom. Just how far this salvation will go and just what that will look like in the future is still mysterious:

> For just as you [Gentiles] once were disobedient to God, but now have been shown mercy because of their [the Jews'] disobedience, so these also now have been disobedient, that because of the mercy shown to you they also may now be shown mercy. For God has shut up all in disobedience so that He may show mercy to all. Oh, the depth of the riches both of the wisdom and knowledge of God! How unsearchable are His judgments and unfathomable His ways![74]

I won't try to unpack this text of holy Scripture. If Paul says that God's ways in this matter are ultimately "unfathomable," who am I to indicate otherwise? On the other hand, Paul tells the Roman Gentiles just before this that there are two things that are certainly true about ethnic Israel—two things that seem contradictory:

> From the standpoint of the gospel they are enemies for your sake, but from the standpoint of God's choice they are beloved for the sake of the fathers; for the gifts and the calling of God are irrevocable.[75]

To speak here of anything other than Paul's revelation that many Jews (some would say *all* Jews) will be saved in the end feels to me a little bit like defiling what is holy. Yet I can't help but think that Paul's understanding of "the gifts and the calling of God" included all that God originally promised, both figuratively *and* literally, when he spoke to the ancient patriarchs. There is no doubt here that Paul simply speaks about the ethnic Jewish people. They are, by and large, enemies of Christ—and thus enemies of the Church—and, at the same time, "beloved for the sake of the fathers." Because "the gifts and the calling of God are irrevocable" and in view of the OT witness, it seems to me that God will fulfill for the ethnic Jews, in complete spiritual *and* literal fullness, all that he has promised.

[74.] Romans 11:30–33
[75.] Romans 11:28–29

KINDNESS TOWARDS ISRAEL

It's time to bring this discussion of Paul to a close. But there is one more thing that I should illuminate. From what we've seen so far, it's clear that this apostle to the Gentiles cared deeply about the Gentiles and, specifically, about their salvation. This is reflected in his mission as recorded in Acts and in his letters to the churches. But there are signs—especially from what he said in Romans 9–11—that he continued to care deeply about his Jewish brothers even while he recognized that they were "enemies" of the Gospel and, as he said to the Thessalonians, that "wrath [had] come upon them to the utmost."[76] His concern for them was so profound that he suffered "great sorrow and unceasing grief" to the point that he even wished that he could suffer eternally in their place.[77] What was the reality with the Jews that prompted this anguish? It's pretty clear that it was the fact that in his day, most of the Jews were dying unsaved, and it looked like that would continue "until" God finished his saving work among the Gentiles and unhardened the hearts of the Jews.

Paul was distraught at the thought of most Jews dying in their sins. But that concern is not the main point of Romans 9–11. That some Jews all along had been saved and that some would be saved in the future was sufficient for Paul to believe that God had kept his promises to the Jews, even while he seemed to be fulfilling those promises in the Church—for the Church consists of not only Gentiles but Jews too. But if God really has fulfilled his promises to the Jews in this way, why does Paul, at the end of his discourse, still appear to be in some anguish of heart and declare in conclusion that the full answer which he hoped to apprehend is still lacking and thus the ways of God in this matter are yet "unfathomable"?

How the promises of God given to the Jews, as interpreted *spiritually*, can still be fulfilled in the Jews, Paul has answered successfully: there has always been a remnant, and always will be, who believe and are saved. Could it be that part of the mystery that Paul perceives has to do with how the ancient promises and prophecies might be *literally* fulfilled? In other words, Paul the Pharisee could not help but observe what appeared like the beginning of a slow disappearance of Jews and Judaism, and marvel with sorrowful amazement at how Israel, as the blood descendants of Abraham, Isaac, and Jacob, as "the apple of [God's] eye," could now be discarded like a bloody rag on the garbage heap of history. How could this be? For, as Paul testified, theirs are "the adoption as sons, and the glory and the covenants and the giving of the law and

---

[76.] 1 Thessalonians 2:16
[77.] Romans 9:1–3

the temple service and the promises"—*literally* and, praise be to God, figuratively.[78]

I just wish that Dr. Luke would have told us what Paul told the Jews in Ephesus when, as Luke records, "he entered the synagogue and continued speaking out boldly for three months, reasoning and persuading them about the kingdom of God."[79]

Well, maybe the Lord will one day inform his resurrected children of what Paul said during those three months. In any case, while it is true that Paul told us that he "forget[s] what is behind" and "press[es] onward toward the goal," he cannot help but glance over his shoulder at the Jews and all the traditions that made them the most unique and blessed people in the world. I believe that the Holy Spirit would not allow him to let go completely of the thought that God would one day again work directly with Israel and make good on his plainly stated promises and prophecies.

In his letters, Paul far and away presents the spiritual fulfillment side of the Old Testament: to be "blessed" means to be saved; to have "seed" means that people will come after Abraham who will believe like him and be saved; circumcision is taken as circumcision of the heart, which occurs when men are drawn by the Spirit and thereby saved; the Law given to Moses in the course of the Exodus, with expiatory sacrifices at its cult center, is spiritually fulfilled in Jesus Christ, who is the "Lamb of God who takes away the sin of the world";[80] and finally, the book of Hebrews—some believe written by Paul—indicates that the land promised to the patriarchs figuratively represents salvation and heaven, for Abraham looked forward to a "better country, that is, a heavenly one," where there is a "city which has foundations, whose architect and builder is God."[81]

With all this in mind, one would think that Paul had no reason whatsoever to look back longingly at Jerusalem, the Jews, and the Mosaic religion with its ceremonies and sacrifices practiced at the temple. Paul told us that his only intention was to "press on toward the goal" and that he considered everything that he had previously been and done to be "rubbish."[82] Yet, as we have just seen, what Paul said in Romans 9–11 reveals that there remained a tension in his mind regarding the Jews and the Church. And what Paul did toward the end of his evangelistic life

---

[78] Romans 9:3
[79] Acts 19:8
[80] John 1:29
[81] Hebrews 11:10, 16
[82] Philippians 3:8, 14

mission also showed that he could be a great man of the Church and yet still love his "brothers according to the flesh" and still honor their religion and their world.

After Paul completed his third main missionary journey, the Holy Spirit set in Paul's heart the intention of going to Jerusalem in time for the Pentecost festival.[83] On the way there, he met the leaders of the Ephesian Church in Miletus and said to them:

> And now, behold, bound by the Spirit, I am on my way to Jerusalem, not knowing what will happen to me there, except that the Holy Spirit solemnly testifies to me in every city, saying that bonds and afflictions await me.[84]

The Spirit urged Paul on yet warned him of troubles to come. He then sailed on to Tyre where the disciples "kept telling Paul through the Spirit not to set foot in Jerusalem."[85] And once in Caesarea, the Holy Spirit told Paul, via the prophet Agabus, that in Jerusalem he would be bound and handed over to the Gentiles. Luke and the disciples there, full of the Spirit just like Paul, begged him not to go. But Paul, full of the Spirit, would not agree, and the only thing that his dear friends could say was "the will of the Lord be done!"[86] We have already observed Paul's general ambivalence regarding the future of the Jews. Notice here also the apparent ambivalence of the Holy Spirit regarding Paul and Jerusalem: the Spirit in Paul prompted him to go; the Spirit in Paul's dear friends prompted them to urge him not to go.

Nevertheless, Paul went up to Jerusalem and greeted the leaders of the Church of Christ there. After Paul gave them a mission update, James informed him that there were there at that time many Jewish Christians who were "zealous for the Law." James then said:

> [T]hey have been told about you, that you are teaching all the Jews who are among the Gentiles to forsake Moses, telling them not to circumcise their children nor to walk according to the customs.[87]

---

[83]. Acts 20:16
[84]. Acts 20:22–23
[85]. Acts 21:4
[86]. Acts 21:10–14
[87]. Acts 21:21

THE NEW TESTAMENT CASE: ACTS AND EPISTLES

In other words, James let Paul know that in the minds of many, Paul was denigrating and dismissing the very heart of what it meant to be a Jew and be pleasing to God.

Now Paul, at this point, could have replied to James,

> Being in Christ, neither ethnicity nor circumcision nor the keeping of the law means anything, for we are saved by grace through faith alone. This is absolutely true for the Gentiles, and I'm growing in the opinion that it's true for Jewish Christians too. I'm guilty as charged!

But Paul didn't say anything like this. Instead, he acquiesced to James's request that Paul demonstrate unity with his Jewish brothers and his fidelity to the Mosaic Law by participating with four Jewish-Christian men in their final stage of, what was certainly, a Nazarite vow. He was to "purify" himself along with them for several days at the temple and then pay the cost for the shaving of their heads accomplished at the vow's completion.[88] If he could do this, James told Paul that "all will know that there is nothing to the things which they have been told about you, but that you yourself also walk orderly, keeping the law."[89] So this is what Paul did. Was this a case of Paul being, as he says elsewhere, "all things to all men"?[90] Or was this a case of hypocrisy? Or was it the case that there was some "mysterious" non-contradiction about a Jewish Christian continuing to identify with the Jews and their ways as literally decreed by God? That it was the latter is indicated by subsequent events.

At the temple, some Jews from Asia recognized Paul and cried out,

> Men of Israel, come to our aid! This is the man who preaches to all men everywhere against our people and the Law and this place; and besides he has even brought Greeks into the temple and has defiled this holy place.[91]

The latter charge about Paul bringing Greeks into the forbidden zone was untrue, but the former charge was not entirely unfounded: Paul "preaches...against our people and the law and this place." That is, Paul is against what it means to be Jewish. They then began beating Paul until Roman soldiers wrestled him out of their hands. As the soldiers were

---

[88.] Acts 21:22–26. The rules for the Nazarite are first spelled out in Numbers 6. Paul possibly also shared in the cost of the men's bloody sacrifices due at the end of the vow.
[89.] Acts 21:24
[90.] 1 Corinthians 9:22
[91.] Acts 21:28

taking him up the stairs into the Antonia Fortress, Paul was allowed to speak to the angry crowd. Here, Paul did not say if the accusations were true or false but witnessed to them about how Jesus had commissioned him to take the Gospel to the Gentiles. As soon as he mentioned the Gentiles, the mob renewed their outrage and cried out, "Away with such a fellow from the earth, for he should not be allowed to live!"[92]

The original plan was for Paul to stand trial there, but because a Jewish plot to kill Paul became known to the Roman commander, he was taken to Caesarea. There, the Roman governor Antonius Felix had him stand trial before a small delegation of accusers. Paul maintained his innocence, saying:

> I confess to you, that according to the Way, which they call a sect, I worship the God of our fathers, believing everything laid down by the Law and written in the Prophets.[93]

The mob at the temple accused Paul of denying "the Law," but he testified here to his belief in and fidelity to the Law and to what was written by the prophets as well.

After languishing for two years there (Felix hoped Paul would bribe him), Porcius Festus took over and soon thereafter convened a court to hear Paul's defense. Again, Paul maintained his innocence, saying, "I have committed no offense either against the Law of the Jews or against the temple or against Caesar."[94] Because Festus wanted him to return to Jerusalem to stand trial (where Paul knew men still wanted to kill him), Paul appealed to Caesar. So he was taken "through many dangers, toils and snares"—including a horrible shipwreck—to Rome. Acts ends with Paul holding an audience (in rented quarters, under guard) with the leading Jews of Rome. Among other things, Paul said to them:

> Brethren, though I had done nothing against our people or the customs of our fathers, yet I was delivered as a prisoner from Jerusalem into the hands of the Romans.[95]

So Paul, in various ways, denied that he was in any way against the Jews or the Law of Moses or the center of Jewish life, the temple. Positively speaking, he demonstrated his fidelity to the Law by partnering with the Nazarite Christian brothers in the completion of their vow. Before Felix,

---

[92.] Acts 22:22
[93.] Acts 24:14 (ESV)
[94.] Acts 25:8
[95.] Acts 28:17

he also confessed that it had been his intention in coming to Jerusalem to bring "alms" and to "present offerings," which may have included bloody sacrifices.[96] In any case, he financially assisted the Nazarites, as James advised, which is remarkable considering all that Paul by then had written, or would shortly write, about the Law and about what it really means to be a true son of Abraham.

[96.] Acts 24:17

THE NEW TESTAMENT CASE:
Revelation

INTRODUCTION

The OT looks down to earth with occasional glances up to eternal things. The NT Gospels, Acts, and the epistles look up to eternal things with occasional glances down to earth. Revelation continues the NT focus although, as with the NT in general, there are indications that God's end-time "Day of the Lord" will play out on earth—with Jerusalem as ground zero—and that Jesus will return to earth and defeat his remaining enemies there. The kingdom that he then establishes upon earth will last, according to Revelation 20, one thousand years. After this "Millennium" will come the final judgment, the consignment of all God's enemies to the "lake of fire," and, lastly, the establishment of the final state. In that final state, God's people will live within the "New Jerusalem" where there "will no longer be any death; there will no longer be any mourning, or crying, or pain."[1]

All this comes out plainly enough when Revelation is read straightforwardly. The events that, as John was told, "must soon take place" are, from John's standpoint, to take place in the future.[2] The fact that these events would "*soon* take place" notwithstanding (we're now nearly two thousand years beyond John's time), the general prophetic narrative of the events that play out as parts of the seals, trumpets, and

---

[1.] Revelation 21:4
[2.] Revelation 1:1, 19, 4:1, 22:6

bowls judgments gives the impression that those events occur *shortly before* the second coming of Christ.

In other words, Revelation, when read plainly, does not give the impression that the apocalypse lasts all the way from near John's time clear to the end (like many replacement theologians believe), but it only comprises a time span shortly before Christ's coming. This is especially apparent, as I'll show in some detail later, in view of the fact that the critical events of Revelation are indicated by the book to happen within a three-and-a-half years time span. And this, along with other facts, conclusively identifies these events with the final 3 ½ years of Daniel's prophetic time line in which the "little horn" runs amok and is at last killed by God. The death of the little horn—or as Revelation calls him, "the beast"—ushers in the omnipotent reign of the "Son of Man" along with his saints, which Revelation 20 limits to one thousand years. Christ's capitol city during the Millennium is most likely Jerusalem, and it may be the case that a physical temple will once again be up and running with rites that are somewhat based upon the Mosaic Law.

THE TRIBULATION EVENTS OF REVELATION OCCUR JUST BEFORE CHRIST'S SECOND COMING

That the Church during the Church age is not in view in the yet future (from John's time) events portrayed in chapters 5–19 is made likely by this simple fact: in chapters 1–4, which depict earthly and heavenly scenes/situations *at* John's time, *ekklesia* ("Church"), whether singular or plural, is mentioned some nineteen times; but in the following chapters that describe Tribulation events *after* John's time, the word is nowhere to be found.[3] Instead, the focus is upon the whole world convulsed by the Tribulation although there is some attention given to the Jews and their land.

Dispensationalists claim that the Church is taken up to heaven at the beginning of the Tribulation ("the rapture") and remains there protected during this 3 ½ years outpouring of God's wrath. When Jesus returns, it is almost certainly the case that he returns, along with his saints, to Jerusalem. That Jerusalem is the capital city during the Millennium is not overtly stated; but the fact that the end-of-the-Millennium final

---

[3.] Revelation 4–21 has no mention of the Church. Jesus at the end of the book (Rev 22:16) says that the vision given to John is intended for the "churches."

THE NEW TESTAMENT CASE: REVELATION

rebellion, led by Satan himself, comes against "the beloved city," surely confirms that Jesus's millennial throne city has been Jerusalem all along.[4]

As I showed in the book's introduction, leading men of the first century or two of the Church understood Revelation to teach that Jesus would return and reign for a thousand years on earth. But later churchmen, because they understood that the OT promises and prophecies were fulfilled in the Church, could not accept the notion that Christ would establish in the future an earthly and somewhat Jewish millennial kingdom. So they came to believe that the Tribulation and millennial events described in Revelation occur during the present Church age.

As I have shown before, this view of churchmen then and now makes the mistake of assuming that the OT promises really only have spiritual meaning and therefore can only be fulfilled in the Church. Israel lived under the Mosaic Law, and because the NT plainly teaches that the Law cannot save (only faith in Christ can save), Israel has no possible prospect of an eschatological blessed future. Thus, if the eschatological-themed book of Revelation describes anything of Jews, Israel, or the temple in the eschaton, it must be interpreted to figuratively represent the Church. With this accepted, and in view of the fact that the OT prophecies of the Day of the LORD and of the final restoration began to be fulfilled, as Peter declared, with the coming of the Holy Spirit at Pentecost, then whatever Revelation says about the Day of the LORD (= the Great Tribulation) and Christ's establishment of his kingdom (= the Millennium), must apply not to the end of time, but to the entire Church age.

This, however, is the predictable result of insisting from the start that the OT promises and prophecies are only about salvation and eternally blessed life in Christ. If the Church allowed for literal fulfillments also, then this would allow for the possibility of a literal earthly Millennium at the end of the Church age when the OT promises and prophecies of literal "seed" and land and material blessings for Israel are fulfilled.

I will now briefly lay out an argument that will, I hope, provide some justification for the view that the Tribulation occurs just before the return of Christ. If the Tribulation does not correspond to the Church age, then it is very difficult to say that the Millennium—which Revelation shows to come after the Tribulation—corresponds to the Church age. There are a number of details in Revelation that give strong evidence that key Tribulation events occur shortly before the Lord's return. These details can

---
[4.] Rev 20:9

be compared to details in the book of Daniel concerning the Tribulation that strongly indicate the same. Between the two testimonies, it is likely that these key Tribulation events do indeed occur just before Jesus returns. The diabolical career of the "beast"—or "the lawless one," "little horn," "Antichrist" as he is also called—is the key to understanding this.[5]

Right after the seals and trumpets judgments, the narrative in Revelation continues on to depict the advent of a profoundly wicked and powerful man who is called throughout the book, "the beast." The several verses that describe his personage and his evildoings pertain to the second half (3 ½ years) of Daniel's seventieth week, and the account of him ends with his demise at the coming of Christ.[6] That the beast is the same as the "little horn" in Daniel is easily discerned; both are described in terms of the features of a leopard, bear, and lion.[7] John, in the vision, sees the beast for the first time rising from the ocean. After noting the animal-like features just mentioned, that he was terribly wounded (probably killed) yet recovered, and that he is empowered by Satan (the "dragon"), John records this:

> There was given to him a mouth speaking arrogant words and blasphemies, and authority to act for forty-two months was given to him. And he opened his mouth in blasphemies against God, to blaspheme His name and His tabernacle, that is, those who dwell in heaven. It was also given to him to make war with the saints and to overcome them, and authority over every tribe and people and tongue and nation was given to him.[8]

Important to note here is that the beast is an arrogant blasphemer par excellence, that he hates and persecutes the saints, and that his term of wicked disservice lasts for 3 ½ years (42 months).

Further on in Revelation, we discover that he facilitates the gathering of an enormous army to fight against God and God's people; but as Christ returns to earth along with his saints, all on white horses, the beast and his army are destroyed:

[5.] 2 Thessalonians 2:8. Here, Paul speaks obviously of Revelation's beast. John elsewhere (1 John 2:18) probably refers to this final world ruler when he speaks of the "Antichrist."

[6.] Revelation 19:20

[7.] Revelation 13:2; Daniel 7:4–6

[8.] Revelation 13:5–7

> These will wage war against the Lamb, and the Lamb will overcome them, because He is Lord of lords and King of kings, and those who are with Him are the called and chosen and faithful.[9]

> And I saw the beast and the kings of the earth and their armies assembled to make war against Him who sat on the horse and against His army. And the beast was seized, and with him the false prophet who performed the signs in his presence, by which he deceived those who had received the mark of the beast and those who worshiped his image; these two were thrown alive into the lake of fire which burns with brimstone. And the rest were killed with the sword which came from the mouth of Him who sat on the horse, and all the birds were filled with their flesh.[10]

With this archenemy now defeated and consigned eternally to the lake of fire, Christ sets up his thousand-year kingdom, a kingdom in which his saints rule alongside him.[11]

Now here, the replacement theologians will say that this thousand-year reign is really not a literal thousand years but an indefinite length of time during which the Church grows on earth as Christ, her head, rules at the right hand of the Father from heaven. The Revelation 20 Millennium is the same era as the Revelation 6–18 Tribulation era. They say that Christ indeed did "come" on the "white horse" and, as Daniel has it, "on the clouds of heaven," when his wrath was displayed against the Christ-killing Jews in AD 70, and his power was manifested in the early Church. But this is highly questionable. Has Jesus really returned in bodily glory just like he himself foretold and Revelation 19 anticipates? The very words of Jesus on this question surely deny the possibility that he has, in some way or another, already returned:

> So if they say to you, "Behold, He is in the wilderness," do not go out, or, "Behold, He is in the inner rooms," do not believe them. For just as the lightning comes from the east and flashes even to the west, so will the coming of the Son of Man be.[12]

---

[9] Revelation 17:14
[10] Revelation 19:19–21
[11] Revelation 20:4
[12] Matthew 24:26–27

In other words, when Jesus returns, there will be no doubt about it. If the replacement theologians are right and Jesus has returned a long time ago, then not a soul on earth would disagree with them, for it would have been spectacularly obvious. But many do disagree, which necessarily means (in view of Jesus's words just quoted) that they are not right. The world has yet to see Jesus coming on the clouds riding a white horse in spectacular glory. And, of course, the worldwide cataclysmic Tribulation events depicted in Revelation and the horrible persecution prompted by the beast (directed at those who do not take his "666" mark) have not yet happened.

Let us now link the beast of Revelation with the little horn of Daniel in order to emphasize the fact that all this happens at the end of time. Daniel, like Revelation, has several features that plainly indicate that the Antichrist appears only a few years before the return of Christ.

Daniel served the Babylonian kings at the highest levels of government for about sixty years, then served Persian kings till the end of his earthly life. Early in his ministry—which began after he was brought from Judah and schooled in the ancient Babylonian cultic and imperial customs—Daniel was miraculously enabled to know the dream that King Nebuchadnezzar had dreamed (up till then the king had not told anyone the contents of the dream) and then went on to interpret that dream.[13] The king dreamed of an enormous and glorious statue that consisted of sections, from top to bottom, of gold, silver, bronze, steel, and finally, feet of steel mixed with clay. At the end of the dream, a great stone smashed the statue and only the stone remained. We know the statue's symbolic meaning from what Daniel said or from subsequent history. The four metals represented four kingdoms in successive order: Babylon, Persia, Greece, and Rome. The great stone that destroyed them all was understood by Daniel to represent the kingdom of God, which would then be permanently established upon the earth:

> In the days of those kings the God of heaven will set up a kingdom which will never be destroyed, and that kingdom will not be left for another people; it will crush and put an end to all these kingdoms, but it will itself endure forever.[14]

Some half century later, as Daniel served under the last Babylonian king, Belshazzar, the prophet had a dream (chapter 7) depicting the same four human kingdoms, but these kingdoms were represented by

---

[13.] Daniel 2
[14.] Daniel 2:44

four animals—a lion, bear, leopard, and, in the prophet's words, "a fourth beast, dreadful and terrifying and extremely strong; and it had large iron teeth."[15] Nebuchadnezzar's dream moved swiftly from the Roman empire to God's permanent empire; Daniel's dream in chapter 7, however, showed that significant events would occur between the Roman epoch and the establishment of God's kingdom. There would arise ten kingdoms from the Roman empire, and out of them would come a diabolical and extremely powerful king—the little horn—who would persecute God's people but would come to his end when God would establish his permanent kingdom.

As I now show the similarities between Daniel's little horn and the beast of Revelation, I will consider verses not only from Daniel 7 but also from chapters 8, 9, and 11. Chapters 8 and 11 are a little tricky because the final world ruler—called the "little horn" in chapter 8 and "the king of the north" in chapter 11—in the more short-term prophetical context is the Greek-Seleucid King Antiochus IV Epiphanes who intensely persecuted the Jews for about four years (roughly two centuries before Christ's ministry). He forced Jews, under pain of death, to eat pork, and he converted the temple into the worship of "Olympian Zeus" and the offering up of swine.[16] In Daniel 8 and 11, it is clear that the prophetical horizon eventually moves beyond Antiochus to the final Antiochus-like world ruler—i.e., the little horn—who is killed at the coming of the Lord.

The following comparison should make it plain enough that the beast of Revelation is the same person as the little horn of Daniel. Revelation 13:5 tells us that the beast is supremely arrogant and speaks blasphemies against God. Daniel, in speaking of the little horn, tells of his self-magnifying boasting. He thinks so highly of himself that he speaks "monstrous things against the God of gods."[17] In his mind, he is "equal with the Commander of the host"[18] and, in truth, probably considers himself better than God for he, as Daniel says, "will show no regard for the gods of his fathers...nor will he show regard for any other god; for he will magnify himself above them all."[19]

Because he is so wicked, Revelation 13:7 tells us that "it was... given to [the beast] to make war with the saints and to overcome them." The Holy Spirit speaking through John here surely had Daniel 7:21 in mind, for there, the prophet says: "I kept looking, and [the little] horn

---

[15] Daniel 7:7
[16] 1 Maccabees 1; 2 Maccabees 6–7
[17] Daniel 11:36
[18] Daniel 8:11
[19] Daniel 11:37

was waging war with the saints and overpowering them." Daniel also says that "he will destroy mighty men and the holy people."[20] The beast, according to Revelation 13:5, was given 42 months to carry out his malevolent plans, and this is exactly the time span that Daniel specified that the saints would endure under his murderous hand: "He will... wear down the saints of the Highest One…and they will be given into his hand for a time, times, and half a time," i.e., 3 ½ years, which is 42 months.[21]

During this time, Daniel shows in several ways that the little horn brings about a desolation and defilement of the temple.[22] Revelation does not mention this, but it is apparent that the Jerusalem Temple exists at this time, for during the Tribulation, John is told to measure the temple's inner and outer courts.[23] Because the beast rampages over all the earth, hates God, and kills God's people, it only makes sense that he would target the temple.

There is one more commonality between Revelation and Daniel that makes the identity between the beast and the little horn even more sure. When God and Christ come in glory and establish the kingdom of God, both John and Daniel record the demise of the beast/little horn. John tells us that he and a coalition of lesser kings "wage war against the Lamb" and "against Him who [sits] on the horse and against His army,"[24] which is the scene of Christ—the "King of kings, and Lord of lords"—returning in glory along with his saints to earth. The beast (as well as his right-hand man, the "false prophet"), as has already been mentioned, is "seized" and immediately "thrown alive into the lake of fire which burns with brimstone."[25] In the lake of fire, as John says earlier of the fate of the followers of the beast, "the smoke of their torment goes up forever and ever."[26]

Similarly, Daniel notices the following in the course of the "Ancient of Days" taking his seat in final judgment, and the "Son of Man" coming on "the clouds of heaven" and being presented before him:

---

[20] Daniel 8:24

[21] Daniel 7:25. See also Daniel 8:13–14, 9:27, 12:11.

[22] Daniel 8:11–14, 9:27, 11:31, 12:11

[23] Revelation 11:1–2. Jesus and Paul spoke about this future defilement of the temple. See Matthew 24:15 and 2 Thessalonians 2:3-4.

[24] Revelation 19:19

[25] Revelation 19:20

[26] Revelation 14:11

THE NEW TESTAMENT CASE: REVELATION

> I kept looking because of the sound of the boastful words which the [little] horn was speaking; I kept looking until the beast was slain, and its body was destroyed and given to the burning fire.[27]

Note here that Daniel calls the little horn "the beast." All this goes to show, along with other features of Daniel and Revelation, that the final world rulers that they respectively depict are one and the same.

The fact that Daniel depicts the final world ruler and his terrible persecution against the saints during the few years just before God's judgment and Christ's return makes it doubly likely that the era of the beast and the Tribulation as recorded in Revelation indeed occurs just before Christ's second coming.

In Revelation 19, as we have just noted, Christ returns upon his white horse and defeats and consigns to the lake of fire the beast who, along with his great army, has defied the armies of the living God. The killing and burning of the little horn in Daniel 7 also occurs in the context of God's judgment and the coming of the Son of Man. In the similar vision of Daniel in chapter 8, God's judgment and the coming of the Messiah are not mentioned, but we do read that the little horn is "broken without human agency" and that this "pertains to the time of the end."[28] We could notice too Daniel 9:27, which, while admittedly enigmatic, seems to have the final world ruler—"the prince"—wreaking havoc at the temple during the last 3 1/2 years of world history immediately after which he comes to a "complete destruction." Finally, the king of the north of chapter 11—who "will exalt and magnify himself above every god and will speak monstrous things against the God of gods"—after rampaging up and down through "the beautiful land" will "come to his end, and no one will help him."[29]

The very next words of the Lord to Daniel are these:

> Now at that time Michael, the great prince who stands guard over the sons of your people, will arise. And there will be a time of distress such as never occurred since there was a nation until that time; and at that time your people, everyone who is found written in the book, will be rescued. Many of those who sleep in the dust of the ground will awake, these to everlasting life, but the others to disgrace and everlasting

---

[27] Daniel 7:11
[28] Daniel 8:25, 17
[29] Daniel 11:36, 41, 45

contempt. Those who have insight will shine brightly like the brightness of the expanse of heaven, and those who lead the many to righteousness, like the stars forever and ever.[30]

After the demise of the king of the north comes the final judgment and the general resurrection. Similarly, in Revelation 19–20 we see the demise of the beast, Christ's return to earth, his wrath poured out, and the resurrection of the righteous—called "the first resurrection."[31] When all this is honestly considered, it is hard to believe that the Tribulation events involving the final world ruler should be nebulously understood as occurring over much or all of the Church era.

The preexilic prophets before Daniel spoke much about the final return of God's people to Jerusalem, where God's perfect kingdom, ruled by the Messiah, would be permanently established. These prophets, as we've seen, provided many wonderful details about this kingdom: the nations will submit to it, the wolf will lie down with the lamb, there will be amazing material abundance, people will live much longer than now, and Isaiah even seems to show (Isa. 25:6–8) that death in that kingdom will finally be overcome. But they didn't say *when* this final return from exile would be. Some, no doubt, thought that the return from Babylon would commence God's permanent kingdom, but the experience on the ground by Zerubbabel, Joshua, and later, Ezra and Nehemiah refuted this view (life was anything but the life of the promised Millennial Kingdom), and this view was also refuted by the prophetic truths revealed to Daniel.

Between his day (at the time of the Babylonian exile) and the setting up of the kingdom of God, there would arise and fall large-scale human kingdoms. And just before God's kingdom would come, a wicked world ruler—the little horn—would run roughshod over God's people for 3 ½ years. Immediately following, God and the Son of Man would establish a kingdom, as Daniel told Nebuchadnezzar, that would fill "the whole earth."

Unlike the previous prophets, Daniel says little about the characteristics of this kingdom other than the facts that it would last forever and never be destroyed and (praise the Lord!) that its commencement would happen more or less at the time of the general resurrection of the dead—some "to everlasting life, but…others to disgrace and everlasting contempt."[32]

The prophets before Daniel made this kingdom out to be very Jewish, but Daniel attached no Jewishness to it at all although, with only

---

[30] Daniel 12:1–3
[31] Revelation 20:5–6
[32] Daniel 12:2

THE NEW TESTAMENT CASE: REVELATION

one indicator (Dan. 2:39), he confirmed the fact that it would exist on earth. The "stone not made by hands"—i.e., God's kingdom that would pulverize all preceding kingdoms—would be a kingdom that would fill "the whole earth." For Daniel and the prophets before him, this kingdom that fills "the whole earth" is permanent and, it seems, unchanging. But John in his Revelation shows us that this kingdom does experience several major changes. After a thousand years, there will be a general rebellion against God and Christ led by the devil himself. After this rebellion is put down and the devil condemned to the lake of fire, the heavens and earth are destroyed and remade, the wicked dead are resurrected to judgment and condemnation, and the "new Jerusalem" coming down "out of heaven, as a bride prepared for her husband" becomes the new center of God's universe.[33]

Because these changes seem to be at odds with the steady state of the restored kingdom of the OT prophets, many Christian theologians have understood that the eternal kingdom of the prophets corresponds to the eternal state of Revelation 21's New Jerusalem. Revelation 20's Millennium, on the other hand, is believed to be an unknown, but substantial, span of time during which the Church grows upon earth while Christ rules at the right hand of the Father and while Satan is bound in the abyss. Of course, much could be said about this, pro and con. Yet Christ, in his words to John as recorded in Revelation 20, put such an emphasis upon the precise span of a thousand years that it makes it very difficult for us to understand it as anything other than just what it says repeatedly: after Christ returns, the devil is bound for a thousand years and confined to the abyss for a thousand years; the nations are thus free from being deceived for a thousand years; the Tribulation era martyrs are resurrected and reign with Christ for a thousand years;[34] the wicked dead are resurrected at the end of the thousand years; and finally, at the end of the thousand years, the devil is freed from the abyss and organizes a worldwide rebellion against Christ and his saints which fails. Satan is then thrown into the lake of fire, and the wicked dead from all ages are judged and also thrown into the lake of fire.

For those who think that the Millennium is the Church age, I would ask, "Is Satan really fully bound now? Is not the evidence of his presence and power all around us?" I would also ask: "Have we already

---

[33.] Revelation 20–22

[34.] It seems to be the case that all the righteous dead—apparently from the creation to the second coming of Christ—are resurrected at the beginning of the Millennium and reign with Christ for a thousand years.

been resurrected and are we now truly reigning along with Christ with all enemies under our feet?" I'm just a simple man, but it seems to me that the conditions described in the Revelation 20 Millennium are far different than the conditions today.

THE MILLENNIAL REIGN OF CHRIST IS EARTHLY AND SUBSTANTIALLY JEWISH

That the restored perfect kingdom of the Messiah is Jerusalem-based and substantially Jewish has already been shown from the OT prophets. Although the gaze of the NT is mainly upward to heaven and eternal life, we still see flashes of concern for the Jews and for the promises made to them. Jesus foretold the time when he would return in glory—and there would be no doubt about his return—to rule on his "glorious throne" along with his apostles who would themselves "sit upon twelve thrones, judging the twelve tribes of Israel."[35]

As to the exact location of Christ's reign, we are not told by Jesus (it was probably simply assumed to be Jerusalem); but the two angels who spoke to the disciples at Christ's ascension told them that Jesus would return just like he had gone up, which surely—especially in view of Zechariah 14:4—meant that he would descend from the cloud back to the Mount of Olives, or generally speaking, Jerusalem.[36] When Christ returns as a mighty warrior riding a white horse, as described in Revelation 19, we are not told where he returns to, only that he first appears on the horse in heaven and that he and the saints who come with him defeat the beast as well as the kings in league with him. That Jesus's millennial reign is earth focused, even Jerusalem focused, can be made certain by the consideration of not a few verses in Revelation that in general show that the Jews and their land continue to stand in some prominence in God's end-time plans. Let us consider these briefly.

We must first keep in mind that Revelation is centered upon the "Lamb" who, as Revelation 5:5 says, is "the Lion that is from the tribe of Judah, the Root of David." The Jewishness of Jesus's kingdom may be debatable, but there is no doubt about the Jewishness of the king, which will surely always be of treasured value to him.

Now notice that the 144,000 men who are sealed and protected from the wrath of God during the Tribulation are not from twelve nations

---

[35.] Matthew 19:28, 24:27, 25:31
[36.] Acts 1:11

but are "sealed from every tribe of the sons of Israel"—the individual tribes being named one by one.[37]

Apparently, the temple exists during the Tribulation period. Although most of John's mentions of the temple in Revelation are of the temple in heaven, he is told at one point to measure what appears to be the physical temple in Jerusalem.[38] These measurements did not include the outer temple court for, as John was told, "it has been given to the nations, and they will tread underfoot the holy city for forty-two months."[39] Note that these can only be the "nations" of the earth and that the "holy city" can only be Jerusalem. We also might recall that the heavenly messengers told Daniel that the temple would be desolated and defiled for 3 ½ years, but after that, "the holy place [would] be properly restored."[40]

If the temple is "properly restored" more or less at the end of that time, then it is probably the case that it exists when Christ returns immediately following those forty-two months. We should also consider the fact that toward the end of the Tribulation, the "kings of the whole world" are gathered by demonic forces to "Har-Magedon," often rendered "Armageddon," for "the war of the great day of God, the Almighty."[41] The name "Har-Magedon," although taken from the hill ("Har") of Megiddo that is situated on the southwest edge of the Jezreel Valley, here represents this valley where armies have, through the ages, from time to time joined in battle.[42] Now when the Lord returns, he does not fight against evil forces in heaven but attacks, according to Revelation 19, from heaven against "the beast and the kings of the earth and their armies" who are all, obviously, on earth.[43]

As the battle rages, the blood from the wicked slain rises up to the horses' bridles.[44] Those who die are not "the spiritual forces of wickedness in the heavenly places"[45] but "the flesh of kings and the flesh

---

[37] Revelation 7:4–8
[38] Revelation 11:1–2
[39] Revelation 11:2
[40] Daniel 8:14. See also Daniel 7:25, 8:13, 9:26–27, 12:11.
[41] Revelation 16:12–16
[42] Deborah and Barak were victorious there against the army of Jabin, king of Canaan (Judg. 4). Necho, the king of Egypt, defeated the army of Judah there and killed King Josiah (2 Kings 23; 2 Chron. 35).
[43] Revelation 19:19
[44] Revelation 14:20, 19:15. See also Isaiah 63:1–6.
[45] Ephesians 6:12

of commanders and the flesh of mighty men and the flesh of horses and of those who sit on them."[46] This fulfills Psalm 110:5–6:

> The Lord is at Your [i.e., Yahweh's] right hand; He will shatter kings in the day of His wrath. He will judge among the nations, He will fill them with corpses, He will shatter the chief men over a broad country.

Once victorious, Christ rules, according to Revelation 20, for a thousand years. Where he rules is not stated. The saints also sit on thrones and judge, and the righteous Tribulation martyrs rule along with Christ as well. Where the saints rule is also not stated in Revelation 20, but the general location is made clear in Revelation 5:10: "They will reign upon the earth." It is apropos here to quote Paul's words to the Corinthians: "Do you not know that the saints will judge the world?"[47]

At the end of the Millennium, Satan will be released from the abyss and "deceive the nations which are in the four corners of the earth, Gog and Magog," in order to marshal them for war against "the saints and the beloved city."[48] This is certainly an earthly scene, and the "beloved city" is surely Jerusalem. But God destroys them by fire from heaven, and Satan is straightaway cast into the lake of fire wherein already reside the beast and his false prophet. And just after that is the "great white throne" judgment where all the wicked dead are resurrected, judged guilty, and condemned to the lake of fire.[49]

Worthy of note is that both the earth and the heavens disappear at the time when God sits on the great white throne for the final judgment. From that time on, Jerusalem and the Holy Land and the temple as we have known them are no more, for God makes all things new—even a "New Jerusalem" in which there is no temple, and there is no sun or moon, for God is the temple of men and God is their light.[50]

So Revelation does not tell us too much about what happens during the Millennium, but as we have seen, the OT prophets told us a lot. There we learned that there is a terrible "Day of the Lord" judgment that immediately precedes the great regathering of the Jews to their homeland, and once the Messiah's kingdom is established, Edenic conditions will then prevail and the nations of the earth will bring their

---

[46] Revelation 19:18
[47] 1 Corinthians 6:2
[48] Revelation 20:7–9
[49] Revelation 20:11–15
[50] Revelation 21

wealth to Zion and offer their allegiance to the God and Messiah of Israel. The picture that the prophets literally painted of this time was consistently earthly. The greatest feature of that earthliness was their portrayals of human life—admittedly greatly improved—proceeding on *mortally*: men and women would live longer but still die.[51]

The only *clear* prophetic exceptions to this were Isaiah's declaration (Isa. 25:6–8) that "on this mountain" (probably Mount Zion [Isa. 24:23]) death would finally be abolished, and Daniel's prophecy (Dan. 12:1–3) of the eventual resurrection of both the righteous and unrighteous dead.[52] Daniel's prophecy indicates that this resurrection will happen not long after the "king of the north" (i.e., the "little horn"/"beast") is killed, but Isaiah's prophecy is not time specific.

The OT thus gave us a robust picture of the eschatological situation of *mortal* men but only an extremely faint picture of the eschatological situation of *immortal* men. And this "robust picture" presented mainly the Jewish situation, but the "extremely faint picture" was ethnically unlimited. The NT is just the opposite. The "robust picture" concerns the eternal afterlife, and an "extremely faint picture" can be discerned that involves the "eschatological situation of *mortal* men," i.e., their situation after Christ returns to earth and during his millennial reign there.

The OT told us much about the final earthly Jewish kingdom and hinted at the fact that there is much beyond that, i.e., immortal life. The NT tells us much about immortal life and hinted at the conditions of mortal life once Jesus returns. So when we consider the *big* biblical picture, the OT and the NT are really not that much different. They both tell of the culmination of temporal life during the reign of the Messiah in Jerusalem, and they both tell of the eternal life to come.

The OT far and away emphasizes the former, the NT the latter. Thus, when Revelation gets to the point of telling us about the return of the Messiah, we, after having studied the OT prophets, are not surprised to find that there is a long span of time given—the "thousand years" of Revelation 20—during which the Messiah rules on earth along with his saints.

Then from Revelation 20:11 on to the end, we have presented to us a "robust picture" of the eternal state—vastly richer than what the OT only hinted at: the evil dead are raised, finally judged, and condemned to eternal suffering in the lake of fire; the old heaven is replaced by a "new heaven" that has no sun or moon, and the old earth is replaced by a "new earth" that has no ocean or temple; and the eternal home of saved

---

[51.] Isaiah 65:20
[52.] Daniel 12:3

men and women is the "New Jerusalem," which has twelve gates named after the twelve Israelite tribes and twelve foundation stones named after the twelve Israelite apostles of Christ. The organic and foundational connection of Israel with the "bride of Christ" is thus memorialized forever.

Let us now briefly consider the Millennium proper, mainly from the little bit of information that Revelation 20 gives us but also from some corresponding facts provided by OT prophets. Christ's coming is presented in Revelation 19. John saw the Lord coming, as "heaven opened," on a white horse followed by his saints who also rode white horses. He is called the "Word of God" and the "King of kings, and Lord of Lords." John says in 19:15:

> From His mouth comes a sharp sword, so that with it He may strike down the nations, and He will rule them with a rod of iron; and He treads the wine press of the fierce wrath of God, the Almighty.

This fulfills several OT prophecies concerning the coming of the LORD—the great "Day of the LORD"—that immediately precedes the messianic kingdom. Isaiah, for example, told us that the Messiah would "strike the earth with the rod of His mouth" and that he, in "anger" and "wrath," would tread "the wine trough alone."[53] And David said that the Messiah would one day "break" the nations "with a rod of iron."[54] We also might recall that Jesus's coming upon the white horse is the same as Daniel's vision of the Messiah coming "with the clouds of heaven."[55]

Now proceeding on to Revelation 20, we first learn that the devil is taken out of commission for the entire thousand years. This is not specifically mentioned by the prophets, but we do know from them that once the messianic kingdom begins, there is such a level of peace and commitment to the LORD that it is hard to picture the devil during that time "prowling around like a roaring lion seeking whom he may devour." Satan specializes in lies, murder, mayhem, and rebellion against God, but the prophets don't show these being manifested in the messianic kingdom—although according to Ezekiel, enough sin will still be present to warrant expiatory sacrifices (more about this a little later).

Next, we are told that Christ rules during the Millennium in concert with saints, who themselves sit on thrones, some of them being

---

[53.] Isaiah 11:4, 63:3
[54.] Psalm 2:9. The NT—Acts 4:25–26—attributes Psalm 2 to David.
[55.] Daniel 7:13; Matthew 24:30, 26:64

THE NEW TESTAMENT CASE: REVELATION

righteous and resurrected martyrs who died during the Tribulation. This, of course, matches perfectly the prophecy of Daniel that showed that Christ's followers will reign with him in his kingdom:

> Then the sovereignty, the dominion and the greatness of all the kingdoms under the whole heaven will be given to the people of the saints of the Highest One; His kingdom will be an everlasting kingdom, and all the dominions will serve and obey Him.[56]

Daniel wasn't the only one who predicted that the saints would one day function in a royal capacity. Moses, for example, informed the Israelites that if they loved and obeyed God, they would be the "head" of the nations and not the "tail."[57] This promise certainly applies to Israel during the Millennium when everyone will know the LORD:

> For the LORD your God will bless you as He has promised you, and you will lend to many nations, but you will not borrow; and you will rule over many nations, but they will not rule over you.[58]

And God, through Isaiah, had this to say about Israel's millennial role in the world:

> Kings will be your guardians, and their princesses your nurses. They will bow down to you with their faces to the earth and lick the dust of your feet; and you will know that I am the LORD; those who hopefully wait for Me will not be put to shame.[59]

Just after the end of the Millennium, Satan is released from his bondage in the abyss and then leads a worldwide rebellion against "the saints and the beloved city."[60] This rebellion is immediately put down by God, and the devil is thrown into the lake of fire.

The Revelation 20 Millennium description fits fairly well with what the OT prophets foretold, but there are a couple of significant difficulties. First, the prophets gave no indication that post-death

---

[56] Daniel 7:27
[57] Deuteronomy 28:13
[58] Deuteronomy 15:6
[59] Isaiah 49:23
[60] Revelation 20:9

resurrected saints would occupy the Millennium. Isaiah 65:20 says that people would then live longer than normal, but there is no mention of immortality. Also, the prophets indicated in various ways that the perfect restored kingdom ruled over by the LORD and his Son, the Messiah, would endure indefinitely, with no further rebellion and disasters of the kind that had repeatedly occurred in the past.

Replacement theologians take these features as evidence that the prophesied messianic kingdom is not an earthly "Millennium" but is the heavenly eternal state. Isaiah 65:20's depiction of lengthy, but mortal, life spans is to be taken as figurative of eternal life. If the replacement theologians are right, it comes at the very high cost of spiritualizing such a large portion of OT Scripture, that the plain meaning of the rest of Scripture is put in doubt. Their main defect is that they, in general, spiritualize the whole corpus of OT eschatological prophecy and, in the process, dismiss the literal meaning of these prophecies.

If there were substantial indications in the prophecies themselves that this should be done, that would be one thing; but the prophets do not show any sign that this *wholesale* spiritualization should be the rightful interpretive mode. In my view, the far more reasonable and biblical and meaningful mode is to first take these prophecies literally, then be open to the possibility of further figurative meaning. Taking this much more literally coherent route, we can be open, for example, to the possibility that Isaiah 65:20's prophecy of unusually long life in the Millennial Kingdom can mean just that while at the same time hinting at unending life. Perhaps as the messianic kingdom commences, one is fulfilled as well as the other.

Regarding the messianic kingdom's duration, it may also be the case that the prophecies of the literal earthly messianic kingdom are to be taken both literally and figuratively. The kingdom is truly earthly, for a season, and it can be figuratively taken for the permanent "better country" to come. As far as the post-Millennium final rebellion is concerned (Rev. 20:7–10), it may not be that big of a conflict with the OT prophecies. For while it is true that the prophets said that, from the commencement of the messianic kingdom-onward, there would be no more major disasters for God's people, they did not say that there would be no sin at all. Zechariah, for example, warned that nations that failed to attend the Feast of Booths would be punished by God with severe drought.⁶¹ Assumed here is that some nations will hesitate to obey God in the Millennium.⁶²

In any case, Satan's final rebellion at the end of the Millennium may not harm any of God's children, for it seems to be the case from the Revelation 20 text that Satan and the rebellious hordes with him at that time will be destroyed by fire from God *before* they attack "the camp of the saints and the beloved city." There's not enough information given here to be dogmatic, but if it is so that the saints during Satan's final rebellion are kept safe, then the unending peace and security of the messianic Jerusalem described by the prophets is in harmony with Revelation 20–22 because the Millennium will transition peaceably— for God's people—to the eternal New Jerusalem.

Now one more thing before I proceed to the book's conclusion. Because the Jerusalem Temple exists during the Tribulation and is "restored" at the end of the Tribulation,⁶³ then it is probable, as I said earlier, that it exists at the beginning of the Millennium.⁶⁴ Even if it is destroyed in the Tribulation, it will be rebuilt as soon as Christ begins reigning from Jerusalem.

John in Revelation 20 does not say anything about the temple, but Ezekiel, as we've already seen, describes the Millennial Temple in minute detail. The main reason why replacement theologians interpret all the details of this temple figuratively of heaven and eternal life (which is a big stretch, literally speaking) is because they absolutely cannot allow any sort of temple wherein is practiced the Mosaic Law, for that would mean that in the future, men must earn their way to heaven through works of the Law, including expiatory sacrifices, which makes the cross of Christ count for nothing. I have already handled this issue, and related issues,

---

⁶¹· Zechariah 14:16–19. Robert Saucy writes: "[Under the millennial reign of the Messiah] the nations will not engage in war, and the world will live in peace (Ps 46:9; Isa 2:4; 9:5; Mic 4:3; Hos 2:18; Zec 9:10). This messianic reign of peace does not immediately involve the exclusion of all sin; that will take place only with the making of all things new. That sin is present during the Messiah's reign is evident in his settling disputes among the nations (cf. Isa 2:4) and in the possibility of punishing the disobedient (Zec 14:16–19). But that sin will never be able to thwart the righteous, powerful reign of the Messiah" (Robert Saucy, *The Case for Progressive Dispensationalism* [Grand Rapids: Zondervan, 1993], 234).

⁶²· See also Isaiah 60:12.

⁶³· Daniel 8:14

⁶⁴· Multiple passages speak of a Millennial Temple and/or sacrifices, including: Isaiah 2:2–3, 56:4–7, 60:7, 13; Jeremiah 33:14–22; Ezekiel 40–48; Daniel 9:24; Joel 3:18; Haggai 2:7–9; and Zechariah 14:16–21.

before, but let me spend a few moments dealing with this subject in relation to the possible future temple in the Millennium.

As Revelation 20 shows, there will be resurrected saints reigning with Christ in the Millennium. They will initially rule over living, but mortal, saints who survive the Tribulation. Revelation 19 and not a few OT prophecies give the impression that no Christ-rejecters survive the Tribulation and the coming of Christ.[65] But maybe there will be a few infidels who come crawling through only to find themselves suddenly under the iron rule of Christ. Be that as it may, it is most likely the case that the mortal survivors of the Tribulation will rapidly multiply during the peaceful and productive days of the Millennium, especially in view of the fact that they will live very long lives. Even though all men will know the LORD then,[66] not all men will fully worship or obey the LORD. The massive rebellion that occurs at Millennium's end is proof that not all hearts will be *fully* devoted to the LORD during the Millennium.

All will probably be well at the beginning, but as the centuries roll on, a desire for freedom will build up that will finally reach a boiling point just in time for Satan's release from the abyss. And so, he will easily then "deceive the nations" and put them in a worldwide state of insurrection.[67] The point is that during the Millennium, there will be many regular mortal men and women upon the earth. Yes, they will possess God's Spirit, but that will not make them absolutely impervious to sin.

The trend, therefore, will be roughly similar to that which obtained during the era of the First Temple in Israel. Things started off with a bang with Solomon at the helm—his people were "joyful and glad of heart"[68]—but the situation went rapidly downhill from there, such that ten tribes rebelled right after Solomon died, and Judah and Israel after that eventually became so idolatrous and corrupt that God destroyed them both.

So if there is a temple during the Millennium, its function might not be all that much different than the First Temple. The thought that I'm

---

[65] Dwight Pentecost, regarding the mortal people who transition into the Millennium, says this: "The earthly theocratic kingdom, instituted by the Lord Jesus Christ at His second advent, will include all the saved of Israel and the saved of the Gentiles, who are living at the time of His return. Scripture makes it very clear that all sinners will be cut off before the institution of the Kingdom (Isa. 1:19–31; 65:11–16; 66:15–18; Jer. 25:27–33; 30:23–24; Ezek. 11:21; 20:33–44; Mic. 5:9–15; Zech. 13:9; Mal. 3:2–6; 3:18; 4:3)" (Pentecost, *Things to Come*, section entitled "The Subjects in the Millennium").

[66] Jeremiah 31:34

[67] Revelation 20:8

[68] 2 Chronicles 7:10

THE NEW TESTAMENT CASE: REVELATION

moving toward is this: if the people of Israel under the Mosaic Law and the people of the Millennium are *fundamentally* the same (i.e., they are both prone to sin although the latter much less so), and if the Mosaic Law, especially its substitutionary sacrifices, had a legitimate function, then it may be the case that Mosaic Law-like rites, including substitutionary sacrifices, could have a legitimate function in the Millennial Temple.

Before discussing the possible legitimacy of the Millennial Temple and sacrifices offered there, we must understand several critical truths that are often misunderstood and thus lead to an unnecessary total dismissal of the notion that a temple and sacrifices might exist in the future. The knowledge of these truths is necessary to fully understand the NT teaching about the relationship of the Mosaic Law and the atonement provided by Jesus Christ.

The apostle Paul and the author of Hebrews earnestly taught that works of the Law (Paul emphasizing circumcision, Hebrews emphasizing sacrifices) could do nothing to add to the salvation that a Christian has in Christ.[69] Their teaching here was intended for those Christians, many of them Jews, who assumed that works done under the Law before Christ could save a man eternally, and therefore, those necessary works must continue on into the Christian era—even in view of Christ's all-sufficient sacrifice. The fact is that Paul's and the Hebrews author's understanding of this was not that the saving work of Christ supersedes the saving work of the Law but that the saving work of Christ makes the works of the Law, *which never could save men*, utterly superfluous. To understand this fully and how this relates to the Millennial Temple, the following truths must be known.

The first truth, as made clear in the NT, is that the atonement of Christ eliminates the sins of all faithful men, regardless of when they live.[70] Abraham's sins are paid for, through Christ's substitutionary atonement, because he "believed in God"; your sins, if you are a true Christian, are paid for, through Christ's substitutionary atonement, because you believe in God as he is revealed in the person of the Son of God, Jesus Christ.[71]

The next truth, also fully revealed in the NT, is that "it is impossible for the blood of bulls and goats to take away sins."[72] In other words, the sacrifices accomplished under the Law could not "take away sins"; that is, they were not valuable nor pure enough to satisfy God such that

---

[69] Acts 13:39, 15:1–35; Romans 3–7; Galatians 1–6; Hebrews 10:1–18
[70] Genesis 15:6; Isaiah 53:6; Zechariah 3:9; John 3:16; Romans 4:3; 1 Peter 2:24
[71] John 14:1
[72] Hebrews 10:4

he would annul the eternal condemnation that a man deserved from a lifetime of sinning. To put it more simply, regular sacrificing of animals could not save a man from damnation.

This brings us to another critical truth: animal sacrifices made under the Mosaic Law, and sometimes even before, did provide, so to speak, a very *limited* atonement.[73] These animals functioned as substitutes that God accepted, but they only bought the offerors limited reprieve from God's wrath—and this only for unintentional sins. To use theological language, their sins were "covered" but not "taken away."[74] The animal offered by a man who sinned unintentionally would prompt God to grant temporal clemency to the man, but this alone could not relieve him of his guilt in the final judgment. Only repentance and faith in God could do that.[75]

King David, for example, offered countless animals to the LORD on behalf of himself and the people, and this was pleasing to God. But when David committed the high-handed sin of adultery with Bathsheba and the subsequent murder of her husband Uriah, he did not offer any animal. All he could do was repent, confess, and throw himself upon God's mercy.[76] At the moment that David confessed and humbled himself before God, the LORD forgave him—although he suffered the consequences of the sins for the rest of his life. David repented, but the standard always remains the same: "The soul that sinneth, it shall die."[77]

[73.] That sacrifices made under the Law atoned for the sins of those who offered them is plainly stated by many OT texts (mostly in Leviticus), e.g., Leviticus 1:4, 4:27–31, 16 (Day of Atonement) and Numbers 6:11. But nowhere is it said that these sacrifices atoned for sins sufficient to save a man from final eternal punishment.

[74.] My understanding of the function of Mosaic Law sacrifices, both before and after Jesus's death, is based on the following articles: Jerry M. Hullinger, "The Compatibility of the New Covenant and Future Animal Sacrifice," *Journal of Dispensational Theology* 17:50 (Spring 2013), 47–66; "The Function of the Millennial Sacrifices in Ezekiel's Temple, part 1," *Bibliotheca Sacra* 167:665 (January 2010), 40–57; "The Function of the Millennial Sacrifices in Ezekiel's Temple, part 2," *Bibliotheca Sacra* 167:666 (April 2010), 166–179; Charles C. Ryrie, "Why Sacrifices in the Millennium?" *Emmaus Journal* 11:2 (Winter 2002), 229–310; and John C. Whitcomb, "Christ's Atonement and Animal Sacrifices in Israel," *Grace Theological Journal* 06:2 (Fall 1985), 201–208.

[75.] The general teaching in the Law shows that unintentional sins were forgivable (e.g., Lev 4:2–3, 5:15; Num 15:22-29), and intentional sins were unforgivable (Num 15:30-31). Yet the guilt offering, it seems, could be offered by men who had sinned intentionally (see Leviticus 6:1–7). And the Day of Atonement seemed to cover "all" outstandng sins of the people committed since the last Day of Atonement (Lev. 16:34), although Hebrews 9:7 says that only sins "committed in ignorance" were covered.

[76.] 2 Samuel 11–12. See also Psalm 51, especially verses 16–17.

[77.] Ezekiel 18:20 (KJV)

THE NEW TESTAMENT CASE: REVELATION

There must be justice, and there was justice: God offered up his "only begotten Son" but not David.[78] Jesus took David's place, "and with his wounds," David was "healed"—eternally.[79] It was this way with him; it is the same way with us—if, like him, we repent and have faith. Now let's take all this into consideration as we ponder how the temple might function in the Millennium.

The Mosaic Law was no contradiction of Christ's shed blood, for the sacrifices made under the Law could not satisfy God *for salvation purposes*. If a man sinned, he could offer up the required sacrifice for that sin, and God would cover that sin—but only for the duration of that man's mortal life. As soon as he sinned again, however, he was once again guilty. Between the apparent unavailability of covering for intentional sins and the reality that most, if not all, men could not offer sacrifices at the pace that their unintentional sins required, we can say with some certainty that all men under the Law were most of their lives considered to be unclean and guilty before God. Their only recourse, if they wanted to be saved from eternal punishment, was to do like David did and throw themselves upon the mercy of God.[80] The only difference between now and then was that their faith in God did not have to contain an understanding of the way that God would come in the flesh one day as the Messiah. Once God did come in the flesh, men and women were required, as always, to repent and believe in God, but also to believe in him as he had come to them in the form of the Son of God.[81]

This could be seen as a major difference, but as to *substance*, it is not. Abraham "believed in God" *and* graciously received God when he came to the patriarch at the Trees of Mamre; we believe in God and graciously receive God as he has come to us as Jesus, the Son of God. Because Abraham believed in God, he accepted God when God came to him in the flesh. Likewise, we believe in God and therefore accept the Son of God who has come to us in the flesh.[82]

Should the temple and its rites exist in the Millennium, it may be the case that they will function approximately the same as in olden

---

[78.] Isaiah 53:10; John 3:16, 5:19, 14:10; Acts 2:23; Psalms 51:14; 2 Samuel 12:13

[79.] Isaiah 53:5 (ESV)

[80.] "There was only one recourse for sins committed deliberately and knowingly. The sinners could humble themselves, entreat the grace of God and plead for his mercy. David is the example of one who appealed to God in this way because of his great sin of lust, adultery, and murder (2 Sam 12:13; Ps 32:1; 51:1)" (Lamar E. Cooper, *Ezekiel*, vol. 17 of *The New American Commentary* [Nashville: Broadman & Holman, 1994], 400).

[81.] John 6:29, 10:30

[82.] John 8:42

days. This is the impression that Ezekiel gives in his Millennial Temple vision.[83] The main components that existed in the old dispensation will exist in the new: there will be a similar temple; there will exist mortal, sinful people who need their sins atoned for; the Levites and (a much shrunken) priesthood will minster there (although there seems to be no Aaronic High Priest);[84] all the various offering types will be made;[85] and several of the feasts will be practiced, although the Day of Atonement is conspicuously absent.

As it was under the Mosaic Law, none of the Millennial Temple rites will have anything to do with saving a man from eternal damnation. Until a man's heart is fully repentant and fully faithful to God, limited grace will be extended to him by God through the means of the practice of presenting animal sacrifices. Like under the Law, his sins will be "covered" but not "taken away." For the purpose of getting on with life under the iron reign of the Messiah, the sacrifices will offer him some "breathing room" to get his act together.[86] If he does, then God will see in him only Christ when he dies, not his sins, and he will be saved.

But perhaps more important than this "breathing room" will be the *memorial* value of these sacrifices. The Mosaic Law sacrifices prompted the offerors to develop a *faint* idea of the future atonement of the Messiah that would save them from their sins—eternally. The millennial sacrifices will be a *blatant* reminder that Jesus, their king and Messiah, was tortured and killed for their sins. Every one of them will have a Bible, and every one of them, when making a sacrifice, will be painfully aware that their lives were "bought with a price…with precious blood, as of a

---

[83]. Ezekiel 40–47

[84]. "One of the problems accompanying the literal interpretation of the Old Testament presentation of the millennium is the problem surrounding the interpretation of such passages as Ezekiel 43:18, 46:24; Zechariah 14:16; Isaiah 56:6–8; 66:21; Jeremiah 33:15–18 and Ezekiel 20:40–41, all of which teach the restoration of a priesthood and the reinstitution of a bloody sacrificial system during that age" (Pentecost, *Things to Come*, section entitled, "Will there be Literal Sacrifices in the Millennium").

[85]. "Ezekiel, however, does not say that animals will be offered for a 'memorial' of Messiah's death. Rather, they will be for 'atonement' (45:15, 17, 20; cf. 43:20, 26)" (Whitcomb, "Christ's Atonement and Animal Sacrifices in Israel," 211).

[86]. Hullinger points out that God's expectation of holiness and obedience will be higher in the Millennium than before, for then the Messiah will rule, as the prophet said, with a "rod of iron." He cites Psalm 2:9, 72:1–4; Isaiah 11:4, 29:20–21; 65:20, 66:24; Jeremiah 31:29–30; Zechariah 14:16–21. Jerry Hullinger, "The Compatibility of the New Covenant and Future Animal Sacrifice," 60.

lamb unblemished and spotless, the blood of Christ."[87] With Jesus right there and with each of millions of sacrifices offering a picture of what the Jews and the rest of mankind did to the Messiah, there will be millions, perhaps billions, of men and women during the Millennium who come to faith in Christ and—according to God's infinitely holy and loving plan—are saved.

---

[87] 1 Corinthians 6:20; 1 Peter 1:19. Clive Thomson has this interesting perspective about sacrifices in the Millennium: "[B]lood sacrifices are necessary. The awful destruction of life preceding the millennium will have become past history: all will be aware of it. So God in His mercy warns unbelievers steadily during the 1,000 years that 'without shedding of blood is no remission' of sins (Heb. 9:22). Each sacrifice shows the shed blood of the victim and reminds all that as all unbelievers were destroyed before the millennium, so will it be again. It refers them to Revelation 20:8–9. For they will have their Bibles, and the warning is plain. Every sacrifice says that sin necessitates blood shed. Therefore, beware of the wrath to come. It is not God's way to punish without warning. The writer believes therefore that the animal sacrifices are a constant warning to the unbelieving, as well as a memorial" (Clive A. Thomson, "The Necessity of Blood Sacrifices in Ezekiel's Temple," in *Bibliotheca Sacra*, 123:491 [July 1966], 247).

CONCLUSION

"When all has been heard," said Solomon, "the conclusion of the matter is this: Fear God and keep His commandments, because this is the whole duty of man. For God will bring every deed into judgment, along with every hidden thing, whether good or evil."[1] Final judgment and having one's name found in the "Lamb's book of life" are the things that should concern human beings the most. The Church's doctrines and concerns certainly should take precedence over any thoughts about God's provision of an earthly kingdom some day for the Jews. In other words, God's intended spiritual meanings of the OT promises and prophecies are vastly more important than their literal meanings. The spiritual has to do with human immortality, the literal with earthly mortal life, which is like "a flower of the field; when the wind passes over, it vanishes, and its place remembers it no more."[2]

Yet we who are immortal-minded should not dismiss Israel's mortal-mindedness, for through the latter, God is bringing about the former. To put this thought as Paul put it, speaking to us Christians: "If you are arrogant, remember that it is not you who supports the root, but the root supports you."[3]

The spiritual meaning of what God said to the Jews is certainly more important than what he said literally to them; but the fact is that what he said to them literally is still God's Word, is Holy Scripture, and therefore of supreme value and fidelity, even while in our immortality-minded Christian minds we might naturally feel that it's not terribly important. We should not disregard the Jews. They are the "apple of His eye,"[4] and he has always considered himself to be a "husband" to them. He poured his love into that family for centuries, and in the miraculous birth in Bethlehem two thousand years ago physically became one of them. Then because of his love for them (and for us), he died so that he might live with them forever in loving unity.

At the Hazor archeological dig (that I mentioned in the preface), we came upon a grave that contained the bones of two Canaanites along

---

[1] Ecclesiastes 12:13–14 (BSB)
[2] Psalm 103:15–16 (BSB)
[3] Romans 11:18
[4] Zechariah 2:8

with their various jewelry trinkets and two short swords. There were plenty of Jewish archeologists and diggers there that day to excitedly witness the sight—but no Canaanites. They are long gone. That fact by itself should be evidence enough that Jehovah has lovingly watched over the Jews through the millennia. "The LORD has done great things for them!"[5]

As I said in the preface and many times throughout the book, there is no contradiction of our *sola fide* doctrine if God continues to provide some measure of literal fulfillment to the Jews, either for a short or a long time. He's arguably doing that now as the Jews flourish worldwide, especially in their own land of Israel. If the Lord has them flourish in an earthly mortal way for some length of time when Christ returns and sits "on his glorious throne," what does that matter to the Christian? We will, in any case, be immortal and be with Jesus. If the Lord does plan to preside over a thousand-year Jerusalem-based kingdom before heaven and earth are remade and mortality is completely a thing of the past, won't it be a tremendous blessing for his resurrected saints to witness the great harvest of Jewish souls during that epoch as we participate in Jesus's administration of that kingdom?

Let me close by reminding ourselves of what the apostle Paul said regarding the mostly unbelieving and unsaved Jewish people: "Theirs is the adoption as sons; theirs the divine glory and the covenants; theirs the giving of the Law, the temple worship, and the promises."[6] These literally belonged to them then, they belong to them now, and they will belong to them "as long as the sun shines, as long as the moon remains."[7] Among the "promises" is the promise of a final restoration of their kingdom. When the Lord returns from the "distant country" to be enthroned over that kingdom, that event will be as awesome as when "lightning comes from the east and flashes even to the west." There will be no doubt about it. And we will all cry out, "Blessed is he who comes in the name of the LORD!"[8]

---

[5] Psalm 126:2
[6] Romans 9:4 (BSB)
[7] Psalm 72:5 (BSB)
[8] Psalm 118:26 (ESV)

BIBLIOGRAPHY

Above all, the Bible, and secondarily:

Allis, Oswald T. *Prophecy and the Church*. Eugene: Wipf and Stock, 2001.

Augustine. *City of God*. In *Nicene and Post-Nicene Fathers*. Vol. 2. Edited by Philip Schaff. Edinburgh: T & T Clark. https://ccel.org/ccel/schaff/npnf102/npnf102.iv.XX.7.html.

Blaising, Craig A. and Darrell L. Bock. *Progressive Dispensationalism*. Grand Rapids: Baker Books, 2000.

Bock, Darrell L. "The Reign of the Lord Christ." In *Israel and the Church*. Edited by Craig A. Blaising and Darrell L. Bock. Zondervan Academic. Kindle eBook.

Brooks, David. "The Tel Aviv Cluster." *New York Times*, January 11, 2010. https://www.nytimes.com/2010/01/12/opinion/12brooks.html.

Carson, Donald A. *The Gospel According to John*. Vol. 4 of *The Pillar New Testament Commentary*. Edited by D. A. Carson. Leicester: Apollos, 1991.

Cooper, Lamar E. *Ezekiel*. Vol. 17 of *The New American Commentary*. Nashville: Broadman & Holman, 1994.

Crutchfield, Larry V. "The Early Church Fathers and the Foundations of Dispensationalism." *Conservative Theological Journal* 2:4 (March 1998): 19–31b.

Darby, John N. *Seven Lectures on the Second Coming of the Lord, Delivered in Toronto in 1863*. Toronto: Gospel Tract Depository, 1863. https://www.brethrenarchive.org/people/john-nelson-darby/pamphlets/seven-lectures-on-the-second-coming-of-the-lord/.

Darby, John N. "The Hope of the Church of God in Connection with the Destiny of the Jews and the Nations, as Revealed in Prophecy, Eleven Lectures delivered in Geneva, 1840." London: G. Morrish. https://www.brethrenarchive.org/people/john-nelson-darby/books/the-hopes-of-the-church-of-god-in-connection-with-the-destiny-of-the-jews-and-the-nations-as-revealed-in-prophecy-eleven-lectures/.

Dio, Cassius. *Dio's Roman History*. Vol. 8/9. Translated by Earnest Cary. London: Wm. Heinemann, 1925. https://archive.org/details/L176Cassius-DioCocceianusRomanHistoryVIII6170/page/n5/mode/2up.

BIBLIOGRAPHY

Eade, Alfred T. *The Second Coming of Christ.* In *The New "Panorama" Bible*, no. 3. Old Tappan: F. H. Revell Co., 1966.

Edersheim, Alfred. *Life and Times of Jesus.* Vol 1. New York: E. R. Herrick & Co., 1866. https://archive.org/details/lifetimesofjesus01eder/page/164/mode/2up.

Eusebius. *The Ecclesiastical History of Eusebius Pamphilus.* Translated by Christian F. Crusé. New York: Thomas N. Stanford, 1856. https://archive.org/details/ecclesiasticalhi00euse/page/n7/mode/2up.

Gibbon, Edward. *The History of the Decline and Fall of the Roman Empire.* Philadelphia: H. T. Coates & Co., 1860. Vol. 1/5. https://catalog.hathitrust.org/Record/000555622.

Hanegraaff, Hank. *The Apocalypse Code.* Nashville: Thomas Nelson, 2007.

Hullinger, Jerry M. "The Compatibility of the New Covenant and Future Animal Sacrifice." *Journal of Dispensational Theology* 17:50 (Spring 2013): 47–66.

Hullinger, Jerry M. "The Function of the Millennial Sacrifices in Ezekiel's Temple, part 1." *Bibliotheca Sacra* 167:665 (January 2010): 40–57.

Hullinger, Jerry M. "The Function of the Millennial Sacrifices in Ezekiel's Temple, part 2." *Bibliotheca Sacra* 167:666 (April 2010): 166–179.

Keil, Carl Friedrich and Franz Delitzsch. *Commentary on the Old Testament.* Peabody, MA: Hendrickson, 1996.

Laqueur, Walter. *The History of Zionism.* New York: Schocken Books, 2003.

Lazare, Bernard. *Antisemitism, Its History and Causes.* New York: The Int'l Library Pub. Co., 1903. https://archive.org/details/antisemitismitsh00lazaiala/page/54/mode/2up.

Martyr, Justin. *Dialogue with Trypho.* http://www.earlychristianwritings.com/text/justinmartyr-dialoguetrypho.html.

Merkley, Paul C. *The Politics of Christian Zionism 1891–1948.* London: Routledge, 2012.

Moo, Douglas J. *The Epistle to the Romans.* Vol 6 of *The New International Commentary on the New Testament.* Edited by Gordon D. Fee. Grand Rapids: Eerdmans, 1996.

Morris, Leon. *The Gospel According to John.* Vol. 4 of *The New International Commentary on the New Testament.* Edited by Gordon D. Fee. Grand Rapids: Wm. B. Eerdmans, 1995.

Oepke, Albrecht. "Ἀποκαθίστημι, Ἀποκατάστασις." In *Theological Dictionary of the New Testament.* Edited by G. Kittel, G. Bromiley, and G. Friedrich. Grand Rapids: Eerdmans, 1964.

Origin. *De Principiis.* In *The Ante-Nicene Fathers: Translations of the Writings of the Fathers Down to A.D. 325.* Vol. 10. Edited by Philip Schaff. Grand Rapids: Wm. B. Eerdmans. https://ccel.org/ccel/origen/works/anf04.vi.v.i.html#fnf_vi.v.i-p26.1.

Pentecost, J. Dwight. *Things to Come.* Grand Rapids: Zondervan, 2010.

Riddlebarger, Kim. *A Case for Amillennialism: Understanding the End Times.* Grand Rapids: Baker Books, 2013.

Ryrie, Charles C. "Why Sacrifices in the Millennium?" *Emmaus Journal* 11:2 (Winter 2002): 229–310.

Ryrie, Charles C. *Dispensationalism.* Chicago: Moody Press, 1995.

Saucy, Robert L. *The Case for Progressive Dispensationalism.* Grand Rapids: Zondervan, 1993.

Saucy, Robert L. *The Church in God's Program.* Chicago: Moody Press, 1972.

Schaff, Phillip. *The History of the Christian Church.* Vol. 2. New York: Charles Scribner, 1914. https://archive.org/details/historyofchris02scha/page/n9/mode/2up.

Sizer, Stephen. *Zion's Christian Soldiers: The Bible, Israel and the Church.* Kindle eBook, 2018.

Taylor, Daniel T. *The Reign of Christ on Earth; or, the Voice of the Church in all Ages.* Boston: S. Bagster & Sons, 1882. https://archive.org/details/reign-christonea00taylgoog.

Thomson, Clive A. "The Necessity of Blood Sacrifices in Ezekiel's Temple." In *Bibliotheca Sacra* 123:491 (July 1966): 237–248.

Weizmann, Chaim. *Trial and Error: The Autobiography of Chaim Weizmann,* book two, 1918–1948. Plunkett Lake Press, 2013. Google eBook.

Whitcomb, John C. "Christ's Atonement and Animal Sacrifices in Israel." *Grace Theological Journal* 06:2 (Fall 1985): 201–208.

SCRIPTURE INDEX

1

1 Chron 16:
- 8 .... **49**
- 9 .... **49**
- 12 .... **49**
- 15–18 .... **49**
- 17 .... **43**

1 Chron 17 .... **61**

1 Chron 17:
- 14 .... **61**

1 Chron 21:
- 29 .... **59**

1 Cor 6:
- 2 .... **119, 166**
- 9–10 .... **131**
- 19 .... **16, 98**
- 20 .... **177**

1 Cor 9:
- 22 .... **149**

1 Cor 11:
- 25 .... **70**

1 Cor 12:
- 27 .... **60**

1 Cor 15:
- 24 .... **131**
- 44 .... **131**
- 50 .... **131**

1 John 2:
- 18 .... **156**

1 John 4:
- 8 .... **134**

1 Kings 1:
- 34 .... **62**
- 45 .... **62**

1 Kings 7:
- 49 .... **92**

1 Kings 8:
- 1 .... **63**

- 51 .... **43**
- 56 .... **101**

1 Kings 11–12 .... **60**

1 Pet 1:
- 19 .... **177**

1 Pet 2:
- 5 .... **98**
- 24 .... **173**

1 Sam 4 .... **59**

1 Sam 6:
- 20 .... **32**

1 Sam 7:
- 15–17 .... **57**

1 Sam 8 .... **58**

1 Sam 8:
- 7 .... **78**
- 7–8 .... **58**

1 Sam 12 .... **78**

1 Sam 12:
- 16–17 .... **58**
- 18 .... **58**

1 Thess 2:
- 16 .... **21, 146**

1 Thess 4:
- 17 .... **131**

1 Tim 2:
- 4 .... **134**

2

2 Chron 7:
- 1–3 .... **90**
- 10 .... **172**
- 13–14 .... **67**

2 Chron 20:
- 6–12 .... **50**
- 20–25 .... **50**

2 Chron 28:
- 3 .... **51**

2 Chron 35 .... **165**

2 Chron 36:
- 22–23 .... **74**

2 Cor 3:
- 6 .... **70**
- 7 .... **127**
- 7–9 .... **133**
- 9 .... **127**

2 Cor 5:
- 21 .... **60**

2 Kings 13:
- 23 .... **50**

2 Kings 17 .... **50**

2 Kings 23 .... **165**

2 Sam 5:
- 1–10 .... **59**
- 7 .... **63**

2 Sam 7 .... **59**

2 Sam 7:
- 10–11a **86**
- 11b–16 .... **60**

2 Sam 11–12 .... **174**

2 Sam 12:
- 13 .... **175**

2 Sam 24 .... **91**

2 Thess 1:
- 5 .... **131**

2 Thess 2:
- 3-4 .... **160**
- 8 .... **156**

2 Tim 3:
- 16 .... **32**

2 Tim 4:
- 18 .... **131**

SCRIPTURE INDEX

A

Acts 1:
  1–8 .... **120**
  6 .... **135**
  11 .... **164**
  11b **121**
Acts 2 .... **98, 144**
Acts 2:
  23 .... **175**
  41 .... **106**
Acts 3 .... **144**
Acts 3:
  19–21 .... **96, 136**
  20–21 .... **132**
  21 .. **73, 137, 139, 144**
  24 .... **132, 136, 137**
Acts 4:
  4 .... **106**
  12 .... **16**
  24–26 .... **61**
  25–26 .... **168**
Acts 7:
  2–4 .... **35**
  4 .... **35**
  42–43 .... **45**
Acts 13:
  39 .... **173**
Acts 14:
  22 .... **131, 132**
Acts 15 .... **128, 132**
Acts 15:
  1 .... **40**
  1–35 .... **173**
  10 .... **128**
  16–18 .... **132**
Acts 16 .... **128**
Acts 19:
  8 .... **132, 147**
Acts 20:
  16 .... **148**
  22–23 .... **148**
  25 .... **132**
Acts 21:
  4 .... **148**
  10–14 .... **148**
  21 .... **148**
  22–26 .... **149**
  24 .... **149**
  28 .... **149**
Acts 22:
  22 .... **150**
Acts 24:
  14 .... **150**
  17 .... **151**
Acts 25:
  8 .... **150**
Acts 28:
  17 .... **150**
  23 .... **132**
  31 .... **132**
Amos 5:
  25–26 .... **45**
Amos 9:
  11–12 .... **132**

C

Col 1:
  13–14 .... **131**
  15 .... **94**
Col 3:
  11 .... **131**

D

Dan 2 .... **158**
Dan 2:
  39 .... **163**
  44 .... **80, 158**
Dan 4:
  34 .... **80**
Dan 6:
  26 .... **80**
Dan 7 .... **114, 119, 158, 159, 161**
Dan 7:
  4–6 .... **156**
  7 .... **159**
  11 .... **161**
  13 .... **122, 168**
  13–14 .... **82, 114, 117**
  18 .... **114**
  21 .... **159**
  25 .... **160, 165**
  27 .... **169**
Dan 8 .... **159, 161**
Dan 8:
  11 .... **159**
  11–14 .... **160**
  13 .... **165**
  13–14 .... **160**
  14 .... **165, 171**
  17 .... **161**
  24 .... **160**
  25 .... **161**
Dan 9 .... **102, 159**
Dan 9:
  1–5a **53**
  24 .... **171**
  26–27 .... **165**
  27 .... **160, 161**
Dan 11 .... **159, 161**
Dan 11:
  31 .... **160**
  36 .... **159, 161**
  37 .... **159**
  41 .... **161**
  45 .... **161**
Dan 12 .... **102**
Dan 12:
  1 .... **69**
  1–3 .... **72, 162, 167**
  2 .... **103, 162**
  3 .... **167**
  11 .... **160, 165**
Deut 1:
  8 .... **41, 43**

SCRIPTURE INDEX

Deut 4:
  19 45
  20 43
  27 52
Deut 6:
  5 .... 108, 134
  10 43
Deut 9 101
Deut 9:
  3–7 46
  5 43
Deut 15:
  6 169
Deut 26:
  5 130
Deut 28 ....50, 66
Deut 28:
  13 169
  64 52
  65 66
Deut 29:
  13 55
Deut 29–30 53
Deut 30 50
Deut 30:
  6 54
  19–20 .... 55, 67
  20 43
Deut 34:
  4 43
  6 48

E

Eccl 12:
  13–14 179
Eph 2:
  8–9 129
  13–16 131
Eph 5:
  5 131
Eph 6:
  12 165

Exod 3:
  13–14 112
  15 65
Exod 6:
  8 43
Exod 12:
  48 40
Exod 20:
  13 134
Exod 24 123
Exod 28:
  1 93
Exod 32:
  12 44
  13 .... 41, 44, 54, 89
Exod 33:
  1 .... 41, 43
Ezek 1 94
Ezek 1:
  2 96
  26–28 95
Ezek 3:
  15 .... 94, 95
Ezek 8:
  4 94
Ezek 10:
  15 94
Ezek 10–11 94
Ezek 11:
  21 172
Ezek 12:
  10–13 96
Ezek 17:
  12 96
  22–24 113
Ezek 18:
  20 174
Ezek 20 94
Ezek 20:
  9 44
  14 44
  22 44
  33-34 79
  33–44 172

34–38 69
40–41 176
42 79
Ezek 21:
  25 96
Ezek 22 94
Ezek 22:
  26 94
Ezek 26:
  7 96
Ezek 29:
  2 96
Ezek 34 58
Ezek 34:
  11–13 80
  12 82
  15 82
  22–24 82
  23 .... 58, 96
  24 96
  28 80
Ezek 36:
  20–23 44
  22 123
  22–24 76
  26–28 71
  27 70
  27–28 123
Ezek 37 ....58, 71
Ezek 37:
  12–14 72
  14 70
  15–28 65
  24 .... 58, 83, 96
  24–26 65
  24–28 66
Ezek 38:
  2–3 96
Ezek 39:
  27–29 75
  29 70
Ezek 40:
  1–2 90
  1–4 90
  4 .... 90, 91

187

SCRIPTURE INDEX

Ezek 40–47 .... **15**, **176**
Ezek 40–48 .... **171**
Ezek 41:
   22 .... **92**
Ezek 43:
   1–4 .... **95**
   1–7 .... **90**
   7a **96**
   10–11 .... **91**
   18 .... **176**
   20 .... **176**
   26 .... **176**
Ezek 44:
   5 .... **90**
   10–16 .... **93**
Ezek 44–46 .... **94**
Ezek 45:
   8–9 .... **94**
   13–17 .... **96**
   15 .... **176**
   17 .... **176**
   20 .... **176**
   22 .... **94**
   22–25 .... **96**
Ezek 46:
   1–18 .... **94**
   24 .... **176**
Ezek 47 .... **89**, **97**, **106**
Ezek 47:
   8–9 .... **97**
   10 .... **99**
   12–48:29 .... **89**
   13–14 .... **89**
Ezek 48:
   35 .... **84**
Ezra 1:
   1–4 .... **74**
Ezra 3:
   12 .... **84**

G

Gal 1–6 .... **173**
Gal 2:
   19 .... **133**

Gal 3 .... **92**
Gal 3:
   6 .... **102**, **128**
   7 .... **37**, **41**
   7–9 .... **130**
   10–13 .... **133**
   16 .... **37**
   19–25 .... **133**
   24 .... **106**
   29 .... **41**, **130**
Gal 5:
   12 .... **128**
   21 .... **131**
Gen 1:
   1 .... **32**
Gen 3:
   15 .... **32**
Gen 6:
   5 .... **33**
Gen 8:
   21 .... **33**
Gen 9:
   8–17 .... **33**
Gen 11 .... **33**
Gen 11:
   31–12:5 .... **35**
Gen 12 .... **35**
Gen 12:
   1–3 .... **35**, **56**
   1–4a **35**
   2–3 .... **125**
   7 .... **35**, **125**
Gen 13:
   14–17 .... **36**
   15 .... **43**
Gen 14:
   17–20 .... **62**
Gen 15 .... **36**, **38**, **43**
Gen 15:
   1 .... **38**
   5–7 .... **36**
   6 .... **102**, **173**
   12–18 .... **38**
Gen 17 .... **35**, **39**

Gen 17:
   1 .... **129**
   4 .... **56**
   5 .... **56**
   7 .... **43**
   9–11 .... **40**
   10 .... **46**
   13 .... **43**
   19 .... **43**
Gen 22 .... **40**
Gen 22:
   16–18 .... **41**, **76**, **89**
   18 .... **36**, **77**
Gen 23:
   6 .... **56**
Gen 26:
   3 .... **41**
   3–5 .... **41**, **76**, **89**
Gen 48:
   5 .... **57**

H

Hag 2:
   3 .... **84**
   6–9 .... **85**
   7–9 .... **171**
Heb 4:
   14 .... **133**
Heb 6:
   13–18 .... **41**
Heb 7 .... **62**
Heb 7:
   3 .... **62**
   9–10 .... **62**
   25 .... **85**
   27 .... **133**
Heb 8:
   8 .... **70**
   13 .... **70**, **91**, **133**
Heb 9:
   7 .... **133**, **174**
   9 .... **133**

15 70
22 177
Heb 10 127
Heb 10:
  1–3 133
  1–4 123
  1–18 173
  4 .... **133**, 173
  11 .... **133**
Heb 11:
  8–16 31
  10 .... **39**, 147
  16 .... **37**, 147
Heb 12:
  24 70
Hos 2:
  16 84
  18 171
  19–20 84

I

Isa 1:
  19–31 172
Isa 2:
  2 .... **90**, 97
  2–3 .... **77, 89**, 171
  4 171
Isa 4 85
Isa 6 83
Isa 6:
  1 95
  5 .... **83**, 95
Isa 7:
  9 134
  10–14 51
  14 58
Isa 9:
  5 171
  6 58
  6–7 81
Isa 11 85
Isa 11:
  2 70

4 .... **168**, 176
6–9 86
11–12 74
Isa 13:
  9–12 68
Isa 24:
  23 167
  23b 87
Isa 25 102
Isa 25:
  6–8 .... **87, 162**, 167
  9 87
Isa 29:
  20–21 176
Isa 32:
  15 70
Isa 35:
  10 75
Isa 42:
  1 70
Isa 44:
  3 70
  3–4 98
  28 74
Isa 49:
  22 74
  23 169
Isa 51:
  3 88
Isa 53:
  5 175
  5–6 33
  6 173
  10 175
Isa 54:
  9 34
Isa 55:
  9 83
Isa 56:
  4–7 171
  6–8 176
  7 93
Isa 60:
  4–5 88

7 .... **93**, 171
12 171
13 171
Isa 61:
  1 70
Isa 62:
  5 84
Isa 63:
  1–6 165
  3 168
Isa 65:
  11–16 172
  19–20 87
  20 .. **97, 167, 170**, 176
Isa 66:
  15–18 172
  20 74
  21 176
  24 176

J

Jer 3:
  17 78
Jer 7:
  3–7 51
Jer 11:
  14 52
Jer 14:
  19 52
  21 52
Jer 23 85
Jer 23:
  5–6 64
  6 58
Jer 25:
  8–9 52
  11 52
  27–33 172
Jer 30:
  3 52
  23–24 172
Jer 31 70

SCRIPTURE INDEX

Jer 31:
　12 88
　29–30 176
　31–34 .... **54, 65, 70**
　34 .... **73, 172**
　36 123
Jer 32:
　37–40 72
Jer 33 85
Jer 33:
　14–22 171
　15–18 176
　18 93
Jer 34:
　18–20 39
Jer 39 61
Job 19:
　25–27 87
Joel 2:
　1–2a 68
　28 70
　32 129
Joel 3:
　1–2 69
　18 .... **97, 171**
John 1:
　11 116
　18 94
　29 147
John 2:
　17 116
　19 .... **16, 60, 98**
John 3:
　3 109
　16 .... **173, 175**
　30 105
John 4 106
John 4:
　10 98
　22 143
John 5:
　19 175
John 6:
　29 175

John 7:
　37–38 98
　39 98
John 8:
　42 175
John 10:
　30 175
John 11:
　25 128
John 12:
　41 .... **83, 95**
John 14:
　1 .... **18, 173**
　10 175
John 15:
　18 118
　20 118
John 16:
　25–30 120
John 18:
　36 .... **109, 111**
John 19:
　11 .... **111, 112**
　15 168
　19 62
　30 112
John 20:
　28 113
Josh 5:
　1–7 46
　2–9 40
Josh 21:
　43–45 .... **42, 48**
　45 101
Josh 23:
　14 .... **53, 101**
Judg 4 165

L

Lev 1:
　4 174
Lev 4:
　2–3 174

　16 174
　27–31 174
Lev 5:
　15 174
Lev 6:
　1–7 174
Lev 9:
　23 90
Lev 16 93
Lev 16:
　34 174
Lev 17:
　7 45
Lev 19:
　18 .... **108, 134**
Lev 23 93
Lev 26:
　12 71
　33 52
　40–42 .... **47, 55**
　44 .... **47, 55**
Luke 1:
　55 43
　72b–73 104
　77 104
Luke 2:
　4 115
　21 40
　30 105
　41–50 115
Luke 3:
　9–10 105
　12 105
　14 105
　22 62
Luke 11:
　14–22 115
Luke 13:
　34 110
　35 144
Luke 14:
　16–24 .... **110, 134**
Luke 17:
　20 126

SCRIPTURE INDEX

Luke 19:
  11 .... **113**
  11–27 .... **113, 134**
  12–27 .... **110**
  17 .... **119**
Luke 20:
  38 .... **48**
Luke 21 .... **112, 113**
Luke 21:
  20–24 .... **117**
  24 .... **139, 144**
  27 .... **114**
  33 .... **133**
Luke 22:
  14–18 .. **108, 118, 126**
  16 .... **119, 139**
  16–18 .... **144**
  18 .... **139**
  20 .... **70, 123**
  28–30 .... **119**
Luke 24:
  45 .... **120**

M

Mal 3:
  1 .... **115**
  2–6 .... **172**
  18 .... **172**
Mal 4:
  3 .... **172**
Mark 4:
  30–32 .... **113**
  33–34 .... **120**
Mark 7:
  27 .... **116**
  31 .... **110**
Mark 8:
  1–9 .... **110**
Mark 11:
  12–14 .... **134**
  20–26 .... **134**
  22 .... **134**

Mark 12:
  28–34 .... **108**
Mark 13 .... **112, 113**
Mark 13:
  32 .... **121**
Mark 14:
  24 .... **123**
  61 .... **112**
  62 .... **112**
Matt 2:
  1–12 .... **89**
Matt 3:
  9 .... **105**
  12 .... **105**
Matt 5:
  18 .... **133**
  20 .... **109**
Matt 6:
  31–33 .... **108**
Matt 7:
  21 .... **109**
Matt 8:
  5–13 .... **110**
  10 .... **110**
  11–12 .... **110**
Matt 10:
  5–7 .... **109**
Matt 13:
  24–30 .... **109**
  31–33 .... **109**
  36–43 .... **109**
  43–45 .... **109**
Matt 15:
  24 .... **109, 116**
  26 .... **143**
Matt 17:
  1–8 .... **48**
  1–13 .... **95**
Matt 18:
  1–4 .... **109**
  23-35 .... **109**
Matt 19:
  13–14 .... **109**
  27 .... **137**

  28 ... **19, 96, 114, 137, 164**
Matt 21:
  28–32 .... **109**
  33–44 .... **110**
  33–46 .... **134**
  43 .... **109, 110**
Matt 22:
  2–14 .... **110**
  34–40 .... **108**
  37–40 .... **18**
Matt 23:
  37 .... **140**
  37–39 .... **116**
  39 .... **12**
Matt 24:
  15 .... **160**
  26–27 .... **157**
  27 .... **114, 164**
  30 .... **168**
  31 .... **114**
Matt 24–25 .... **112, 113**
Matt 25:
  14–30 .... **114**
  21 .... **115**
  31 .... **164**
  32 .... **115**
  34 .... **115**
  41 .... **115**
Matt 26:
  28 .... **123**
  64 .... **168**
Matt 27:
  25 .... **111, 112**
Mic 4:
  1 .... **97**
  1–2 .... **77**
  3 .... **86, 171**
  4 .... **51**
  7 .... **51**
Mic 5:
  2 .... **58**
  2–4 .... **81**
  9–15 .... **172**

SCRIPTURE INDEX

Mic 7:
  18–19 73
  18–20 51

N

Neh 9:
  7–8 .... **42**, **48**, **101**
  8 53
  23 42
Num 3:
  5–10 93
Num 6 149
Num 6:
  11 174
Num 12:
  3 47
Num 13–14 75
Num 14:
  3 75
  15–16 .... **44**, 76
  16 44
  23 41
Num 15:
  22-29 174
  30-31 174
Num 18:
  1–7 93
  6 57
  20–24 57
Num 20:
  2–13 47
Num 32:
  11 .... **41**, **43**
Num 35:
  1–8 57

P

Phil 3:
  2 128
  3 130
  8 147

  14 147
Ps 2 .... **61**, **62**, **63**, **168**
Ps 2:
  6 63
  8 64
  8–9 63
  9 .... **168**, **176**
  10–12 63
Ps 23:
  1 83
Ps 32:
  1 175
Ps 45:
  6 58
Ps 46:
  9 171
Ps 51 174
Ps 51:
  1 175
  14 175
  16–17 174
Ps 69:
  9 116
Ps 72 64
Ps 72:
  1–4 176
  5 180
  8–11 64
Ps 103:
  15–16 179
Ps 105 49
Ps 105:
  10 43
Ps 110 .... **61**, **62**, 64
Ps 110:
  2 63
  5 63
  5–6 .... **63**, **166**
Ps 118:
  26 180
Ps 126:
  2 180

R

Rev 1:
  1 153
  19 153
Rev 1–4 154
Rev 4:
  1 153
Rev 4–21 154
Rev 5:
  5 164
  10 166
Rev 5–19 154
Rev 6–18 157
Rev 7:
  4–8 165
Rev 11:
  1–2 .... **160**, **165**
  2 165
Rev 13:
  2 156
  5 .... **159**, **160**
  5–7 156
  7 159
Rev 14:
  11 160
  20 165
Rev 16:
  12–16 165
Rev 17:
  14 157
Rev 19 ..... **157**, **161**, **164**,
       165, **168**, **172**
Rev 19:
  15 165
  18 166
  19 .... **160**, **165**
  19–21 157
  20 .... **156**, **160**
Rev 19–20 162
Rev 20 ..... **18**, **19**, **24**, **97**,
       119, **153**, **154**, **157**,
       163, **164**, **166**, **167**,
       168, **169**, **171**, **172**

Rev 20:
  4 157
  5–6 162
  7–9 166
  7–10 170
  8 172
  8–9 177
  9 .... 155, 169
  11 167
  11–15 166
Rev 20–22 .... 163, 171
Rev 21 .... 163, 166
Rev 21:
  4 153
Rev 22 98
Rev 22:
  1–2 98
  6 153
  16 154
Rom 1:
  16 143
Rom 1–7 63
Rom 2:
  11 143
Rom 2–3 129
Rom 3:
  20 133
Rom 3–7 173
Rom 4:
  3 173
  11 130
Rom 5:
  20 133
Rom 7:
  5–13 133
  7–13 92
Rom 8:
  1–4 133
  28 39
Rom 9 .... 140, 141
Rom 9:
  1–3 146
  3 147

  4 .... 141, 180
  4–5 140
  5 128
  6 .... 139, 140
  32 138
Rom 9–11 111,
  129, 138, 139, 143,
  144, 146, 147
Rom 10 141
Rom 10:
  13 129
  28 143
Rom 11 ...... 16, 139, 142
Rom 11:
  1 140
  4 140
  11–12 142
  14 142
  15 142
  16–25 135
  17–18 143
  17–24 142
  18 179
  25 139
  25–26a 144
  26 135
  28 .... 47, 140
  28–29 .... 13, 145
  29 16
  30–33 145
  33–36 61
  34 .... 83, 139
Rom 14:
  17 .... 126, 131

Z

Zech 2:
  8 179
Zech 3 85
Zech 3:
  9 173
Zech 6 85

Zech 6:
  11–13 85
Zech 8:
  1–3 84
  22–23 77
Zech 9:
  10 171
Zech 12:
  10 .... 58, 70
Zech 13:
  9 172
Zech 14:
  4 .... 122, 164
  8 97
  8–10 122
  9 .... 80, 83
  10 97
  16 .... 93, 176
  16–19 ...... 78, 93, 171
  16–21 .... 171, 176
Zeph 1:
  14–16 68
Zeph 3:
  14–17 79

www.ingramcontent.com/pod-product-compliance
Lightning Source LLC
Chambersburg PA
CBHW060726110426
42738CB00056B/1711